MW00809193

JOHN HENRY NEWMAN

IDA FRIEDERIKE GÖRRES

John Henry Newman

A Life Sacrificed

Edited and with an introduction by
Hanna-Barbara Gerl-Falkovitz

TRANSLATED BY
JENNIFER S. BRYSON

IGNATIUS PRESS   SAN FRANCISCO

Translated from the German:
John Henry Newman—der Geopferte:
Ein anderer Blick auf ein großes Leben
by Ida Friederike Görres, ed. Hanna-Barbara Gerl-Falkovitz, 4th edition
Vallendar-Schönstatt: Patris Verlag, 2015

Unless otherwise indicated, Scripture quotations are from the Revised Standard Version of the Bible—Second Catholic Edition (Ignatius Edition), copyright © 2006 National Council of the Churches of Christ in the United States of America. Used by permission. All rights reserved worldwide.

Cover photograph of John Henry Newman
by Herbert Rose Barraud
carbon print, 1887, published 1888
(detail from full portrait)
© National Portrait Gallery, London

Cover design by Roxanne Mei Lum

© 2024 by Ignatius Press, San Francisco
All rights reserved
ISBN 978-1-62164-698-3 (PB)
ISBN 978-1-64229-309-8 (eBook)
Library of Congress Control Number 2024942599
Printed in the United States of America ∞

CONTENTS

TRANSLATOR'S PREFACE

by Jennifer S. Bryson

Why, in 2022, does one translate a book about Saint John Henry Newman that was written in German mostly in the 1940s? After all, when Ida Friederike Görres wrote *John Henry Newman: A Life Sacrificed*, she had only partial access to the works of Newman and only partial access to the relatively limited secondary literature of the time. Since then, the complete works of Newman have been published in annotated editions and secondary literature about Newman now abounds. One might, therefore, dismiss Görres' book as out-of-date or superfluous at this point. But I believe this would be a mistake.

In this book, Görres offers her own distinct perspective on the life and work of Newman. She shares her insights into the life of this great saint in chapters 1−8 and 11 and her rich reflections about Newman on conscience in chapter 10. Chapter 9 consists of two poems by Newman; Görres' selection of these two poems in particular reflects the arc of the narrative in chapters 1−8 and thus the particular way she understood the life of Newman.

Görres did not write this book as an academic study of Newman. As with all her works, she wrote this for a general readership, for the enrichment of faith in the lives of Catholics. They and other nonspecialists who want to learn about Newman are the primary audience for whom I have translated this book. I will be happy, however, if this book may also be of use in some way to scholars of Newman.

Another aspect of the significance of this book—and part of my motivation to translate it—is that it is also a book about Ida Friederike Görres. This book is an example of her great love of the saints, her keen observations about sanctity, and her particular devotion to Newman, even decades before his canonization. Also, like Newman, she herself knew the dreams, trials, and disappointments of trying to support, enliven, and contribute to the life of the

Church. For Görres, this started during her active involvement with the Catholic Youth Movement in Germany in the 1920s and 1930s and continued throughout her years as a writer up to 1946, when she appears to have (more or less) completed the draft manuscript for chapters 1–8 of this book. It is clear that, while these experiences were enriching for her, she lived through more than a few disappointments along the way and, over time, came to sobering realizations about the Church.[1] In this book, I see hints that her own experiences contributed both to the empathy she had for Newman's struggles and to her insights about the significance of them and how Newman handled them.

Another reason I translated this book is that it offers English-speaking readers a window into the reception of the works of Newman in German-speaking Europe in the twentieth century.[2] Hanna-Barbara Gerl-Falkovitz's excellent introduction aids in this regard as well as in introducing Görres to the reader.

The translation of this book into English, however, proved to be complicated in unusual ways. If you are interested in the technical challenges that influenced how I translated and how I annotated this book, read on. If you want to get on to Newman, skip ahead to the introduction by Gerl-Falkovitz or even to chapter 1.

Quotations and Citations: Hunting and Reverse Engineering

Even after the excellent work of Gerl-Falkovitz to transform a stack of papers, sometimes out of order, and note cards into a book for publication, in the German edition there remained scores of quota-

---

[1] The examples of this in her work are too numerous to list here. But to start with, see the essay she wrote in 1941, "Vom Optimismus zur Hoffnung" ("From Optimism to Hope"), about being part of the Catholic Youth Movement; see also her reflections on her childhood and her involvement in the Catholic Youth Movement in Ida Friederike Görres, "Reinhold Schneiders 'Unglaube' oder die negative Mystik", in *Der göttliche Bettler* (Frankfurt am Main: Josef Knecht, 1959), 122–29. See also some of her works written near the end of her life; they reflect a sobriety about reform and the Church that one does not see in her earlier works. For example, see "Demolition Troops in the Church" and "Trusting the Church", in Ida Friederike Görres, *Bread Grows in Winter*, trans. Jennifer S. Bryson (San Francisco: Ignatius Press, forthcoming).

[2] For an overview, see Claus Arnold, "Newman's Reception in Germany: From Döllinger to Ratzinger", *Newman Studies Journal* 18, no. 1 (2021): 5–23. See also Hanna-Barbara Gerl-Falkovitz's introduction to this volume.

tions from Newman and other authors without citations. As Gerl-Falkovitz explains in her introduction, this book "was created from the available manuscripts and notes. . . . The quotations are based on the contemporary literature used by Görres. However, around half of all the quotations in the original manuscript lacked citation. Unfortunately, it was not possible to make up for this in every single case."

What I had before me was a text in *German* not only containing what Görres herself wrote about Newman but also full of quotations from Newman and other English-speaking figures, largely with no citations. Because I was translating this book into *English*, it was imperative for me to find not merely sources for the citations but, even more importantly, the original *English text* of these quotations. This proved to be quite a bit more difficult than one might imagine. Trying to tease out, from the German text, which English words to search for in the works of Newman and other authors was a long process of trial and error but ending, most of the time, in eureka moments.

I compiled a detailed spreadsheet of all the quotations lacking citations. In the end, I whittled this list down to only a few short phrases and short sentences for which I could not find an English (or German) source. Thus, in almost every instance in this book, when you read, "Newman wrote . . .", you are reading the original words of Newman, not Jennifer Bryson's translation back into English of someone else's former translation from English into German.

As for the very few words and short phrases quoted for which I could not identify sources, you will recognize these by the presence of quotation marks around the words or phrases (and in some cases, sentences) with the absence of a citation. In a few other cases where Görres quotes only short phrases and where I do not have full confidence that I have identified the correct original text in English, I have noted my uncertainty in the citation. Fortunately, there are few such passages in this book.

Next came the question of which editions of the works of Newman to cite in my translation. Due to the complicated history of this manuscript, the incomplete annotation of the German edition, and the fact that I was preparing this edition for an English-speaking audience, the works I cite are the works Görres quotes, but my citations are not necessarily from the same editions that Görres used.

My primary concern as translator was not which edition of any given work Görres had used. Thus, my translation is not a study of how Görres used her sources; that would be a different book. Rather, I focused on accuracy in providing the correct English versions of the quotations, while weighing other considerations as well.

And not only did I have to find sources where there were no citations, but I also often had to supplement or simply replace sources provided by Görres (or added by Gerl-Falkovitz) with English-language sources. The citations I provide are for the sources I used for this English edition. My citations are not translations of the citations in the German edition (with a few exceptions, which I indicate).

My criteria in selecting which editions of the works of Newman and secondary sources to cite in this book were based on several factors. Once I determined which work by Newman or another author a quotation originally came from, I had to make a prudential decision about which edition of that particular text to cite.

Here is one example: In chapter 4 there is a quotation from Newman's *The Via Media of the Anglican Church* with no information at all about where Görres found it. In the English edition of *The Via Media*, I was able to find the passage that corresponds exactly to the quotation in Görres' German text. The citation I provide is for the English edition of *The Via Media* by Newman. Does my citation of the English text mean that Görres took the quote from this English text and translated it herself into German? Perhaps, but not necessarily. *The Via Media* is a work she quotes only a few times; I do not know if she even had access to *The Via Media* while she worked on her manuscript. She may have found the quotation in a secondary source. Or perhaps she found the quotation in a German compilation of translated passages drawn from multiple works by Newman. We just do not know.

Another consideration in selecting which editions of Newman's works to cite was pragmatic: namely, I wanted to get this translation into print. Because of the need to search for the original quotations in English and the complicated, copious citations for this book, this translation took much longer than other books by Görres that I have translated into English. I wanted to avoid the risk that my translation of this book might, mirroring the history of the book itself, be left at my death as only a digital "box" of "papers" and "note cards" for someone else to edit several decades later. On top of this, due to the Covid pandemic and geography, when I did this translation, I did not have access to a library with the latest editions of the collected works of Newman in English. Rather than wait until some unknown, perhaps even nonexistent, future point when I would have access to the latest academic works at a major library for an extended period, I used the most reliable sources I could access, primarily at the newmanreader.org website of the National Institute of Newman Studies and at archive.org.

Another consideration was that, where possible, I tried to remain close to the source cited by Görres or the source used by the German translator of the text Görres used. For example, many of the letters quoted by Görres are from the early twentieth-century editions published by Wilfrid Philip Ward and Anne Mozley. It seems clear that Görres had access to both works in English (and she translated passages from them into German herself). Thus, I have cited the letters from these older editions of Ward and Mozley, not from the more recent critical editions of Newman's correspondence. An exception is Newman's important *Apologia pro Vita Sua*, quoted often by Görres, for which I used the most recent critical edition by Ian Ker.

By studying which sources Görres cited, I was able to use those sources to search for the English texts of quotations that lacked citations in the German text. For example, I noticed that Görres repeatedly quotes from Henry Tristram's book *John Henry Newman: Centenary Essays* and that sometimes she cites this book. I am quite certain that Görres had a copy of this in English.[3] In passages in which she quotes from Tristram's book, I found that some of the

---

[3] At present, there is no bibliography of the books in Görres' library. Such a bibliography would have been helpful in preparing this translation. Her personal library is still intact, however, and sits in a room in Freiburg, Germany. One can hope that someone will someday prepare a bibliography of the works in this library and preserve the collection intact. Brother Meinrad Hötzel, O.S.B., mentioned to me that many of the works in this library have handwritten notes by Görres in them; these could be quite helpful for future scholars studying Görres. Brother Meinrad is the nephew of Beatrix Klaiber. Klaiber, an archivist, managed the portion of Görres' estate involving her works, her library, and her unpublished papers, until Klaiber's death in 2020. After Klaiber's death, Brother Meinrad arranged for some of the unpublished papers and letters by Görres that were in Klaiber's possession to be archived in the Archive of the Archdiocese of Freiburg, where they are today. Meinrad Hötzel, in a conversation with the translator, Regensburg, Germany, June 17, 2022.

Newman quotations nearby in Görres' text directly parallel the Newman quotations in Tristram's book. Thus, by studying the text closely, I found indications that, in just a few passages, she likely supplemented her lack of access to primary sources by Newman with quotations by Newman in secondary sources, such as Tristram's book; I note some examples of this in the citations. To be clear, however, this is the exception, not the norm. In almost all cases in which Görres quotes Newman, she is quoting directly from Newman's texts, either from German translations of them or by providing her own German translation from the English text.

One other step in my method to ensure that I provide readers with the English text that corresponds accurately to the passage Görres quotes involved consulting the early- and mid-twentieth-century translations of Newman's works from English to German. Where Görres quoted Newman from someone else's translation of a text into German, access to the German versions of Newman's works—thanks to the library at the Abbey of Heiligenkreuz, Austria—was valuable so that I could verify that I had identified the correct corresponding passage in the original English. Newman repeats some ideas and phrases, sometimes with slight variation in wording in English that does not translate into German; so, in a few instances, a quotation, especially a short phrase, could have come from one of several passages in a work by Newman. As a result, finding the source in English was sometimes quite difficult. Yet by means of reverse engineering this, so to say, when I was able to find such a short phrase *in the context* of a German translation of a work by Newman, I could identify exactly which part of a paragraph Görres was quoting and thus determine the corresponding passage in English.

This process of comparing Görres' text with some of the German translations of Newman yielded a surprise. Görres availed herself of German translations, and, in some cases, she had access to works of Newman only in German, not in English. Yet sometimes, when she had access to a text by Newman in English that was already available in German, she did not quote the existing German translation but instead provided her own translation.[4] This is not as surprising as, at

---

4 In later works by Görres, I have also noticed that she sometimes provides her own translation from English into German, even when an established translation of a text in

first, it might seem, however, when one sees that Görres translated many quotations from works that were available to her only in English, most often from Newman's *Correspondence with John Keble and Others 1839–1845*, Ward's *The Life of John Henry Cardinal Newman*, and Mozley's *Letters and Correspondence of Newman to 1845*. She also translated quotations into German from several secondary works that were in English. Her command of English was excellent.

"Dark, 17" and Detective Work

I am grateful for Gerl-Falkovitz's thoroughness in including citations from the original manuscript of Görres even in cases when Gerl-Falkovitz could not identify what they meant. In doing so, Gerl-Falkovitz left clues in place that I was able to use to take the research a step further. One example is found in chapter 5. In the German edition, one citation reads, "Dark, 17". That is the entire citation, just "Dark, 17", with the (apparent) name "Dark" but no text listed in the bibliography. This one lived up to its name and proved to be a "dark" mystery for Gerl-Falkovitz as well as for me. The lack of information in the citation and the generic name of "Dark" made trying to decipher this difficult. But after two years of wondering about "Dark, 17" and attempting multiple ways to make sense of it, I discovered that Sidney Dark wrote a short biography titled *Newman*, which he published in 1934, thus before Görres wrote her book. At long last, I suspected I might find a light at the end of this, well, *dark* tunnel. Excited by this discovery, I sent my assistant, John Paul Beane, on a mission to obtain a copy of Dark's book via his university's library. In it, he found the quote to which this citation referred (albeit on page 16, not 17; maybe there was more than one edition of Dark's book, or perhaps there was a small error in Görres' notes, or perhaps her handwriting on that note card was hard to read). In any event, Dark was a mystery no more.

German is available. In her book *Bread Grows in Winter*, I found quotations from John Henry Newman's *An Essay on the Development of Christian Doctrine* and C. S. Lewis' *Letters to Malcolm* that are not from the established German translations in print during her lifetime. Here, too, she appears to have been reading these works in English and providing her own translation.

The Citations: Layers of Complications

Annotating this translation was further complicated by the fact that three people contributed to the citations: the author, Görres, in her unfinished manuscript; the editor, Gerl-Falkovitz, in the German edition; and I, who added some 640 citations for this English edition, reformatted the citations that are in the German edition, and modified or added to many of those German citations. Thus, the citations in this translation are different from those in Gerl-Falkovitz's German edition, which, in turn, are different from those in Görres' original unfinished manuscript.

Adding yet one more layer of complexity to the citations in this book, I handled the citations in the introduction by Gerl-Falkovitz differently from the citations in the body of Görres' book. In this English edition, the citations in Gerl-Falkovitz's introduction are, for the most part, my translations of her citations. There are several exceptions to this, however. Where I have added a citation to Gerl-Falkovitz's introduction, there is a note clarifying that the citation came from the translator (indicated by "—Trans."). I reformatted the bibliographic information in her citations to correspond to the *Chicago Manual of Style* so there would be consistency throughout this book. Where possible, to assist the English-speaking readership of this translation, I replaced the German edition of a work Gerl-Falkovitz cited with the English translation or the original English edition of the same work. Lastly, I updated the information in Gerl-Falkovitz's citations to cite recently published editions of works she initially had been able to access only in archives (such as the letters from Ida Görres to Father Paulus Gordan, which she later edited and published).

I initially experimented with several ways to indicate to the reader whether a citation came from Görres, Gerl-Falkovitz, or me—for example, by using various brackets, such as { } for a citation from Görres, < > from Gerl-Falkovitz, and [ ] for mine. But in all of my experiments, the result was a set of complicated citations cluttered with information that would likely be of no interest or use to most readers and, worse, could obscure key information. Sometimes a single citation had three different types of brackets, depending on who contributed which part of the citation. In the interest of clarity (and sanity as well), I abandoned this approach. In the main body of the book, I limit my identification of citations by Gerl-Falkovitz to her observations about what she found in Görres' manuscript. Readers who are interested in the sources that Görres herself used and Gerl-Falkovitz's additional citations should consult a German edition of this book issued prior to the publication of this English translation. (Subsequent editions of the German text may add citations based on my identification of the sources for many of the as-yet unidentified quotations in the German edition.)

Görres wrote this book for a broad audience, not for academic specialists. Throughout her life she was dedicated to writing substantive but nonacademic books and essays on Catholic topics. In omitting details about whether a citation came from Görres, Gerl-Falkovitz, or me and thereby simplifying the citations, I hope that I have been true to the spirit of Görres' intent to make this book accessible to a broad audience.

Orthography: A Patchwork Quilt

After the hurdle of the citations came the challenge of orthography for a translated book comprising so many influences and sources. I chose the following approach.

Where I quote from primary sources, I have respected the original text and left the orthography in those quotations as it appeared in the printed text. This means the reader will find inconsistencies in capitalization as well as between the American orthography in the body of my translation and the British orthography in the many quotations from Newman and others. As a result, sometimes one word appears in the same paragraph with different capitalization. For example, in a quotation from Newman, one reads "Popery", while in the body of the text—that is, in my translation of Görres— I write this word using the standard English orthography of today as "popery". And Newman himself is not consistent. Thus, in one quotation one reads "ordinances" and in another "Ordinances".

Also, there are inconsistencies in orthography in the names and pronouns referring to God when one compares my translation of passages by Görres, the quotations from Newman, and the quotations from the Bible. The quotations from the Bible are, unless otherwise noted, from the Revised Standard Version of the Bible—Second Catholic Edition (RSV2CE). The RSV2CE does not capitalize pronouns referring to God, whereas I do.

I capitalize the word "Church" when referring to the Catholic Church. I use the lowercase "church" when referring to the churches of the Anglicans or Protestants. In the official name of a non-Catholic body, however, such as the Church of Ireland, I use capitalization.

In many of her works, Görres sometimes separates a prefix from the main part of a word by a hyphen to emphasize the meaning of the prefix. This not standard German orthography; it is, rather, simply a quirk in her style. One sees this quirk in this volume, including in the introduction when Gerl-Falkovitz quotes from letters by Görres. For example, one finds "re-sistance" instead of "resistance" (*Wider-Stand* instead of the standard German orthography of *Widerstand*). Where Görres does this, I have placed the word in quotation marks, as with "re-sistance", and noted "[*sic*]" so that the reader will see that this is intentional, not a typographical error.

Görres is inconsistent in how she mentions names of people in this book. Sometimes she mentions only a last name or only a first name. I have left these as she had them in the text. Some of these partial names may have been familiar to readers in German in the mid-twentieth century but may not be familiar to those reading in English today. To assist the reader, I added a register of persons, in which I provide full names along with brief biographical details. In a few cases, in which an individual plays a key role in a passage but is unlikely to be well known to readers, I provide brief details about the person in a citation in addition to listing the person with others in the register of persons.

Overall, it may help the reader to keep in mind that this book is like a patchwork quilt: first came Görres' text, along with many quotations from Newman, secondary sources, and the Bible in her draft; then came the peculiar posthumous origins of the book in a stack of papers along with a box of note cards and Gerl-Falkovitz's meticulous labor in turning this unfinished work into a coherent book; then came the process of translating the resulting volume from German to English. The result is what one might call "patch-work orthography", a "textual quilt".

Acknowledgments

I extend my gratitude to John Paul Beane for his research assistance, to Newman scholar Dr. David Deavel for his advice, and to Hochschule Heiligenkreuz in Austria for the opportunity to be a visiting researcher there during my final year of working on this translation. The access to the joint library of Hochschule Heiligenkreuz and the Abbey of Heiligenkreuz was a tremendous help for this work. I am indebted to the outstanding online collections of digitized texts provided by the National Institute of Newman Studies (among others, at newmanstudies.org) as well as the Internet Archive (archive.org). Ann Aubrey Hanson's fine copyediting skills aided greatly in preparing this manuscript.

Not least of all, I thank Peter Thiel, without whose support this translation would not have been possible. While working on this translation, I enjoyed imagining hosting Peter and John Henry as dinner guests and listening to what would undoubtedly be a fascinating conversation.

Finally, this English translation is dedicated to Hanna-Barbara Gerl-Falkovitz, in gratitude for her scholarship and her effort to keep the memory of Ida Görres alive.

Heiligenkreuz, Austria
Feast of the Immaculate Heart of Mary 2022

INTRODUCTION

A New Discovery
Ida Friederike Görres on Newman

by Hanna-Barbara Gerl-Falkovitz

Hagiography: A Segment of Görres' Life's Work

In 1998, a previously unknown manuscript about John Henry New-man in the possession of psychologists Albert and Silvia Görres surfaced unexpectedly in Munich.[1] Evidently, during and just af-ter World War II, Ida Friederike Görres wrote a book about the "Church Father of the Twentieth Century", as she called him. Newman was just being discovered in her generation for intellec-tual German Catholicism through Theodor Haecker, Josef Wei-ger, Romano Guardini, and Erich Przywara.[2] Conversely, today's

---

An excerpt from "A New Discovery: Ida Friederike Görres on Newman" in English translation was published previously as Hanna-Barbara Gerl-Falkovitz, " 'Only the Lover Discerns': A Brief Introduction to Ida Friederike Görres", trans. Jennifer S. Bryson, *Logos* 23, no. 4 (September 9, 2020): 121–22. This excerpt has been edited lightly for this volume.

[1] Albert Görres, well-known psychologist and writer, was the youngest brother of Carl-Josef Görres, the husband of Ida Friederike Görres, and was considered a son by his sister-in-law [Ida] because of their age difference. Albert's wife, Silvia Görres, was also a psychologist. She reported to the editor of this book [Gerl-Falkovitz] that a manuscript about Newman had been sent to her husband, Albert, by Beatrix Klaiber of Freiburg, the administrator of the estate of Ida Friederike Görres. In 1997, the Newman manuscript, together with the related note cards, was first given to Heinrich Fries, ecumenist and Newman researcher in Munich after whose death in 1998 the materials were passed on to the editor [Gerl-Falkovitz].

[2] Hanna-Barbara Gerl-Falkovitz, "Die Newman-Rezeption in den 20er Jahren in Deut-schland: Edith Stein im Umkreis von Maria Knoepfler, Romano Guardini und Erich Przywara", *Communio* 5 (2001): 434–49.

generation has almost forgotten the once-famous author of the German *renouveau catholique* (Catholic renewal): Ida Friederike Görres (1901–1971). In the meantime, this historian and theologian, who was born Countess Friederike Maria Anna von Coudenhove[-Kalergi] and belonged to the European nobility, was effectively overtaken by silence thirty years after her death and one hundred years after her birth. This silence not only came from the "classic" loss of memory in the next generation but was also due to the cultural break after 1968, which she witnessed with anguish.[3] At that time, nothing seemed as remote as the themes of her work: the Church, the saints, marriage and virginity, woman in a taut juxtaposition to man. Concern for the transmission of the Truth of Christ consumed her toward the end of her life; she died in the heated atmosphere of the Synod of Würzburg in 1971, where she collapsed after passionately submitting her statement for the proposed measure on "Sacrament".[4] Her friends and those who met her, those who were even mentored or led by her, certainly remember her, to the extent they are still alive, with an admiration that shows the reverberation of the deep impression she left.[5]

---

[3] [Most of] Ida Görres' letters are still awaiting publication. Especially in her letters to Father Paulus Gordan, O.S.B. (Beuron [Archabbey, Germany]), her commentary on the social and ecclesiastical demolition of what is "old" is vehement and on target. [After Gerl-Falkovitz published this book, she edited and published Görres' letters to Paulus Gordan: Ida Friederike Görres, *"Wirklich die neue Phönixgestalt?" Ida Friederike Görres über Kirche und Konzil: Unbekannte Briefe 1962–1971 an Paulus Gordan*, ed. Hanna-Barbara Gerl-Falkovitz. I have updated the citations of these letters with the page numbers from the published edition.—TRANS.]

[4] Görres was a member of the committee on marriage for the synod. The statement she presented was a defense of the Catholic teaching on marriage, which she expanded into a short book. Eight days before her death, she submitted the manuscript for this book, her final publication, to the publisher. It appeared as Ida Friederike Görres, *Was Ehe auf immer bindet: Unsystematische Meditation zur Unlösbarkeit der Ehe, anthropologisch betrachtet*. [See Ida Friederike Görres, *What Binds Marriage Forever: Reflections on the Indissolubility of Marriage*, trans. Jennifer S. Bryson (Washington, D.C.: Catholic University of America Press, forthcoming).—TRANS.]

[5] The editor [Gerl-Falkovitz], who was the director of study at Burg Rothenfels at the time, remembers the participants, including Alfons Rosenberg, Father Manfred Hörhammer, Beatrix Klaiber, and Dr. Maria Kallab, and the conversations on the occasion of the conference there about Ida Friederike Görres in May 1980, documented

Nevertheless, some harbingers of a new awareness of Görres are emerging today: Theological doctoral theses were written in Innsbruck and Vienna;[6] in Mooshausen, a location filled with memories,[7] her centenary was commemorated;[8] following several brief portrayals of her life,[9] new editions of her poems have appeared,[10] an edition of letters is planned,[11] and the beginnings of an archive

---

in *Burgbrief Burg Rothenfels*, no. 3, 1980. Conversations between the editor and Father Paulus Gordan in the 1990s and with Erik von Kuehnelt-Leddihn in 2000, who called her "the cleverest woman" he had ever met, confirm the impression from 1980. See the references to Görres in Erik von Kuehnelt-Leddihn, *Weltweite Kirche, Begegnungen und Erfahrungen in sechs Kontinenten 1909–1999* (Stein am Rhein, Germany: Christiana, 2000), 202–203, 211, 488, 495, 556n550.

[6] Anna Findl-Ludescher, *"Stützen kann nur, was widersteht": Ida Friederike Görres—ihr Leben und ihre Kirchenschriften*, Salzburger Theologische Studien 9 (Innsbruck: Tyrolia, 1999); this was Findl-Ludescher's dissertation at the University of Innsbruck, Austria, in 1998. Michael Kleinert, *Es wächst viel Brot in der Winternacht: Theologische Grundlinien im Werk von Ida Friederike Görres*, Studien zur systematischen und spirituellen Theologie 36 (Würzburg: Echter Verlag, 2002); this was Kleinert's dissertation at the University of Vienna in 2000.

[7] ["From 1917 to 1966, Mooshausen was the residence of parish priest Josef Weiger (1883–1966), [Father Romano] Guardini's best friend. A large circle of friends gathered in this rectory, and Guardini himself lived in the rectory from 1943 to 1945, when he had to leave Berlin. . . . Ida Görres knew Fr. Weiger. . . . Her sister Olga, who is buried near M[ooshausen] in Altenstadt an der Iller, may also have been acquainted with Father Weiger." Hanna-Barbara Gerl-Falkovitz, email to the translator, March 16, 2020.]

[8] There was a conference September 28–30, 2001, on the topic "Piety and Revolution". Andreas Batlogg discussed the conference in "Zwischen Pietät und Revolution: Neuentdeckung von Ida Friederike Görres?" *Stimmen der Zeit* 219, no. 12 (2001): 857–60.

[9] Hanna-Barbara Gerl-Falkovitz, "Görres, Ida Friederike", in *Baden-Württembergische Biographien*, ed. B. Ottnad (Stuttgart: Kohlhammer, 1999), 161–63. Hanna-Barbara Gerl-Falkovitz, "Zwischen den Zeiten: Ida Friederike Görres (1901–1971)", in *Freundinnen: Christliche Frauen aus zwei Jahrtausenden* (Munich: Pfeiffer, 1994), 121–32. Susanna Schmidt, "Ida Friederike Görres (1901–1971)", in *Zeitgeschichte in Lebensbildern: Aus dem deutschen Katholizismus des 19. und 20. Jahrhunderts*, ed. Jürgen Aretz et al. (Münster, Germany: Aschendorff Verlag, 2001), 10:179–90.

[10] Ida Friederike Görres, *Gedichte*, ed. and with an introduction by Hanna-Barbara Gerl-Falkovitz (Dresden: Thelem, 2008).

[11] [This collection of letters has since been published as Ida Friederike Görres, *"Wirklich die neue Phönixgestalt?" Ida Friederike Görres über Kirche und Konzil: Unbekannte Briefe 1962–1971 an Paulus Gordan*, ed. Hanna-Barbara Gerl-Falkovitz (Heiligenkreuz, Austria: Be+Be Verlag, 2015)—TRANS.]

are underway.[12] What is available, by no means exhausted, testifies to passionate yet restrained thinking, a supple and sparkling intellect, a piety that was at first romantic and later purified and tested by suffering.

The new significance of Ida Friederike Görres lies—apart from her sometimes-enchanting language and analytical sharpness—without a doubt in her hagiographical achievement, which includes an image of the Church that is both firmly established and open to development. Since the 1930s, she has come to the public's attention through striking biographies of saints, especially women— Elizabeth of Hungary, Mary Ward, Radegund, Hedwig of Silesia; among the male figures she dealt with are Francis of Assisi and Henry Suso, as well as [another, who was not a saint] Teilhard de Chardin. Her books were standard holdings in Catholic libraries. With her masterpiece on Thérèse of Lisieux,[13] Görres had opened the door not only to a new way of looking at the "big little ones" but also to a complex approach to the phenomenon of holiness. If it were not for the fact that she would presumably disdain the word "modern", it could be said that she initiated "modern hagiography", a comprehension of the inner, "human" face of the saints. Or, in words from her diary: "The story of a person goes from being a 'cultural Catholic' to one who becomes a Christian; a path *inside* the Church from the exterior of the 'communion' to the interior of the Divine Reality."[14]

---

[12] There are archives in Germany in Freiburg, Burg Rothenfels, and Erlangen. The archive in Erlangen is the private archive of Hanna-Barbara Gerl-Falkovitz, referred to hereafter as Gerl-Falkovitz Private Archive.

[13] *Das verborgene Antlitz: Eine Studie über Therese von Lisieux* (this first edition [titled simply *Eine Studie über Therese von Lisieux*] burned [in an air raid in 1944]; a second edition [was published as *Das verborgene Antlitz: Eine Studie über Therese von Lisieux* in] 1946, later revised and published in 1958 under the title *Das Senfkorn von Lisieux: Neue Deutungen*. [The English translation appeared in 1959 and is available today as Ida Friederike Görres, *The Hidden Face: A Study of St. Thérèse of Lisieux.*—Trans.]

[14] *Nocturnen: Tagebuch und Aufzeichnungen* (Frankfurt am Main: Knecht, 1949), 102.

The New Discovery: A Newman Draft

That Ida Görres also dealt with Newman was evidenced by five slim but dense pages in her later book *Aus der Welt der Heiligen* (From the world of the saints, 1955).[15] The attentive reader could also find some remarks about reading Newman in her journal *Nocturnen* (1949), her insightful notes mostly from the years of World War II.[16] Görres records in November or December 1944, for example, reading the sermons [of Newman] in the translation by Guido Maria Dreves, which she valued more highly than the translation by Theodor Haecker.[17] The sermons led her to critical self-examination:

> They are so dense, so original, so existential that all my writing about religious matters by comparison seems like pure sulfur to me. He "takes the tone deeper" than I ever dare—beyond all objections . . . says the most outrageous things in proper English, understating, matter-of-factly, without paradox. He, too [like Kierkegaard], emphasizes self-denial, penance, asceticism, "being vigilant", taking risk. . . . But how *differently!* How *gently*, how "politely", really *courtois* [courteous], without bitterness, sweetly, critical only in spirit, not emotionally, without hatred, without any polemics.[18]

The now-discovered, unfortunately fragmentary bundle [containing the manuscript for this book] consists of pasted, trimmed, variously paginated sheets in several folders that explore different themes of her book but also contain several versions of the same theme. Most of it is handwritten, with passages crossed out and with corrections; little of it is typewritten. At the end of one such typed version, here as chapter 8, is the date "18 6 46" (June 18, 1946). On a handwritten sheet of paper, the back of a printed page, is

---

[15] "Über J. H. Newman," in *Aus der Welt der Heiligen* (Frankfurt am Main: Josef Knecht, 1955), 54–62. [This essay is included in this volume as chapter 11.—TRANS.]

[16] *Nocturnen.*

[17] *Nocturnen*, 149, referring to Johann Heinrich [*sic*] Newman, *Ausgewählte Predigten auf alle Sonntage des Kirchenjahres und für die Feste des Herrn von Johann Heinrich Kardinal Newman*, trans. Guido Maria Dreves (Kempten and Munich: Kösel Verlag, 1907).

[18] *Nocturnen*, 149–50. And she refers to Newman briefly on page 83 of *Nocturnen*.

the date "3.8.1947" (August 3, 1947). Another handwritten draft, some of which contains only keywords, is written "28. 8. 48 [August 28, 1948] Weingarten", which appears to indicate the date of a presentation.[19] In the Benedictine Abbey of Weingarten, Newman's sermons were translated into German from 1948 onward.[20] Furthermore, a letter dated November 20, 1948, contains the handwritten addition: "On the 26th, I'm speaking in Heidelberg (students) about Newman!"[21]

In addition, the backs of the notes for the draft of the book are not unimportant: as a rule, the pages are on printed matter or forms from the business mail of her husband, Carl-Josef Görres, but there are also drafts or copies of her own works (and those of others?), such as text fragments on Francis of Assisi and Joan of Arc as well as a sketch for two theatrical plays with biblical subjects, what today would be called bibliodramas.

This bundle of many kinds of notes (and types of paper) scattered over a long period was accompanied by a note-card box of the type common at the time: hundreds of A6 format [4.1 x 5.8 inch] note cards of cut-up paper, mostly business documents, are covered with keywords and excerpts from English and German works of Newman as well as secondary literature. This made it easier (unfortunately, only partially) to annotate the mostly uncited quotations of the text, and it led to a further chronological ordering: the latest date on a piece of business stationery is December 2, 1946; quite a few others also date from 1946. An undated draft letter has been preserved in French, headed "M et RP"; these letters probably stand for "Monseigneur et Révérend Père", since the letter extends thanks for "his" large volume—namely, the complete edition of the letters

---

[19] Weingarten was where Mr. and Mrs. Helmut Kämpf lived (Helmut Kämpf was rector of a school there); they were converts who received instruction for converts from Ida Görres. The letters to Marili Kämpf are in the Gerl-Falkovitz Private Archive.

[20] They appeared in the series *Deutsche Predigtausgabe* (DP) as John Henry Newman, *Predigten: Gesamtausgabe* (Stuttgart, 1948–1962). DP vols. I–VIII: *Pfarr- und Volkspredigten*; DP IX: *Predigten zu Tagesfragen*; DP X: *Predigten zu verschiedenen Anlässen*; DP XI: *Predigten vor Katholiken und Andersgläubigen*, and DP XII: *Der Anruf Gottes. Neun bisher unveröffentlichte Predigten aus der katholischen Zeit* (Stuttgart, 1965).

[21] Carl-Josef Görres to Klara and Hilde Neles, November 20, 1948, with a handwritten greeting from Ida Friederike Görres, Gerl-Falkovitz Private Archive.

of the Little Thérèse. It is therefore for Abbé André Combes, professor of Christian Spirituality at the Institut Catholique in Paris, who first published Thérèse's collection of letters (a few were added later) in 1947. At the end of the year unidentified [in the letter], Görres apologized for her long silence, as she had spent a month in England researching "C N" (Cardinal Newman) and then went to Switzerland.[22] She also felt that her hagiographic interpretation of Thérèse was confirmed by the letters—her significant book on Thérèse came out in 1943. Another note, from a letter, documents her (only) stay in England[23]—namely, at the Oratory in Birmingham,[24] in August 1949, which, by the way, was the centenary of its foundation.

Overall, her main period of work on a planned publication about Newman seems to have been between 1944 and 1949. In addition, there is an undated sketched outline on the back of the letter to Abbé Combes, that is, at the end of 1949 (or was the outline originally on the front and could therefore be dated earlier?). The ten planned chapter headings show the original overall scope and thus reveal the parts that were not written.

---

[22] A passport in Görres' estate (archive of Beatrix Klaiber, Freiburg) contains a stamp for Harwich/England: entry August 5, 1949, exit August 25, 1949, as well as a stamp for the one-day transit through the Netherlands, issued on August 22, 1949, in Birmingham; then a Swiss stamp of entry October 5, 1949, and exit November 1, 1949.

[23] Ida Friederike Görres to Annalies Stiglocher, September 7, 1949, Gerl-Falkovitz Private Archive, 1, front side of page: "I even wanted to take your letter to England at the beginning of August to answer it there!"

[24] Sister Lutgard Govaert, F.S.O., to the editor [Gerl-Falkovitz], March 23, 2002, Gerl-Falkovitz Private Archive. The letter characterizes the research that was common in Birmingham in the 1950s: The Oratorians would "look for a room in a B&B-inn or with a family from the parish. A room for consultation was then made available to them in the Oratory during the day, and the archivist then brought them the desired manuscripts and texts from the archive. . . . Ida F. Görres can only have been in Birmingham in 1949 for Newman studies: 'The College' at Littlemore was still owned at the time by the Anglican Diocese of Oxford, and all the cottages were rented—it was a poor house. The beatification process was not opened until the 1950s, so there was still no particular interest in Newman research." In fact, there are still forty-four handwritten DIN-A5-size excerpts with the side note "Ms. Orat." (manuscript from the Oratory) on which the diaries not yet published at that time, especially from the early period, are excerpted.

But why was this work that was so far along, for which she spent a month of study—previously unknown—in England in August 1949, not completed?

The Postwar Period: Exiting the Ark, Friendship with Newman Specialist Father Breucha

In the years in which she was presumably reading and taking notes on Newman, Ida Görres' productivity was astonishing. In 1943, in the middle of the war, her significant book on Thérèse appeared,[25] and in 1946, the momentous "Letter on the Church" appeared in the November issue of the newly founded *Frankfurter Hefte*.[26] Incidentally, Newman's passage about "The Gentleman" (translated [into German] by Wilhelm Gulde) was printed in its first issue; this may have bothered Görres as an "incorrect categorization" of Newman, as will become clear in the following text, with her own verdict on him as a gentleman.[27] In 1949, three books followed in one fell swoop, all of which had matured during the past few years: *Der verborgene Schatz* (The hidden treasure), a collection of poetry, as well as *Nocturnen* and *Von Ehe und von Einsamkeit* (*On Marriage and on Being Single*),[28] a "litter" that was continued in 1950 with *The Church in the Flesh*.[29] This astonishing, even exuberant work was curbed beginning in October 1950 by severe episodes of illness that left Görres almost entirely bedridden for years, though this does not completely interrupt her creative power and is perceived by her as a purification.

---

[25] Parts of Görres' Newman draft are written on the back of the typed pages of her Thérèse book *The Hidden Face*.

[26] Ida Friederike Görres, "Brief über die Kirche", *Frankfurter Hefte* 1, no. 8 (November 1946): 716–33. [An English translation, albeit incomplete, was published in 1949: Ida Friederike Görres, "A Letter on the Church (1946)", trans. Ida Friederike Görres, *Dublin Review* 223 (Winter 1949): 71–89. Görres describes this 1949 version in English as an "adaptation" of the German text. I am preparing a new, complete translation of this letter into English for a future publication.—TRANS.]

[27] John Henry Newman, "Der Gentleman", trans. William Gulde, *Frankfurter Hefte* 1, no. 1 (1946): 89–90. [This is a translation of the first paragraph of section 10, Discourse 8 in John Henry Newman, *The Idea of a University* (London: Longmans, Green, 1907), 208–10.—TRANS.]

[28] Ida Friederike Görres, *Von Ehe und von Einsamkeit*. [This book has been translated into English by Jennifer S. Bryson as *On Marriage and on Being Single*, forthcoming.]

[29] Ida Friederike Görres, *The Church in the Flesh*, trans. Jennifer S. Bryson (Providence: Cluny Media, 2023).

If one takes a closer look at these fertile postwar years, one sees they are guided by a resolution to set out across the ruins, with wounds that are still immeasurably deep and not healed:

We, too, stepped out of the mysterious, invisible ark—how often have we called it that!—those of us who had been kept secure for six or even twelve years during the rising flood of deaths. We stepped out into the ruins of a world that was drowned not in water but in fire, blood, and tears, in a judgment that may well be viewed alongside that expiatory flood from early human history. We, too, are still in a world full of mud and corpses, full of carrion and horror that is visible as well as invisible, under the busy parasitic swarm of all the darkness that feeds on decomposition and thrives on destruction. And above us, the same sky spans, blue as ever above the most recent and at the same time first human of a new creation; above our heads as well shines the rainbow of God's promises in the clouds. . . . We must never allow the thought to enter our minds that our being spared was a "sign" of our special worth. We know only one thing: since we remain, God still wants something from us. That we are still alive means there is a calling. What is to come is entrusted to us. We have to prepare the path on which God will again draw near to our people. . . . We have to break through again to the roots and foundations of our existence, to the entrusted and unadulterated inheritance of our faith.[30]

Work on Newman is situated in this spiritual space. As early as October 1945, on the hundredth anniversary of his conversion, a Newman Congress was held in Cologne, chaired by Robert Grosche and Paul Simon; in September 1946, a symposium followed in Nuremberg.[31] That same year, Hugo Rahner wrote in a letter from Innsbruck to Otto Karrer: "Consider that the people here are all inexpressibly longing for something spiritual . . . and that there is a

---

[30] Ida Friederike Görres, "Was wir wollen", in *Kristall: Bild und Ebenbild. Werkheft für Mädchen*, ed. Ida Friederike Görres (Frankfurt am Main: Josef Knecht, 1947), 4–5.

[31] Then the journal *Die Internationale Cardinal-Newman-Studien* (International Cardinal Newman studies) and the associated Newman-Kuratorium (Newman Board of Trustees) were founded. The German Newman Society was founded in 1990 by Günter Biemer, the chair of Religious Education and Catechetics at [the University of] Freiburg. Simon's lecture was revised and expanded as Paul Simon, "Newman und der englische Katholizismus", in *Newman Studien* 1, eds. Heinrich Fries and Werner Becker (Nuremberg: Glock and Lutz, 1948), 13–28.

great deal of interest in Newman; everybody has a voracious appetite for your two volumes, which I have been constantly lending out here and there."[32] At the end of the 1940s, Heinrich Fries,[33] Werner Becker, Johannes Artz, Franz Michel Willam, and Nicolas Theis began a lifetime of work on Newman;[34] in 1948, Joseph Lutz published a work on the "Life and Times of Newman".[35]

Görres' studies, however, are undoubtedly stimulated by her significant, inspiring friendship with Father Hermann Breucha from the Degerloch area of Stuttgart, to whose congregation the Görres couple had belonged since 1939. This bond with Father Breucha (1902–1972), one year removed from Görres in both birth and death, is one of the male friendships—or more precisely, friendships with the male intellect—with which her life was rich.[36] Approvingly, she quoted the words of Annette Kolb about Catherine of Siena regarding her "Diana-like man-loving soul"[37]—and this struck her too. "She once told us about her friendship with Father Breucha that only her love for her husband had moved her as deeply

---

[32] Roman Siebenrock, "Wahrheit, Gewissen und Geschichte: Eine systematisch-theologische Rekonstruktion des Wirkens John Henry Kardinal Newmans", in *Internationale Cardinal-Newman-Studien* 15 (Sigmaringendorf, Germany: Regio-Verlag Glock und Lutz, 1996), 68n233.

[33] To mention just one of many publications: Heinrich Fries, *Die Religionsphilosophie Newmans* (Stuttgart: Schwabenverlag, 1948).

[34] Compare the characterization by Siebenrock, in the section "Wiederentdeckung Newmans vor dem Zweiten Vatikanischen Konzil", in "Wahrheit, Gewissen und Geschichte", 68–71.

[35] Joseph A. Lutz, *Kardinal John Henry Newman: Ein Zeit- und Lebensbild* (Einsiedeln, Germany, 1948).

[36] These include Gustav Siewerth, Werner Bergengruen, Alfons Rosenberg, Father Manfred Hörhammer, Father Paulus Gordan, Walter Nigg, Heinrich Kahlefeld, Hans Asmussen, Werner Becker, Bishop Otto Spülbeck, and in the 1960s also Joseph Ratzinger. Strangely enough, Romano Guardini remained distant from her, even though she admired him. For a description of her promising encounter with Guardini, which was then disrupted by someone else, see her letter to Paulus Gordan dated October 12, 1968, in Görres, *"Wirklich die neue Phönixgestalt?"*, 385–87. To women, she made less pronounced, meaning fewer, intellectual references; exceptions were Josepha Fischer and Birgitta zu Münster. The latter published, for her part, John Henry Newman, *Maria im Heilsplan*, trans. and with an introduction by Birgitta zu Münster, O.S.B. (Freiburg im Breisgau: Herder, 1953).

[37] Letter to Paulus Gordan, September 12, 1968, in *"Wirklich die neue Phönixgestalt?"*, 376. [In this letter, Görres mentions in passing that this is something Annette Kolb said about Catherine of Siena, but there is no information about where Kolb said this.—Trans.]

as the relationship with Father Breucha. She could be jealous of either of them. . . . With Father Breucha, she exchanged views on her writing. She wrote the 'Letter on the Church', published in the *Frankfurter Hefte* in consultation with Father Breucha."[38] Görres also notes, however, a "conflict with Breucha that went on for four to five years" around 1948, which she even described in an unpublished account as "*very* much *cum ira et studio* [with anger and verve], even, unfortunately, grim resentment"[39]—without the core of the conflict being known.

Franziska Werfer's sensitive, detailed picture of Breucha's life conveys the portrait of a truly important theologian who had been schooled in Augustine, Newman, Möhler, Sailer, Scheeben, Adam, and Guardini, and in 1967 Breucha received an honorary doctor of Catholic Theology from the University of Tübingen.[40] In the war and postwar years, he was one of the most important Catholic minds of the time. He was part of Una Sancta (which he cofounded in 1941), was on the radio (starting in 1945), and above all was involved in higher education (starting in 1934, increasingly after 1945).[41] He was also a thought leader of the Second Vatican

---

[38] Letter from Bärbel Wintersinger to Hanna-Barbara Gerl-Falkovitz, March 11, 1991, Gerl-Falkovitz Private Archive.

[39] Letter to Paulus Gordan, Wednesday of Holy Week [March 29,] 1967, in *"Wirklich die neue Phönixgestalt?"*, 266.

[40] Franziska Werfer, *Hermann Breucha (1902–1972): Aufbruch der Kirche im Bild eines Priesters* (Weißenhorn, Germany: Konrad Verlag, 1982). From 1938 to 1970, Breucha worked as a liturgist. He was the preacher and pastor in the parish of the Assumption of the Virgin Mary in Degerloch [Germany], which Ida Görres and her husband joined in 1939 when the war broke out. Regarding Werfer herself as a colleague of Breucha, see Maria Glaser-Fürst, *Franziska Werfer 1906–1985. Die erste katholische Theologin und Religionslehrerin im Dienst der Kirche in der Diözese Rottenburg—Zeugnis eines Lebens aus Glaube, Wahrheit, Liebe* (Weissenhorn, Germany: Konrad Verlag, 2001).

[41] Werfer lists demanding, high-level educational events (Werfer, *Hermann Breucha*, 318–23). Görres lectured, for example, in the [19]40s about Thérèse of Lisieux. During the week of prayer for the reunification of Christianity in January 1957, Breucha had Norbert Schiffers speak about Newman (Werfer, *Hermann Breucha*, 321); Schiffers had done his doctorate with Heinrich Fries in Tübingen on "The Unity of the Church according to John Henry Newman", [later published as] Norbert Schiffers, *Die Einheit der Kirche nach John Henry Newman* (Düsseldorf: Patmos Verlag, 1956). In a letter of April 30–May 1, 1964, to Father Paulus Gordan, Görres writes about "the priest [of our city] Breucha, who was our priest for 20 years, for my husband for 25 [years] until now— and in his educational work, I was a pillar, so to speak, full-time". Görres, *"Wirklich die neue Phönixgestalt?"*, 40.

Council who, however, almost had a breakdown under the painful upheavals of 1968 and in regard to the discussion about *Humanae vitae*.[42] Görres, at that time already living in Freiburg, wrote to him in October 1968:

> The news of your illness upset me very much—however, strangely enough (or not!) with mixed feelings, namely, in addition to the sadness yet also a great joy that there *are* still people who are so touched and worried by concern about the Church that they can collapse from it. . . . It also makes me ill inside, it disturbs me day and night, it can only be drowned out by something else for an hour, never extinguished, never really alleviated. . . .
>
> With outright horror one realizes what enormous cavities must have already been present under seemingly solid stretches of the foundation that suddenly collapse and then one stands in front of the rubble.[43]

This second "perishing" as a result of the era actually was a seal of death, so to speak, for both of them. The first "perishing", however, was overcome by a new beginning, by the graceful possibilities of the "zero hour" in 1945. For both, Newman, the Church Father of the Modern Era, belonged to this grace of a new beginning; when they left the ark, they brought Newman out with them.

Breucha had known and loved Newman since his theology studies in Tübingen, where he wrote a thesis on *An Essay on the Development of Christian Doctrine*—which defined his image of the Church and shaped it forever.[44] For his Sunday evening meditations in Degerloch, he—himself a great preacher—used Newman as a ba-

---

[42] See Werfer, *Hermann Breucha*, 280, where Breucha defends the encyclical and deeply regrets the "great confusion of minds".

[43] Werfer, *Hermann Breucha*, 281–82. Since there is no edition of Görres' letters yet, [I will] quote the follow-on point as well: "But even so it still says: 'Lift up your heads!' We're sitting now right in the middle of the assault at the gates of Hell, that's evident to me—and we can test whether we ourselves believe the promise that these will not triumph. This drives me again and again—even if I have to admit that I feel almost schizophrenically split between this drive and that other drive to be completely silent." Compare this with her letter to Father Paulus Gordan on July 27, 1968: "Pastor Breucha, the poor good man, had a serious nervous breakdown last week *due to anguish about the Church*—first he cried day and night, now he is in the hospital. I can understand it, though I'm of tougher Japanese stock, thank God." *"Wirklich die neue Phönixgestalt?"*, 364.

[44] Werfer, *Hermann Breucha*, 21.

sis,[45] as he also owned the famous edition of Newman's selected works [in German] published by Grünewald Verlag in the 1920s.[46] Incidentally, no fewer than eight new (partial) translations were published in Germany between 1945 and 1948; among them was a small edition, completely anonymous: John Henry Newman, *Gespräche mit Gott. Ausgewählte Worte* [Conversations with God: selected passages].[47] Everything points to Breucha as the editor.

Görres seems to have borrowed from him works related to Newman.[48] In addition, she had many valuable discussions with Father Breucha and suggestions from him.

"That is what is irreplaceable about male conversation—the female is at best an echo or material enrichment of information, but always 'soft' (a cloud, a feather bed, at best rubber—a bit springy!), but the other is always 're-sistance' [*sic*], even if it is not a contradiction, nor is it critically determining, tone-setting, etc., in confirmation."[49]

And vice versa: she gave him a small crimson strip from Newman's cardinal's robe as a "precious possession"; she had brought it

---

[45] See Hermann Breucha, "Newman als Prediger", in *Newman Studien* 1, 157–77.

[46] Werfer, *Hermann Breucha*, 21ff. See also Hermann Breucha, *Hoffnung auf das Ewige: Ausgewählte Predigten* (Weissenhorn, Germany: Konrad Verlag, 1983). Of the planned ten volumes of selected works [of Newman], edited by Matthias Laros at Grünewald Verlag in Mainz, [Germany], only volumes 1–6 and 9–10 were published.

[47] Werner Becker, "Chronologie von Übersetzungen der Werke Newmans", in *Newman Studien* 1, 295–300 (see in particular page 300). Newman's book *Gespräche mit Gott* contains translations from his *Meditations and Devotions*.

[48] Görres wrote, "I am reading in a hurry now, because I should actually return the Newman sermons in the Dreves edition." *Nocturnen*, 149. There is not yet an inventory of the library of the Görres couple along with their possessions, insofar as these can be reconstructed.

[49] Görres, letter to Father Paulus Gordan, June 14, 1965, in *"Wirklich die neue Phönixgestalt?"*, 108. See also her letter to him of April 30–May 1, 1964: "It's curious how much one wants to talk to men—even very nice and beloved girlfriends (how I hate that insipid word! I use it only when really necessary) can, at least in my experience, always only either confirm one's own point of view or offer factual information from what they already know. Both are good and useful, but they don't get oneself one iota further in what's actually on one's mind. Authentic, 'fermenting' suggestions, whether through supplementation = [which equals] confirmation or through critical, goading contradiction that forces revision and correction, I get this only from men. That is why I need fraternal collaboration so much; however rare it may be." *"Wirklich die neue Phönixgestalt?"*, 42–43.

back from her research visit to Birmingham in 1949.[50] Who could have bestowed this honor on her there?

All the preparations and all the inspiration seemed to have been in place to carry out the work that had begun—yet it remained just partially chiseled. In this regard, some things can be conjectured, but nothing can be proven definitively. The first obstacle to be mentioned is the unpleasant, even hurtful, response to the "Letter on the Church" at the end of 1946, which so thoroughly misunderstood the inner motivation from which she wrote this reproach against the clergy.[51] There are some substantive indications that the example of the great English theologian plays a direct role in her "Letter on the Church"[52]—his tense, difficult-to-balance attitude of criticism and approval [of the Church], with the latter being the real source of criticism:

> The most important thing about the Newman letters for me is the insight into how far back our dichotomy between modern, somehow "reformist", and "reactionary" Catholics goes back: in fact, a full hundred years. . . . Newman is really "our" patron; he has the only possible attitude, and at the same time the one that is so difficult to implement—the clearest, coolest critical insight into the thousands of grievances and undesirable developments in the Church and the absolutely inevitable need for many reforms, as well as the

[50] Maria Glaser-Fürst, administrator of the estate of Father Breucha and Franziska Werfer, wrote to the editor [Gerl-Falkovitz] on March 6, 2002: "Mrs. Görres once gave a small strip of crimson fabric measuring 4 x 1 cm together with a framed picture with a photo of the Oratory in Birmingham, a photo of his [Newman's] grave in Birmingham in the Oratory cemetery, and various dried plants to the parish priest Breucha. She brought everything from Birmingham; I do not know when."

[51] [Görres's 1946 "Letter on the Church" unleashed a storm of responses, some of them quite harsh. An anthology of merely a selection of the responses to her letter is more than nine hundred pages long: Jean-Yves Paraïso, ed., "Brief über die Kirche", *Die Kontroverse um Ida Friederike Görres Aufsatz—Ein Dokumentationsband* (Cologne: Böhlau Verlag, 2005).—TRANS.]

[52] In fact, her "Letter on the Church" is introduced, as a sort of motto for the letter, with Newman's letter to John Keble on September 6, 1843: "P.S.—You must bear in mind that, if I speak strongly in various places in the Sermons against the existing state of things, it is not wantonly, but to show *I feel the difficulties* that certain minds are distressed with." Görres, "Brief über die Kirche", 71. This quotation is from John Henry Newman, *Correspondence of John Henry Newman with John Keble and Others, 1839–1845* (London: Longmans, Green, 1917), 260.

passionate one, devotion and loyalty to "Rome", which touches and stirs the whole person in all the heavy burden of this term "Rome".[53]

It is precisely this innermost, unshakable affection for the Church that Ida Görres herself has that she encounters with Newman without contradiction. Even in the persistence of stormy criticism, which was felt to be unjustified, a wonderful mirroring of Newman is at work:

And I was alone out on a limb and the thunderstorm of indignation pelted down on my presumptuous head. . . . For the other [negative letters] I took Newman as an example, who never responded to being knocked about; half out of arrogance, half out of indolence (as he even says of himself)—and with a bit of good intention along the way.[54]

Despite this brave soldierly attitude—to which Ida Görres tended already as it was, "brave as a cherry blossom"[55]—it is possible that the long-lasting consequences of her ominous "Letter on the Church" led to her illness, which developed in the fall of 1950. But her activity did not halt immediately; at least, in 1946–1947, she helped establish "quasi-university courses" in Stuttgart.

A second obstacle can also only be surmised. It is possible that her other publications of these years, already mentioned, were evidently more manageable in terms of the subject matter. Regarding Newman, new knowledge aplenty was rolling in; it was increased and accelerated by Werner Becker, who published [the journal] [Internationale Cardinal-] Newman-Studien, together with Heinrich Fries, from 1948 onward. In a letter, albeit after 1951, Görres noted:

Most interesting discussion with W. B. about Newman. Pity I can't think of resuming my book about him. But I could never catch up with all the newly discovered, or rather newly published, material that would certainly alter the current picture profoundly. W. B. himself

[53] Nocturnen, 237–38.
[54] Letter to Hermann Stenger, March 29, 1955; the quotation was provided by Anna Findl-Ludescher.
[55] Görres used to quote this Japanese saying.

has already unearthed 250 hitherto unknown manuscripts of sermons dating from his Anglican days.[56]

The Church in the Flesh, published [in German] in 1950, shows traces that are infused with her previous work on Newman. He is cited and quoted more than twenty times, and he supports her thought in a prominent passage in which she borrows a section from the Newman manuscript about the dawn of the years after the [First World] War, in which the Catholic intellectual life regained prestige.[57]

About twenty years later, again, Walter Nigg—who found in relation to his own work [on hagiography] that Görres' hagiographical achievement was groundbreaking[58]—tried to persuade her to resume her book on Newman—but this did not come to be.[59] Her book remained just partially chiseled; in spite of everything, however, it appears to be complete in its sketch of Newman's character and in its treatment of individual topics.

---

[56] *Broken Lights*, 348. Unfortunately, neither the addressees nor the dates of the letters in *Broken Lights* are noted. [W. B. is most likely Werner Becker.] Werner Becker was acquainted with Görres—apart from their common background of Burg Rothenfels— through the Leipzig Oratory, where [Görres and her husband] had married at Easter 1935.

[57] In chapter 3 of *The Church in the Flesh*, Görres writes: "'The tide will turn.' We have experienced it. The splendor of those postwar [post–WWI] years, when the first reports from the Academic Conference in Ulm, from Burg Rothenfels and Maria Laach, flew through the country and new stars rose up in our skies, can never diminish for us who were there: Haecker and Guardini, Przywara and Lippert, Abbot Ildefons Herwegen, Gertrud von Le Fort, and Sigrid Undset! One no longer belonged to the disinherited; one had reentered the Western community of the Living Spirit" (p. 97). Compare this with the opening passage of chapter 10 of this volume.

[58] See his beautiful obituary: Walter Nigg, "Eine unter tausend: Ida Friederike Görres", in *Heilige und Dichter* (Freiburg: Olten Verlag, 1982), 227–49.

[59] Letter from Carl-Josef Görres to Fr. Paulus Gordan, June 19, 1971: "Newman (regarding whom Nigg again offered her encouragement) . . ." It is possible that Görres and Nigg exchanged views on this at the conference on "Holiness Today" in Freiburg at the end of April 1971 (shortly before her death on May 15, 1971). [Ida] Görres remarked in retrospect, "Lion's share contested by Nigg—I am always as well as more and more delighted by his genuine, simply deep piety" (letter to Father Paulus Gordan, May 11, 1971). *"Wirklich die neue Phönixgestalt?"*, 500 and 494–95, respectively.

Searching for What Is Distinctive about This Book

[Görres writes:]

> If you ask me what really moves and captivates me most about the
> great figure of our "Father Newman", as we call him with love and
> adoration, I do not need to think long about the answer: it is not his
> noble humanistic harmony, not his embodying the form of gentle-
> man transfigured by Christianity, not the vastness of his gaze into the
> future beyond what his contemporaries saw, his carefully reasoned
> sharpness of judgment, his impartiality and independence of con-
> science, not the soul-stirring power of his sermons, not the compre-
> hensive scholarship of the consummate scholar, not the incorruptibly
> heart-searching vision of a great psychologist, educator, and spiritual
> guide, which reveals itself in his sermons as well as in his letters—one
> could go on for a long time and enumerate merits, gifts, and virtues
> that radiate toward us captivatingly from his truly noble image. But
> it is none of that. Rather, it is this one realization: that Newman was
> a man who was sacrificed.[60]

In contrast to an ostensibly familiar image of Newman as a "gentleman", as the representative of high and even the highest culture,
Görres' draft reveals a distinctive view—which perhaps grew out
of her own painful experiences—of the man who led the English
Catholics out of their ghetto. Astonishingly, Görres draws out the
âme détruite, the "shattered soul"—an expression she borrows from
the description of Thérèse of Lisieux.[61] In a surprising application of
this to Newman, it means the mental attitude by which passion for
Truth pays the price of lasting, thoroughly saturating bitterness—
but without loss of "sweetness" in human interactions and with
the unbreakable love for the true flock of Christ. Newman thus
left the Anglican church to suffer multiple humiliations unexpectedly from fellow Catholics and from Rome itself. Görres traces
Newman's long years of being written off, in which he is denied
public and so-greatly-needed effectiveness—such as the failure of
his conception for a Catholic university in Dublin—and in which
he is left to be directed only toward an incomprehensible humility

---

[60] Chapter 1, 51.

[61] [For a discussion about how Görres understands the phrase *âme détruite*, "a shattered
soul", see the citations for chapter 1.—TRANS.]

and piety, understood in a very masculine sense. He is in constant contradiction to his era. On one of Görres' note cards, one reads: "Wordsworth, Coleridge, Shelley—all the *ingenious young men* of his era praised and proclaimed freedom, whatever was new and emerging—among them N peculiarly lonely, *strictly proclaiming commitment*, even *divine. Byron: moral autonomy!* the most-read poet! N's audience!"; on another: "In a way, he dies 'naked' like [Saint] Francis."

But this "sacrifice" is not carried out in the outside world alone. In Görres' view, Newman himself had to remain mysteriously incomplete, despite the abundance of his talents—no, precisely because of them. On a page with an outline, one reads under the heading "Newman Notes—Plan":

> Preface: Riddle of Biogr[aphy]—cloudy glass[62]—shimmer emanating from his character—stronger and weaker through the lack of embodiment
> Großsedlitz Park
> large-scale plan . . . empty sites—large sketch, only partially executed
> Old age: character *not* stunted—the same width at the base, *in the middle* something destroyed—why?
> 19th cent.—"Golden Apple"

Two things stand out: "embodiment" and "Großsedlitz Park" (the symbol of the "Golden Apple" is explained in chapter 1). Regarding "embodiment", a note that is not included [in this volume] mentions the keyword "Nature—Newman Goethe-like?" with the following reflection:

> A nature of Goethe-like abundance? . . . It was precisely a *talent* that is recognizable, but not actualized, through N's authentic celibacy. The G'[oethe-]like side: a relationship to nature, beauty, etc., would, of course, have come about only through eros, more precisely: realized and made incarnate through women; encounter and fertility (Dartmoor—Hurrell Froude's sister ??); that is why it is so peculiarly lit, as by moonlight; with N, it is there, like a faint glow, transfiguring, transparent, but not really tangible—potency, not actuality.—But

---

[62] "Cloudy" does not refer to Newman but to the gap between him and the view of him by those who came later.

also, not 'repression'. In his life and his character there is, therefore, room for the *anima*—romantics are not afraid of their own feminine component.

Another piece of paper noted:

Noct[urnen]. II. 94 Newman "androgynous"?

With Berdj<ajew> [Nikolai Berdyaev] quote. What is bodily and warm comes into what is masc[uline] life through women—which, for example, one cannot imagine in Goethe, even where he has nothing *directly* to do with the feminine, *that* is completely absent. The air is very thin—and his lyrics are also very "moon-like", like the music of Bach played on the spinet and harpsichord: like crystal, without earthy heaviness. But is it actually a *deficiency* to see the "soul" at some point so "pure", not in the moral sense, unfurled in its own sphere—"as if it existed alone"? N's effect on people, especially the young, may have been in and of itself something like that of an angel.

The reference to "Großsedlitz Park" refers to a group of four poems that originate from Görres' ministry work with girls during her time in Dresden (1931–1935) and is a reference to the half-finished landscape park of a royal castle in Saxon Switzerland near Pirna. In the first poem are the lines:

Conceived very grand, with a princely motion of the hand
A contour cast far across the terrain—
which now decays into nameless soil,
clearly never to be completed toil,
already without a wish and still caught in a dream
of what never was or will be
as if a glass bears a pale trace on its plane
of a face of which it once bore a gleam.[63]

It is precisely this puzzling imperfection that Görres sees in herself as well—"Isn't my deepest image trapped in you?"[64]—and she catches the scent of the same thing in Newman, in the secret kinship of those who "thought big" but were broken. There was also a note card in the box of note cards she left behind, headed "*Noct[urnen]*. May 1946, II, 75" with the following content:

---

[63] "Park von Großsedlitz", in *Gedichte*, 24. [Translation by Jennifer S. Bryson.]
[64] "Park von Großsedlitz", 24.

In this, I feel such a kindred sense to N: this is exactly the burden
on his Cath. life—the keen knowledge of what he could actually
achieve and accomplish if—and at the same time, one floor below,
before God alone, the complaint that he lacks "zeal" (sm[all]. prayer
book 166f), and somewhere too, that "cowardice", as he calls it, is
allegedly the root of all failure with him.

In any case, Görres does not view him—in spite of his early fame
and late dignity as cardinal—as having the distinction of standing
out, but rather the distinction of veiled holiness:

> Since then, perhaps our eyes have sharpened to recognize the sign of
> the face of Christ, which is holiness, not only in the prophet, mar-
> tyr, or miracle worker. And is this mysterious radiance not also com-
> pellingly revealed in the life of this great misunderstood and tested
> man—in the way that he faces his prolonged, burdensome cross and
> matures and perfects himself through this?
>
> It seems like a miracle, a miracle of grace, that Newman did not
> succumb to bitterness.[65]

This image of Newman, which Görres captures, shimmers more
compactly, wonderfully laconically from his remark "this fair world
. . . to admire it, while we abstain from it"[66]—reformulated by
her as:

> The theme of this drama can be roughly paraphrased as follows: that
> an extraordinary nature, a Goethe-like abundance of talents, which
> seems destined for a victorious and conquering encounter and expe-
> rience in the world, thwarted by spirit and grace, must accomplish
> triumph over the world in the form of renunciation and precisely
> in this wreckage, in the fate of failure, the triumph over the world
> achieves its peculiar human and Christian perfection.[67]

Her observations on Newman's concept of conscience are rich;
this concept, when grasped concretely, drives him into solitude and

---

[65] Chapter 7, 180. [In the German edition, this citation is for chapter 8. This quotation appears in chapter 7, however.—TRANS.]

[66] The footnote in the German edition reads, "Quote by Newman without citation
in the note box"; underneath is the additional note, "Max Scheler, *Über Ressentiment um
moralisches Wertgefühl* Lpg 1912 p 41." This quotation is from John Henry Newman, "Sermon 19. Present Blessings", in *Parochial and Plain Sermons* (London: Longmans, Green,
1906), 5:273.—TRANS.

[67] Handwritten note card.

is the driving inner force underlying his destiny. Thus, relative to this concept, his notorious toast is even harder to understand: "to the Pope, if you please,—still, to Conscience first"[68]—if this sentence is cited a bit smugly as a quick way out in the event of a conflict with the Magisterium. On the contrary, Görres shows how extremely careful Newman was with formation of conscience:

> In what we call conscience, we love to seek the ally of our weakness, the defense attorney of our failure, the writ of protection for our passions, the accomplice of temptation. Newman wants man to find in his conscience the ally of his highest self, the anchor of his decisions, the guardian of his purest possibility, the confidante and guarantor of his destiny: "As the seed has a tree within it, so men have within them Angels."[69]

The path through Newman's gradually wavering, then crumbling theological conviction shows, according to Görres, that the great drama, the *agere contra* [going against the grain] of the Anglican theologian, lies precisely in following conscience—namely, acting against one's own roots, against one's ancestry, with all-consuming, yes painful, consequences. On this, there is a note on an isolated piece of notepaper:

> Here it is perhaps most poignantly revealed how little Newman's conversion had to do with feelings, and how everything had to do with deciding on the Truth.—So varied the ways in which God calls souls to His Church are, and how carefully every generalizing statement regarding this must be held in check: It is not uncommon that a person who, for whatever reason, is alienated from and uninvolved in his ancestral religious community, dissatisfied in mind and heart, starts searching and, looking for religion in general, discovers and embraces it in the Catholic Church. That someone who, like Newman, lives with all the fibers of his being embedded in his first church, pulls himself out of such attachment to take on a foreign principle, is— fortunately, one might say—a rare vocation. Others look for beauty,

---

[68] "Certainly, if I am obliged to bring religion into after-dinner toasts . . . I shall drink—to the Pope, if you please,—still, to Conscience first." John Henry Newman, "A Letter Addressed to the Duke of Norfolk", in *Certain Difficulties Felt by Anglicans in Catholic Teaching* (London: Longmans, Green, 1901), 2:261.

[69] Chapter 10, 233. The final sentence of this paragraph is from Newman, "Sermon 24. The Power of the Will", in *Parochial and Plain Sermons*, 5:351.

abundance, art, warmth, and a home in Catholicism; Newman, already endowed with all this, is looking for nothing in her but the Truth.

Görres writes underneath this in red: "Fairy tales of false vs. real bride"—that story in which the real bride, only after all-consuming erroneous paths and agonies, turns out to be the one always meant to be and sought after.

Nevertheless, Görres disagrees with the interpretations of Bremond[70] and Laros, who see in Newman from the beginning a withdrawn, mysterious man who is set apart; and this brings to the fore her interesting, capacious view. In Newman, there is an authentic, astonishing ability to love and worthiness to be loved—in spite of everything and in everything—and it is only from this that his surrender of himself comes at such a high price: "N like a tree— with a protruding crown; providing shade, solitary, but hidden in the ground: carried by a dense network of roots that is even more branched out, from which it lives, blossoms, and is fruitful. 'The great solitary one'? Bremond, Laros—overlook this man's amazingly strong and diverse bond to community." The page of notes includes references to Newman as the "tutor" of his family, to "friendship like bread" with Froude, Keble, Pusey, to the saints of the early Church (Chrysostom)—from which what is given away becomes understandable in the first place: "Who can describe the sacrifice, the tearing out of the roots of the heart? Not a dispassionate scholar. Man between 2 loves. Romantic. Screams of love and pain 7 years— 3 years 'agony'—"

Circling Back Later On

In Görres' two published journals, especially *Broken Lights* starting in 1951, there are crumbs regarding Newman that reveal further thinking about or circling around this mountain range.[71] Görres considers some "fragmentary thoughts"; they continue to grind

---

[70] Henri Bremond, *Newman. Essai de biographie psychologique* (Paris: Bloud, 1906); English: *The Mystery of Newman*, trans. H. C. Corrance (London: Williams and Norgate, 1907). Bremond gave an important initial spark for the engagement with Newman on the continent, albeit in a very psychologizing manner.

[71] [The first of the two journals Gerl-Falkovitz mentions is Görres, *Nocturnen*. The second, which has been translated into English, is Görres, *Broken Lights: Diaries and Let-*

the previous facets in ever-greater reflection. Newman's ability to love, which was still perceived as "moon-like", attracts particular attention; it is modified in a more sensual way, while retaining all its purity. He is now clearly one of the "saints with a special gift for eros" (next to Teresa of Avila, Bernard, Francis, Catherine of Siena, and Henry Suso)[72]—but here, what is really meant is eros in contrast to agape, which appears in the above sense in the "cold, gaunt, straitened (Berdyaev calls it 'glazed') form . . . as 'a duty' ".[73] But Newman's picture shifts into being warm and touching, not least because of newly emerging sources:

> And then all those letters, correspondence with his woman friends, as yet unpublished since they don't fit into the established notion of the cardinal—and "the great solitary". Yet, in reality, he had a genius for friendship—and not only for men—and the few women in his life, not only R[osina] G[iberne], were passionately devoted to him. Biographers to date seem not to have noticed this, going, I suppose, by the strictly or largely spiritual theme of the letters—or did they ignore facts on purpose? But we moderns have sharper ears—and we're less discreet—so that a slightly awkward situation arises. By the way, it's part of the same legend that Newman dismissed everyone from his deathbed with the words: "I can die alone." In fact, his last words were: "William, William!", the name of his last young friend in the Oratory. I think this far more pathetic [or poignant], far more lovable than the fiction.[74]

---

ters, 1951–1959. Görres mentions Newman repeatedly; the page numbers in the English edition are: 17, 19, 27, 43, 76, 119, 142–43, 168, 195, 196–97, 217, 231, 275–76, 302, 305, 309, 314, 340, 343, 348–49, 356, 363, 365. Note: the entry for "Newman" in the index of names (379) is missing more than half a dozen of the passages in which Görres mentions Newman. Gerl-Falkovitz writes of the German edition of *Broken Lights, Zwischen den Zeiten. Aus meinen Tagebüchern, 1951 bis 1959,* "Unfortunately, it does not have an index of names; but Newman is mentioned more than fifteen times: 187, 224, 266ff., 293, 312, 371f., 405, 407, 410, 413, 417, 453, 462, 472, 480, 482".—TRANS.]

[72] Görres, *Broken Lights,* 309.

[73] Görres, *Broken Lights,* 309.

[74] *Broken Lights,* 348–49. [The William referred to in Newman's last words was Father William Neville. The phrase that Waldstein-Wartburg translates here as "far more pathetic, far more lovable", switching the order from the German, is *"viel schöner und ergreifender"*. Waldstein-Wartburg is using "pathetic" in the sense of *pathos*. An alternative translation of this phrase in this context would be "far lovelier and more poignant".—TRANS.]

A second accent, newly discovered, comes to her mind: Newman's thoroughly cautious, even restrained, handling of intelligence, his own and that of others. Because of his incredible talent, Görres sees him as "a typical intellectual of the highest calibre";[75] also as someone deeply familiar with the ambiguity of "intelligence". It is, in his eyes, positioned as something close to unbelief;[76] "only one thing could never be said" of Jesus: "that he was clever!!"[77]; there needs to be an "ascesis as related to brains" that is just as decisive as that for eros.[78]

And finally: the personal, not emphasized, but silently emerging affinity between Newman and herself; Görres, who intellectually still comes from the nineteenth century, is caught up in "constant musings" about it.[79] She describes herself as having not only her own intellectual background in the mentality of this intense, often foolish century; even more, she experiences the otherwise un-

---

[Newman scholar] Günter Biemer, who is sincerely thanked for this and other edits, commented on this passage in a letter to the editor [Gerl-Falkovitz] dated June 19, 2002:

> In order to let reality take the place of the formation of a legend, two things should be noted about this entry by I. F. Görres: In the complete edition of *The Letters and Diaries of John Henry Newman*, edited at the Birmingham Oratory, begun in 1961 . . . all letters to women and—in so far as they are preserved and important—and also some of their letters to him are published. A first study of these letters is provided by the quite witty Newman scholar Joyce Sugg (former professor at Newman College [now University] in Birmingham / Teacher Training) in her volume *Ever Yours Affly. John Henry Newman and His Female Circle*, Leominster 1996 ("affly" = Newman's abbreviation in letters to friends for "affectionately"). By the way, I. F. Görres is probably right that not only Maria Rosina Giberne "passionately loved" Newman. In his last book *Pilgrim Journey: J[ohn] H[enry] Newman 1801–1845*, Vincent F. Blehl, S.J., mentions how Mary Holmes wrote of her affection to him and in what a spiritual way Newman dealt with it and consistently only responded to her spiritual growth (op. cit., 310f., 371ff.).—On the other hand, it is worth knowing that Newman had another "secretary" after the surprising death of Ambrose St. John [in 1875]: William P. Neville (1824–1905), who cared for him until death and whom he, in fact—according to his own records—even called on in his last night, for example. At the age of sixty-six at the time, one would perhaps not describe him [Neville] as a "young friend". Also, he reports that at the death of Newman, "All of us were present." (See Meriol Trevor. *Newman. Light in Winter*, 645).

[75] *Broken Lights*, 305.
[76] *Broken Lights*, 304.
[77] *Broken Lights*, 305.
[78] *Broken Lights*, 365.
[79] *Broken Lights*, 195.

suspected labor pains of "conversion"—Newman was older than forty-five at the time [of his conversion]; she was fifty years old.

> No mother but the Church. I am a daughter of the Church. I loved them all [= the theologians] and clung to them, not only as a daughter and sister, but as a Japanese daughter and sister, in the intensity of unconditional submission which belongs to Japanese filial piety. . . . And so what is happening to me now . . . is real "conversion." Just as converts must break away or at least travel far from the childhood home of their Church, from their brethren in faith and the faith of their fathers with its sweet, familiar habits and ways of thought, so I, too, am now travelling in a certain sense, from Catholicism to the Church, from Catholics to Catholic Christianity, travelling from the small, accustomed vision towards new horizons, huge, awe-ful [sic], unfamiliar. And so, at fifty, I'm gradually becoming a Catholic at last.[80]

This "travelling" also means leaving something behind, and in this, there is a new need: leaving behind not habits but people who are part of one's life—not because they only received but because they gave: Is not the path that has been found thanks to them? Even though they no longer come along? With Görres, it is priests, theologians, with whom she can no longer agree; with Newman, it is the Oxford friends; parting from them means actually tearing apart the heart.

> I am flesh of their flesh, part of their destiny as well, sharing it all in painful, loving responsibility, even if they were no longer to "count" in what is to come . . . ; or like Newman, whose heart was torn for years for his brothers of the Oxford Movement whom he could not take with him on his new way. . . . But it is real separation, a severing, and it hurts—very much.[81]

To the closeness, the related emotional "mood", there also belongs an exclusivity and strict passion that directs one's gaze to God: Newman's "myself and my Creator" becomes an analogous "man and God" for Görres, which is astonishing in view of her "worldly

---

[80] *Broken Lights*, 145.
[81] *Broken Lights*, 314.

piety",[82] in which the world as a third element appears to be only "a side-issue".

Humanism means really *nothing* to me. Ever since I came to use reason, man has been interesting and exciting to me *only* as *capax Dei* [having a capacity for God] and in his God relation—*then*, of course, in the *highest* degree. It has always been difficult for me to find anything outside of these poles "in itself" interesting—and if so, always only as a "side issue," almost as a decoration. It still costs me a violent effort of the will to include "the world" in this pair—"by itself," I do *not* find it in there.[83]

Elective Affinities also affects Newman's overall culture, which for "England" means not so much the country as its transformation into a book, into one's thoughts.[84] "You know that England—not Japan!—is a kind of second adopted home for me,[85] but an England that probably no longer exists. I've only been there once in person, but English books are so natural and familiar to me that everything was really like a reunion back then—in 1949."[86]

The English culture was always familiar to her, a born aristocrat: and this above all as a culture of masculine chivalry (which she also perceived in the noble pilgrim Mary Ward at the beginning of her own journey).[87] In the mid-1930s, she translated the stories about Fionn, the Irish warrior of the pre-Christian saga, into splendid

---

[82] "Worldly piety" (*Weltfrömmigkeit*) was the title of Görres' posthumous work, a term borrowed from Goethe. Ida Friederike Görres, *Weltfrömmigkeit*, ed. Beatrix Klaiber (Frankfurt am Main: Knecht Verlag, 1975).

[83] Letter to Paulus Gordan, January 25, 1969, in *"Wirklich die neue Phönixgestalt?"*, 409.

[84] *Elective Affinities* refers to the ideas developed in the book by Goethe by this title, in German as *Die Wahlverwandtschaften.*—TRANS.

[85] [The German word Görres uses here is *Wahlheimat* (adopted home), a wordplay in German on the title of Goethe's famous book *Die Wahlverwandtschaften* (*Elective Affinities*) in the previous sentence.—TRANS.]

[86] Letter to Paulus Gordan, January 30, 1970, in *"Wirklich die neue Phönixgestalt?"*, 438.

[87] Ida Friederike Görres, *Mary Ward*. From 1923 to 1925, Görres was herself a novice with the English Sisters [founded by Mary Ward, today known as Congregatio Jesu, C.J.—TRANS.] in St. Pölten, where she taught the English language in the same years at the school run by the sisters (record from the school director, January 28, 1927). On November 24, 1920, in Vienna, Görres had acquired a "teaching qualification" for the English language "for all educational establishments in the level of elementary school . . . with distinction" (from documents in the Görres estate, Archive of Beatrix Klaiber, Freiburg).

German—magically beautiful, delightful.[88] The motto of King Alfred (d. 901), represents, in its fearlessness, her understanding of England at its best: "Minds shall be harder, hearts keener, spirit the stronger, as our might lessens", translated by her as *"Härter der Sinn, die Herzen kühner, stärker der Mut, da Macht uns schwindet."* [89] When Görres catches a scent in Froude of the splendid figures of knights among the friends around Newman, then Froude also casts that royal light of early Christian England onto Newman for them.

Unique Approach

At the same time as Görres, Reinhold Schneider wrote a much shorter and historically oriented essay on "Newman's decision", dated September 19, 1945,[90] which was much more distant and staid in its tone. In it, he emphasized the "force of inevitability" that first touched Newman as a person, then world history. "The great difficulty of assessing him lies in the fact that we must understand the personal as historical, the historical as personal, in every phase of his conversion and its effects." [91]

---

[88] [James Stephens, *Fionn, der Held und andere irische Sagen und Märchen*, trans. Ida Friederike Görres (Freiburg im Breisgau: Herder Verlag, 1936). See her letter to Paulus Gordan, O.S.B., feast of the Holy Innocents [December 28] 1966: "Your dear card, still from Freiburg, was one of the greatest Christmas joys on this day: the first time in the 35 (32?) years that my Irish fairy tales exist, that someone noticed the quality!! the indescribable beauty of this book, which I fell so in love with while reading it that I immediately began to translate it—out of sheer enthusiasm, unsolicited, and actually my only book without 'apostolic' motives at the back of my mind. I felt the same way again ten years later with T. S. Eliot's *Murder in the Cathedral*. However, after several unsuccessful attempts, then, during a short flu, during three days of fever, I suddenly scribbled down the whole thing in verse almost in a single torrent." *"Wirklich die neue Phönixgestalt?"*, 234. In a note regarding this letter in the published edition, Gerl-Falkovitz adds, "Görres published a partial translation: 'T. S. Eliot: Weinachtspredigt des Thomas Beckett' in *Werkblätter. Bundesrundbrief des Quickborn* I.12 (Dez. 1948)." Görres, *"Wirklich die neue Phönixgestalt?"*, 234n334.—TRANS.]

[89] [In her lecture "Trusting the Church", Görres translates this quote a bit differently: "Härter der Sinn, die Herzen kühner, stärker der Mut, da Macht uns schwindet." Ida Friederike Görres, "Vertrauen zur Kirche" in *Im Winter Wächst das Brot* (Einsiedeln: Johannes Verlag, 1970), 131.—TRANS.]

[90] Reinhold Schneider, *Das Unzerstörbare: Religiöse Schriften*, in *Gesammelte Werke*, ed. Edwin Maria Landau (Frankfurt am Main: Insel Verlag, 1978), 9:352–75.

[91] Schneider, *Das Unzerstörbare*, 9:354.

Similarly, in his great sketch, an interpretation of imperial England, *Das Inselreich* (The island empire), Schneider reached far beyond the person of Newman into historical continuities: this book "certainly does not want to reconcile what cannot be reconciled, and believes that those who experienced the conflict of powers like Robert Pecham, the unknown, and like John Henry Newman, the great cardinal, knew the nature and fate of their people much better than the most daring fighters on one side or the other. Because whatever England suffered, John Henry Newman endured it once more: just as the cross on the heights of the cliff echoes from the battle unleashed in the valley."[92]

In contrast to the historiographer Reinhold Schneider, Görres remains closer to the person: biography serves as a hermeneutic key; however, [for Görres, the key lies] in plumbing the depths of the inner biography, the critical decisions, struggles, losses, victories, disappointments. Schneider's universal historical overview spans centuries of bygone eras, allowing Newman to appear as the fruit of drawn-out processes. Görres takes a close-up view, and in this, the person himself is much more likely to be a preview of the times ahead. With this, she approaches the interpretation of Otto Karrer, who emphasized in Newman the prophetic anticipation of the difficulties of faith of the twentieth century.[93] Other predecessors of the "first reception of Newman in the German-speaking realm"[94] in the 1920s were Erich Przywara, who helped shape the image of the Church Father of the Modern Age and thus finally released him from suspicion of modernism, as well as Matthias Laros, the biographer and outstanding editor of the selected works [of Newman in German], and ultimately Theodor Haecker as translator, who converted not least of all under the influence of Newman.[95] Przywara and Haecker also appear at the beginning of Görres' reflection [in chapter 10 of this volume] on the new self-confidence of German

---

[92] Reinhold Schneider, *Das Inselreich: Gesetz und Größe der britischen Macht* in *Gesammelte Werke,* ed. Edwin Maria Landau (Frankfurt am Main: Suhrkamp, 1979), 2:590–91.

[93] John Henry Newman, *Christentum: Ein Aufbau,* trans. Otto Karrer, ed. Erich Przywara, vols. 1–8 (Freiburg im Breisgau: Herder, 1922). Otto Karrer, "Zur Einführung: Newmans geistiges Bildnis", in *Kardinal John Henry Newman, Die Kirche,* vol. 1, ed. Otto Karrer (Einsiedeln: Benziger, 1945), 7–23.

[94] Siebenrock, "Wahrheit", 46–67.

[95] See Siebenrock, "Wahrheit", 46–67.

Catholicism alongside Herwegen and Guardini in chapter 1 of this book. Yet her reflection on Newman, although based only on the available sources and translations, is nevertheless original and cannot be compared with the names mentioned because it is significantly sharpened by her previous look at Thérèse of Lisieux. Between the lines of historical information, Görres reads what is human, vulnerable, demanded by God, the bold and the bitter—in short, the face of a saint. As always with her, holiness is interwoven with time; nevertheless, the way she looks at this releases something that transcends the constraint of time. Thus, as demonstrated by her masterful opening in the first chapter, under all the possible outer layers and their interpretations that "somehow" apply in this rich cosmos, she sketches the one decisive factor in Newman's life with the harrowing expression that he is an *âme détruite*. It is the expression that she took directly from her mystical portrait of Saint Thérèse. Such a truly bold interpretation was unique in its time and is still startlingly moving today: like a flash of lightning that surprisingly illuminates and consolidates a broad, spacious landscape.

These pages about Newman may not only make the great, saintly cardinal present to us in a poignant way but may also put Ida Friederike Görres back in the limelight that she has long deserved. In her classic translation [into German] of "The Pillar of the Cloud" (known also as "Lead, Kindly Light"), her extraordinary linguistic power became clear;[96] in the present portrayal of Newman, it

---

[96] [Görres' translation of the poem "The Pillar of the Cloud" appeared as: John Henry Newman, "Führ, liebes Licht", in Ida Friederike Görres, *Der verborgene Schatz* (Frankfurt am Main: Josef Knecht, 1949), 93.—TRANS.] Other translations of [Newman's] poems were also interspersed in the manuscript papers, which, while polished, do not reveal how hard the work was in terms of language. "If only his poetry weren't so terribly difficult to translate." Görres, letter to Paulus Gordan, January 30, 1970, in *"Wirklich die neue Phönixgestalt?"*, 438. In the box of note cards, there was a version of Newman's poem for an occasion of Saint Philip Neri, which was not included in her book:

Wie schäme ich mich meiner, der Tränen, der Zunge,
so eilig gereizt und so selten bezwungen!
Wenn flüchtig und nichtig ein Plunder mich plagt,
wird wütend der Himmel, die Erde verklagt.

[I'm ashamed of myself, of my tears and my tongue,
So easily fretted, so often unstrung;
Mad at trifles, to which a chance moment gives birth,
Complaining of heaven, and complaining of earth.]

is her analytical sharpness as well as her cautious, even reverently bold, look at what was overshadowed, borne painfully, unfulfilled in the life of this rich mind. To be able to do this is an indication of kinship. In her sketch from the 1950s attached as an "Encore" [in chapter 11], she says: "It is becoming increasingly clear to me that if I am going to write any book, it will be on *Newman the Saint*."[97]

Hanna-Barbara Gerl-Falkovitz
Erlangen/Dresden, Germany, June 2002

John Henry Newman, verse 7 of "St. Philip in His Disciples", in *Verses on Various Occasions* (London: Longmans, Green, 1905), 313.

[97] Görres, "Über J. H. Newman", 55. This sketch is appended in this volume as chapter 11.

I

THE LIFE OF NEWMAN

I

THE MAN WHO WAS SACRIFICED

An Initial Reconnaissance of His Life

If you ask me what really moves and captivates me most about the great figure of our "Father Newman", as we call him with love and adoration, I do not need to think long about the answer: it is not his noble humanistic harmony, not his embodying the form of gentleman transfigured by Christianity, not the vastness of his gaze into the future beyond what his contemporaries saw, his carefully reasoned sharpness of judgment, his impartiality and independence of conscience, not the soul-stirring power of his sermons, not the comprehensive scholarship of the consummate scholar, not the incorruptibly heart-searching vision of a great psychologist, educator, and spiritual guide, which reveals itself in his sermons as well as in his letters—one could go on for a long time and enumerate merits, gifts, and virtues that radiate toward us captivatingly from his truly noble image. But it is none of that. Rather, it is this one realization: that Newman was a man who was sacrificed. He was an *âme détruite* [a shattered soul], as the demons revealed to the exorcist about the status of Little Thérèse, this young unknown contemporary of Newman, who survived him by only six years.[1]

---

[1] Little Thérèse, namely, Saint Thérèse of Lisieux (1873–1897). Gerl-Falkovitz writes, "Görres wrote her most significant work about her." Ida Friederike Görres, *Eine Studie über Therese von Lisieux* (1943). After the first edition was burned in an air raid, the book was republished as *Das verborgene Antlitz: Eine Studie über Therese von Lisieux* in 1946 and then, in a second edition, as *Das Senfkorn von Lisieux: Das verborgene Antlitz. Neue Deutungen* (1958), translated into English by Richard and Clara Winston as Ida Friederike Görres, *The Hidden Face: A Study of St. Thérèse of Lisieux*. In this book on Saint Thérèse, Görres calls the *âme détruite*—commonly translated into English as the "shattered soul"—"eine vernichtete, eine zertrümmerte Seele". *Das verborgene Antlitz: Eine Studie über Therese von Lisieux*, 2nd ed. (Freiburg im Breisgau: Herder, 1946), 505. In the English edition, Richard and Clara Winston translate this as "an immolated, a consumed soul". *The Hidden Face: A Study of St. Thérèse of Lisieux* (San Francisco: Ignatius Press, 2003), 407–8.

He is a victim—his whole person, who lays down his entire life on the uncompromising altar of a secret and dreadful calling. At first glance, who would see precisely this harmonious, almost elegant intellectual figure, full of classic simplicity and dignity? He has worked through inner calamity so thoroughly, so virtuously, that it is hidden to every curious eye; this reality reveals itself only very gradually to the contemplative observer of this fate. But once one has noticed this feature, one cannot let it go. Looking at this great man, one might think: here is the classic case of a saint who has climbed to the high peak of Christian perfection without a violent break with the world, without crucifixion of his own being; here is that phrase so dear to our century, that "grace perfects nature, it does not destroy it", grace embodies nature in the most soothing and comforting way, so that Newman is even made to be the crowning example of a religiosity hostile to or at least suspicious of asceticism.

But—who can say who Newman was "in his nature"? More and more, the observer has the impression that we know only the Newman who has already been "disguised", supernaturally "cloaked": the finished bronze cast. His "natural nature" has been shattered into pieces like the earthenware shell of a bell, hardly recognizable even from the remnants and fragments.

The success of a work of art includes, among other things, the impression of the "necessity" of its form: every word of the perfect poem seems to be the only possible one; it cannot be replaced by anything else; every brushstroke of the masterful painting stands there as if there could have been no other. So, too, the moral and religious perfection of some people leaves a similar impression: of course, it looks like nature, and no one notices easily the severe process of cutting, melting, and hewing that the raw material, its nature, went through before the form was finished. That the "real self" afterward standing before us has been refined and shaped, "but only as through fire" (1 Cor 3:15), into a quality that the raw self would never have achieved, is a truism. But is there really only the contrast between the clump of clay and the figurine? Not that of different art forms that different artists would have coaxed out of the same basic material? Could not the same block of marble yield to the face of an Apollo and One resurrected from the dead? Without her divine calling, Little Thérèse might have become a virtuous provincial woman, a radiant young wife and mother—probably a source of happiness for her next of kin but without any meaning for a larger circle. The Holy Spirit alone forms them, far beyond their nature, into the image of saints who can bear the gaze of all Christendom. What would Saint Francis have become without the election of grace? Probably not a successful cloth merchant in Assisi—maybe a troubadour, maybe an adventurer. He is probably also one of those who undoubtedly offer a wonderful point of departure for a vocation, but who, far more than the original measure of their natural gifts, can almost be said to have been raised beyond what is possible: children for whom there are high expectations, in the narrow sense of this phrase. Many of the great penitents belong here, but also among the saints are precisely some sons who "remained at home", who did not go astray. But are there not others who clearly radiate the mark of natural, not supernatural, distinction from the brow—people who seem determined and predestined for a brilliant career path on Earth, to be stars in the natural sky—and then divine election hits them, shattering, like a bolt of lightning?

Just as for the first humans, the bestowing, nourishing, and creative power of God, which does not extinguish the glowing wick, does not let a sparrow fall from the sky, and adorns the lilies of the field more splendidly than Solomon in his glory, so it is in those who came second that the sacrificial majesty reveals itself, the rights of the potter who forms and smashes vessels, and no one is allowed to ask him: Why?

We look at them, and our breath is swept away, cut short before the One who is Wholly Other, who intervenes into His own Creation out of the invisible, tossing in precisely the most precious thing He gives us, as if with a careless flick of the wrist, and jumbling all our standards of important and significant, of high and low, of "disreputable" and "desirable", in order to teach us that this, too, that everything, is only provisional, having only provisional, auspicious, and foreshadowing value.

It seems to me that Newman is one of these witnesses. From the outside, he seems almost enviable, rich in all the good gifts of talent and culture, influence and impact, although, as with everything human, he is subject to the law of the alternation of light and

cloud; his life is a singular death, silent and cruel: a victim who
is cornered, but still a victim. It is only under the incessant, noisy
blows of the ruthless hammer that the lovable and overwhelmingly
beautiful figure is formed, the one we know and who still casts a
spell on us today, as he did on his contemporaries. It is not unlikely
that John Henry Newman will one day be elevated to the honor of
the altars. His long life that filled almost the entire past [nineteenth]
century and even the portion of his continuation in the memory
of the Church show no trace of the splendor of the extraordinary
that belongs to that particular mission. Nevertheless, no one can
approach him and remain under his spell without realizing that this
man is one of the chosen ones, one of those who are continually
given to Christendom as salt and light. His role in the Church is
not that of a martyr or a miracle worker; his charisma is also not the
love generated in a crisis by the great rescuers and helpers: his gift
is wisdom, combined with the other two of the seven gifts that are
particularly related to the sanctification of the human spirit: understanding and knowledge. He is a teacher of the Church like those
Fathers of our faith whom the liturgy addresses as *Doctor optime* (a
Doctor of the Church).

Nevertheless, even those who approach this great figure initially
as the "Church Father of the Twentieth Century" experience more
than a surprise. The figure of Newman grows before their aston-
ished and soon frightened eyes, like a constellation in the night sky.
A constellation—what does this mean? The lights that stand out
against the dark vault are innumerable: we give them names and
group them into figures that we rename and that have nothing to
do with their nature. In this way, against the backdrop of the un-
fathomable depth of this spirit, thoughts and words shine that we
connect—perhaps as arbitrarily as constellations—to systems and
lines of destiny, and we relate them to ourselves and our questions.

Does one dare even try? Is not every attempt at a biography almost outrageous? Even writing something about a living person is
almost necessarily wrong—at a minimum one-sided, limited, inci-
dental. Our judgment is questionable, not only with regard to the
guilt and mistakes of a neighbor. And when one does not experience the tone of voice, the look of the eye, a handshake, and
hand gestures, or what is secret and undisclosed but betrayed in

gait, cadence, and posture of the whole body, in the play of light and shadow in a voice, in folds around the eyes and cheeks, in the expression of the mouth, however restrained: Who dares to paint the portrait of a soul whose living expression in the body one has never known? In his sermons, his soul speaks most openly, like a poet in his poems: they are all "fragments of a creed". But we have them in their entirety only from the first half of his life.[2]

Anyone pursuing the personal, the inner expression of this great sacred soul, does not have it easy. A modesty that is beyond strict, very masculine, and very English is hidden in a silence that is strangely and impenetrably mixed with pride, shyness, sensitivity, and aversion to being in public, and with humility and love of solitude.

"The true life of a man is in his letters",[3] wrote Newman himself and therefore desired that a large selection of his correspondence be published during his lifetime. But what do a hundred letters, or however many there are, tell us compared with the lost sheep of the seventy thousand in the archive? And what does the careful selection convey, still hampered by numerous family considerations?[4] And without [the letters from] Oxford, Birmingham, Rome?[5]

But such is the strange urge that cannot let go of trying to trace the secret of a life in the inadequate sources and fragments of mementos and publications. A face bends near, an image comes to life, a sentence in a letter sounds like a voice, a sermon attracts the heart with a burning finger, and one knows that it is positioned among the others as an affirmation.

Writing a portrait of a life is still a reasonable undertaking. Which years forge a significant destiny can be determined; the places where it happened, the external facts from the existence of a well-known

---

[2] At the time Görres wrote this book, she had only partial access to sermons from the latter part of Newman's life.

[3] Letter to his sister, Mrs. John Mozley, May 18, 1863, in Anne Mozley, ed., *Letters and Correspondence of John Henry Newman during His Life in the English Church: With a Brief Autobiography* (London: Longmans, Green, 1903), 1:3. Newman's sister Jemima Charlotte married John Mozley, and Newman's sister Harriett married John Mozley's brother Thomas. Anne Mozley, the editor of *Letters and Correspondence of Newman*, was the sister of John and Thomas Mozley.

[4] An allusion to Anne Mozley's edition, *Letters and Correspondence of Newman*.

[5] At the time Görres wrote this book, she did not have access to these letters.

personality, family tree, environment, kin, education can be reported precisely and accurately. It may be that a "portrait" is already emerging, unintentionally (and yet the selection, recording,
and transmission of those data and facts were already guided by
an intention), and yet emerging nevertheless convincingly and vi-
brantly.

Things become much more difficult and at the same time questionable as soon as we try to trace the inner shape of a person—
a deceased man, a man whose life ended many years ago. Now
those facts must be interpreted—certainly, they are "eloquent" in
themselves, but their message is initially silent and figurative and
must first be "translated" into the language of the present by the
biographer.

Trying to recreate someone's personality from his "legacy" is a
more daring venture than reconstructing the culture of an ancient,
prehistoric tribe from the runes of a lost script and the ornaments
and incomprehensible devices from discoveries and excavations.
One would often like to know what this or that famous man would
say about the portraits that posterity—especially those who worship—associate with him. John Henry Newman thought that letters give a biographer the necessary documents, but here too—from
the reader doing research who is interested not only in "facts"—
a weighty question mark can be added: the printed correspondence
we received does not make us much wiser if we are not as well
informed about the correspondents. It is well known that a woman
will almost never tell the same story to a man and to a woman in
the same way; often there will be astonishing differences, and yet
it is "true" every time; but in the other mirror, it almost becomes
something else. And does that not also apply to men, to a large
extent? How much does it matter which of the two correspondents
was the superior, which one was the recipient; whether the author
wanted to lighten his heart or to instruct the recipient, whether
he sought or gave advice, comfort, support? So, for example, Newman's own letters from his time at the university in Ireland certainly
had an ambivalence: The hesitant, uncertain, but indispensable em-
ployees must be reassured, encouraged, and cheered on with fresh,
courageous, and confident tones; to his personal friends at home,
he makes no secret of his own deep dejection, disappointment, and

growing hopelessness. So both are "true", and yet the subject matter is situated under completely different lighting every time.

We also know that letters about the most personal relationship between the writing partners can be very "unproductive", downright misleading. The naive researcher of the sources may consider it as a testimony to the increasing disillusionment and objectification, yes, disappointment with the situation, while in reality, it means the exact opposite; everything becomes a cipher, the secret language of the "initiated": every request for laundry to be sent, every short report about events during a trip can contain more intimacy, which is also understandable by the addressee, than the fiery lyrical events of the one touting something, who has to unfold all the peacock's plumage of mind and prose to make the desired, hoped-for good impression.

For one whose heart is full, the mouth does not always overflow. Those of a certain nature even fall silent. The more tender and deeper the relationship, the more inhibited the expression may become, the more strictly limited to the factual and the general. Newman was an Englishman, a son of the nineteenth century, a person of unusual tenderness of the soul, who concealed his unprecedented emotional power in the often "rock-hard" shell of deep reticence.

His correspondence with Maria Rosina Giberne spans about fifty years;[6] presumably the last letters could have been read by the whole circle of friends in the same way as the first ones. Even diaries are not a satisfactory key to a person's secret. These, too, have many faces. Some are the chronicle, mirror, and quintessence of life as experienced; others represent the playground of experiences one never had, of dreams, wishes, enchanted illuminations. There are the records of the hardworking collector, who faithfully and regularly enters note after note into a calendar for work, and the "private" diary, which contains only silent complaint, helplessness, and the endless, sterile, circular discussion of what is unresolved and the hopeless. Newman wrote both, the first sort almost continuously.

---

[6] Gerl-Falkovitz explains, "Maria Rosina Giberne (1802–1885) had been a friend of Newman and his sisters since childhood. She was a follower of the Oxford Movement and a convert to Catholicism, and she entered the Order of the Visitation in Autun, France, under the name of Maria Pia." See Joyce Sugg, *Ever Yours Affly. John Henry Newman and His Female Circle* (Leominster, Herefordshire, UK: Gracewing, 1996).

Of the second sort there are—from ninety years!—four narrow booklets extant. Such records reveal what is most secretive, most intimate, what seeks this way out because it does not even want to reveal itself to one's most loyal friends: But is it really the most important thing, to say nothing of the most valid thing? Who ought to be judged on such notes, which are often referred to as symptoms of temporary conditions?

So, what remains as tangible, reliable material in the hand of the biographer? What is the basis for the biographer's risky venture to depict the face of an unfamiliar—and, on top of this, unworldly—soul in a way that it is not merely grasping at clouds and insolence? How does one who grants such considerations dare to write a biography or even a hagiography?

All of the difficulties listed increase considerably when it comes to the inner guise of a saint. For who can say anything about someone else's relationship with God? Of course, mystical and other—even less—gifted people have filled entire books with the profession and a description of their spiritual experiences, encounters, and states; there are self-testimonials of overwhelming strength, richness, and glory, and those of embarrassing uninhibitedness and trivialities. But the more they are esteemed, the more they assure us of their limitations and helplessness, the more resigned they are as they struggle with the unspeakable, and the more reverently they fall silent before that which is under seal, which is no longer their secret but that of "the King".

Written over each such text, as far as it is genuine, there is the line from *The Story of a Soul*: "Everything I have just written in so few words would require many detailed pages, but these pages will never be read on this earth."[7]

Every saint is, in fact, a "public" figure. As Wilhelm Schamoni emphasizes in his thoughtful introduction to the great work *The True Face of the Saints*, every saint is sent as an image of the Savior and nurtured by God.[8] "Because they are portraits, they should be

---

[7] Thérèse of Lisieux, *Story of a Soul: The Autobiography of St. Thérèse of Lisieux*, trans. John Clarke (Washington, D.C.: Institute of Carmelite Studies, 1996), 160.

[8] Wilhelm Schamoni, *The Face of the Saints*, trans. Anne Fremantle (Freeport, N.Y.: Books for Libraries Press, 1947).

seen"—one could also say that because they are to be seen, they are "portraits", vivid and striking. At the same time, the visible part of his life relates to the invisible, fertile core, as the fruit and flower of the plant to the deeply covered root. So we can at most try to capture the illuminated image that such a person casts forth through the years of remoteness. We may examine the mirrors of hearts that still took on his reflection in their lifetime and the reflection of this great figure in the mirror of our own soul. Perhaps it will be the case that this fabric of external and internal testimonials ultimately results in an outline and a hue that at least neither distorts nor obscures the original image. As a theologian and a philosopher, as one of the last great incarnations of Christian humanism, this English cardinal is situated in the consciousness of our contemporaries as the leader of the Anglican reform movement and the founder of the Anglo-Catholic church, as a cornerstone on which the Roman Catholic Church in England established herself in her "second spring". In the following, we want to try to investigate the person of Newman: the boy, puzzled, who was startled and overwhelmed by God; the active, creative young prophet of his church in crisis; the hermit, who he was and wanted to be all his life; and the fighter, who he was with and against his will: the saint of the Church and the saint of humility, the one perfected in sacrifice.

2

THE GOLDEN APPLE

Like his great contemporary Kierkegaard in Denmark, like Thorvaldsen and Hans Christian Andersen, the man of the 1860s felt like someone buried alive and already forgotten. Like Kierkegaard's, his voice did not ring out loud and clear until a generation after his death: a new generation feels that the person who is almost forgotten speaks to them, and understands and guides them, and they respond with grateful reverence.

One of the main motifs of the nineteenth century, so rich in questions, new beginnings, and experiments, is the act of reaching for the Golden Apple. Decades of invention and discovery; upheaval and repeatedly letting go; dizzying increase in wealth, power, freedom, and pleasure; as well as unlimited belief in progress are condensed, as it were, into this old mythological figure: the abundance of the world, the abundance of pleasure in life, hitherto hovering at an unreachable distance, only now and then to be picked by the chosen one, the one who is rare and called to be a hero—it amasses more and more; it is within human reach; it is available to anyone who is bold enough to reach for it. The Golden Apple appeared in various forms in the nineteenth century: to one it appeared as the abundance of knowledge unfolding without limit for "free" thinking, for "unprejudiced" science; to the other, as the abundance of pleasure, "living out" the free development of one's personality. It is the new vision of the fulfillment of earthly life itself, the new "religious" understanding of man and his world—this-worldly, satisfying, intoxicating. How strange are yesterday and days gone by, how almost childlike, the dream of fulfillment and abundance appears to us in all areas of life today. It seems to us that the believing Christian of the nineteenth century was essentially suspicious, in a strictly defensive manner, of this dazzling wave: this promise was the glittering seduction of the prince of this world; the Golden Apple was the Sodom apple that crumbles to dust and bitterness in the hand grabbing it.[1] In close combat and being pressed into defense from all sides, he felt the attack more than he felt the lure of that challenge. But for the Christians of the following generation, the battle line had already moved. Almost from the turn of the [twentieth] century, first among the youth, the new, much more anxious question arises: whether the Golden Apple is not just a temptation, but a permissible, even necessary goal. May—indeed, should not—we, too, strive for the "abundance of life", to savor and explore the natural glory of this earth?

Is the Golden Apple really forbidden fruit for us because renunciation and self-denial are our "real" food? Or should a new era of Christian mastering of the world, seizing the world, and engaging the world begin with us, with fearless pursuit of knowledge, fearless enjoyment of nature? Should not a new image of the human person emerge, the valid image being the one of the "life-affirming" Christian, who finally possesses and unites nature and grace into perfect harmony? As is well known, this question was one of the major issues of the Youth Movement.[2]

Here Newman confronts us in a strange light. Not so much his language in texts, letters, and sermons as his life and his character give the answer: unsolicited, surprising, perhaps terrifying.

For he was a man of an extraordinary nature, of an almost Goethe-like abundance of faculties, who seemed destined for a victorious and triumphant encounter and experience with the world; certainly, even more so in representing the "new" saint who embodies the joyful "yes to the world". But, thwarted by the Spirit and by grace, he must accomplish the overcoming of the world by way of renunciation, and it is precisely in this rupture, in the fate of nonfulfillment, that he achieves his distinctive human and Christian perfection. However far we look, we hardly find any "world" to be possessed and enjoyed, the Golden Apple snapped back high out of reach.

---

[1] The Sodom apple is "a fruit (now usually identified with that of the mudar, *Calotropis procera* (family Apocynaceae), that, according to legend, appears tempting but dissolves into smoke and ashes when grasped." *Oxford English Dictionary*, s.v. "Sodom apple", September 2023, https://doi.org/10.1093/OED/5502984411.

[2] That is, the Catholic Youth Movement in Germany following World War I into the 1930s, a movement in which Görres played an active role.

What are you doing with us, Father John Henry Newman, you old—
you ancient one?

No, that is exactly what you are not. You are as old as we are.
There, it seems to me, is where your secret lies. You are not older,
and you are not younger than we are, as your contemporaries are.
Let us be honest: our species is incomparably older than you humans were a hundred years ago. We think of the people of the eighteenth century as "grown-up": mature and advanced, erudite, sea-
soned, yes, old, smug, and over-intelligent to the point of depravity
and sophistication. Perhaps there is a deep allegory in even the youth
of that time donning the white wig. One would feel self-conscious
and awkward to meet one of them; on the one side, a person with
powdered hair, with a jabot around the neck or a hooped petticoat;
on the other, a person with a car and a refrigerator; there are the
atomic bomb and media cartels; one of them would feel quite incomplete and like a school pupil. But the people of the nineteenth
century have grown young again, with a charming, touching, and
somewhat risible youthfulness. Would not today's twenty-year-old
feel patronizing, witty, and superior if he were to meet his grandfa-
ther as a young man, who was already a regular husband, employed,
and respected at his age, head of a family under heads of the family? It is the same youthful characteristic that we sense when we
meet people from the outlying provinces of Europe—Croatians or
Romanians, or perhaps, in a different sense, Scandinavians or the
Flemish. They "have not had them yet": the school that we have
long since gone through, the diseases that, oddly enough, we have
survived. They may carry themselves in a serious and solemn manner, talk about their needs and problems—we smile. A little wistful,
maybe a little jealous.

How juvenile is Romanticism, how juvenile is the first exhilara-
tion of democracy, how juvenile is the vehement belief in unlimited
progress, in machines, inventions, and discoveries, in the realm of
freedom, equality, and fraternity! How childish it all is, this exuberant and almost anesthetizing feeling of strength, this lust for adventure, this feverish hunger and thirst for the unknown, this frenzy at
the onset of dominion over the forces of nature! The recklessness
of the experiment; the absolute trust in one's own strengths, the
limits of which are nowhere felt, let alone accounted for; the equally

absolute ignorance of the consequences with which one gets involved; the developments that are conjured; the powers that are called upon and released! How very much Goethe sensed this side of his contemporaries in *The Sorcerer's Apprentice*![3] The cocky contempt for everything from yesterday, for everything conventional, the beaming arrogance of knowing better, the peculiar insolence with which even remarkable spirits believe they can treat the past— this strikes us as being ever so juvenile. Is there not even something almost poignant in the materialism of the middle of the last century that these people develop, just as proud as ethical pathos and virtue in its stubborn, conscientious seriousness, whether in the churches or against them? An "Ethical Society"[4]—who among us would dare to found something like this or to join it—purely out of the sharpened sense of the comical solemnity of such intellectual pomp?

And also, how juvenile is the world-weariness of those past generations, their tears and fainting, their oaths of friendship and cursing their parents, the ceremonial pathos of their declarations of love and grief, their tragic gestures, their posture of contempt for the world and negation of life: all of this seems to us today to be drenched in the gaudy and stormy colors of puberty, full of upheaval, spring fever, and infatuation. Was it because the older culture had until then been borne by the old estates—the nobility and the clergy— who had largely outgrown it or were led by it and shaped by its style, by the old ruling class of Europe, whose day was finally com-

---

[3] See Johann Wolfgang von Goethe, "The Sorcerer's Apprentice", in *103 Great Poems: A Dual-Language Book* = *103 Meistergedichte*, trans. and ed. Stanley Applebaum (Mineola, N.Y.: Dover Publications, 1999), 127–33.

[4] An "Ethical Society" is a chapter of the "Ethical Cultural" movement started by Felix Adler in 1876. "Individual Ethical Society members may or may not believe in a deity." Adler "contended that Judaism and Christianity were mistaken in making ethics dependent on religious doctrine. . . . While Ethical Culturists generally share common beliefs about what constitutes ethical behavior and the good, individuals are encouraged to develop their own personal understanding of these. . . . Since around 1950 the Ethical Culture movement has been increasingly identified as part of the modern Humanist movement." Also, "functionally, Ethical Societies", and some Humanist communities today, "are similar to churches or synagogues, conducting Sunday morning meetings, offering moral instruction . . . , doing charitable work and conducting weddings, baby namings, and memorial services." New World Encyclopedia contributors, "Ethical Culture", *New World Encyclopedia*, https://www.newworldencyclopedia.org/p/index.php?title=Ethical_Culture&oldid=1139299.

ing to an end, whose vitality had run out? The Revolution had freed the Third Estate, the one that previously had no sense of history and had not been devoured by history. Really youthful, unlike the tired upper class, the "new" person of the nineteenth century rose, childlike, dreaming, longing, and believing, hungry for life and without weariness. The nineteenth century, which seemed so sober, practical, and efficient, so mature and realistic, may have pumped more into the future than any other. The land of all five continents would have been too cramped for the castles in the sky it built. And hanging out of the colorful sky of its web of dreams was the ancient symbol of myth: the Golden Apple.

"Abundance of life", "knowledge", "free research", "development of personality", "enjoying life"—there are many terms and names for it. Basically, it always comes down to one thing: knowledge and possession, pleasure and domination have always existed, but, like the golden fruits of myth, they are strictly guarded as a "privilege", as special rights of the elect few, and, as in the myth, protected fiercely from access for the rest by dragons, glass mountains, and fire-breathing maws. But now everyone can, may, and should strive for this—at least those from the Third Estate, the ascending class, to whom, in the new division of the world, the fruit falls; deep underneath the unidentified world of the Fourth Estate, which is just being formed, there is seething and surging, still without faces and form. The golden fruit may just fill the hand of one, while for another it swells to the size of the earth—but "personal happiness" has been discovered, the "right to happiness", the right to "a fulfilling life" and "free development": these are no longer unattainable for him. Origin and legacy alone can no longer determine one's path in life: every drummer boy carries the drum major's staff in his knapsack. Everyone believes the world is taking giant strides toward earthly paradise.

There is still so much to discover: the sources of the Nile and the poles of the globe, the interior of the obscure parts of the world, the secrets behind the Great Wall, and the highest mountains in the world. There are "world travelers", there are still unexplored islands and unknown peoples, deserts and streams, undeciphered pictographic scripts and languages that nobody understands. Cooper's *Leatherstocking Tales*, itself reduced now to a children's book, appeared when Newman was a young professor at Oxford and stirred the Old

World into incredible enthusiasm: "In every city of Europe that I
visited the works of Cooper were conspicuously placed in the windows of every bookshop. They are published, as soon as he produces them, in thirty-four different places in Europe", says his com-
patriot [Samuel] Morse, inventor of the long-distance telegraph.[5]

Of course, there were grumblers and those who sounded the
alarm. But those were mostly people who were on the losing side:
royalists, clergymen, and nobles who were dethroned, pushed aside,
and made redundant by the new era—"reactionaries", as we say today, to whom the "good old days" were and remain the apex, the
world that was made by and for their kind and was by no means
edified by change. They resist and balk with censorship, police, and
all kinds of prohibitions, but there is nowhere to hide: they are on
the defensive, they find themselves more and more in a corner, and
the modern age advances relentlessly.

It is actually strange how very late faithful Christian consciousness recognized the lure of the Golden Apple. The political "youth
movement" of France in the 1930s, the circle around Lamennais
and Lacordaire, discovered that one could be a Catholic and a Re-
publican; Ozanam as well as Bodelschwingh, Kolping, and Bishop
Ketteler, and above all Leo XIII discovered that the "social question" is entrusted to Christians with particular seriousness. Liberal
Protestantism took part in the victory parade of "progress" and
even considered this a special advantage over the point of view of
the obscurantists of Rome. But as for what was called the triumph
of the arts and sciences throughout the nineteenth century, it cannot be denied that the Catholic world stood in opposition, with a
barely concealed distrust and suspicion, locked and loaded, ready
to fire, as it were, especially regarding the sciences. The "spirit of
the age", in which the traits of the Antichrist stand out ever more
clearly, appears to them as *the* great temptation for Christians. The
pious feel more and more like the garrison of a besieged fortress in
a civil war, in which the law is undisputedly on their side, but the
victory is temporarily on the side of the opponent. The "strategic"
relationship to the world becomes increasingly clear: the individual
areas, science or family, art or literature or education, are reduced

---

[5] Morse wrote this about Cooper in 1833. Thomas Raynesford Lounsbury, *James Fenimore Cooper* (Boston: Houghton Mifflin, 1882), 76–77.

more and more to being "positions" that must be maintained or recaptured at all costs. They are becoming more and more means and field deployments in an epic game of power, and the religious educational institutions that shape the young and old, as well as the new upper class, become geared more and more toward the education of this militant "cultural Catholic" in their pedagogy of conservation.

At this point, the Golden Apple is completely disenchanted. It is no longer a dreamy glimmer, sometimes hanging out of the clouds within reach yet always far enough away to call forth all the strength of man in tireless contention. It is the forbidden fruit itself, due to which there would be iniquity for a long time. And yet, in many places, one has to offer careful and often deceptive imitations with one's own brand in order to distract the restless urge of one's own youth from that seductive splendor and to placate them reassuringly. Is it too much to say—even with complete distrust of and reservations against generalizations—that the average attitude of Catholics of that time was a deep resignation, a consciousness of defeat, disinheritance, and being excluded, which, of course, was then displaced in their consciousness by many successes and achievements, by an enormous breadth of religious activity?

But that which dislodged the Christians of the nineteenth century permeated the believers of the twentieth with irresistible force. Whereas others had grasped at the Golden Apple and found it hard and cold and inedible, now it burst open silently like a soap bubble in the rest of the world, its magical splendor beginning to shine in the inner realm of the Church. We reached for it with the usual delay and with the usual fervor of delayed longing. How quickly times change! The questions that kept the liveliest youth of the Church under their spell between the two world wars appear to us today as strangely obsolete and antiquated, almost faintly odd like the past fashion trends of Symbolism or Art Nouveau: "affirmation of life", "devotion to the world", Catholic formation of the world, the new Catholic society, "the world at the gates of the Church", the discovery and rehabilitation of the body and its rights, freedom and maturity of the spirit:[6] see, the Golden Apple had descended

---

[6] These phrases are concepts that animated the Catholic Youth Movement in Germany from 1919 to the early 1930s. The phrase "The world at the gates of the Church"

from the branches of dreams and shimmered temptingly over our foreheads. Not tempting, it seemed to us, but holy and salvific, as God's new challenge for us, as a sign of the new hour of the world. People in the sixteenth century may have felt the same way about their strange preliminary exercise for the nineteenth century, with its blasting of boundaries and expansion of the world. The Golden Apple filled our heads and hearts.

Perhaps at no time has the gospel message "Do not love the world or the things in the world" (1 Jn 2:15) confronted a faithful, indeed a pious, young person as so incomprehensible. One reckoned to conquer, detoxify, and finally sanctify "the world" not from a distance but in embrace and assimilation. One dreamed of the "saint in the world", whose form and fate embodied this mission—of the Christian who was a human being, "independent of body and soul", equal to the "magnificent pagan", knowledgeable and gentlemanly, who knew how to pick the Golden Apple, fearless and reverent at the same time, who offered it to God the Creator and received it in return from God's hands for sanctified, consecrated pleasure. After all, did not we, the redeemed children of God, the gifts of Creation, have the right, before all the magnificent pagans, to pick their most beautiful and most precious fruits, to possess them, and to be happy with them? Should we not form people who would be able and willing to take on such a risk, and would such people not reveal the "other" meaning and value of creation in a much deeper and more convincing way than all fearful warnings and reservations from the edge of life?

Where is he, this saint of the here and now, who shows us how to blend this harmoniously and seamlessly with eternity?

See how fast the world spins! Eight years of war, and the Golden Apple has snapped back into obscurity as if it had never existed.[7]

---

refers both to this idea and to an article from the 1920s by this title: Elisabeth Langgässer, "Die Welt vor den Toren der Kirche," in *Elisabeth Langgässer. Eine biographische Skizze*, by Karlheinz Müller (Darmstadt, Germany: Gesellschaft Hessischer Literaturfreunde, 1990), 102–7.

[7] Gerl-Falkovitz explains that the handwritten manuscript clearly says "eight years of war" instead of the six years from 1939 to 1945. She wonders, "Is Görres including 1937 and 1938 or 1946 and 1947?"

3

NEWMAN'S RELIGIOUS AND HUMAN
CHARACTER IN LETTERS AND SKETCHES

It is odd: Newman, the "Church Father of the Twentieth Century",
seems so closely related to those of us living today that it is difficult
to understand how much he was a child of the past, characterized
by long-gone conditions.[1] His life spans the entire nineteenth century, from 1801 to 1890. His parents were alive during the French
Revolution; his childhood and adolescent years were filled with the
rise, wars, and fall of Napoleon. His first conversion occurred in
the same year as the Battle of Waterloo. His studies in Oxford began while the circle of Catholic Romantics in Vienna—Eichendorff
and Brentano, Friedrich von Schlegel, Veith and Zacharias Werner,
and Stolberg—gathered around Saint Clement Maria Hofbauer; and
how distant and faint these names and figures appear to us! When
Newman preached at St Mary's, Goethe was still living. The Oxford Movement, Littlemore, and conversion—for us this means
Vormärz, Biedermeier, the Romantic paintings by Waldmüller and
Caspar David Friedrich.[2] For Newman, Schubert and Mendelssohn
were "modern"; he could not really find a way to be on friendly

---

[1] Gerl-Falkovitz adds that the beginning of this section in the manuscript reads, "You
have had four lectures on the fate of Cardinal John Henry Newman, his position in
theology, and his importance as a preacher. Now a picture of the human and religious
personality of this great man should complete and round off what you have heard." This
chapter appears to be a lecture Görres gave as part of a series. We do not have information about the series or the other lectures.

[2] Gerl-Falkovitz notes that a different version of this passage reads:

What does all of this matter to us? What are Pusey, Keble, and Rose, what are
Froude, Whately, and Palmer to us? These silhouettes from your youth are much
stranger and paler to us than the figures of German Catholic Romanticism from the
same era—the circle of Eichendorff and Brentano, the siblings Veith and Zacharias
Werner, Adam von Müller and Anton Günther, Friedrich von Schlegel and Graf
von Stolberg, who gathered around the Bohemian Saint Clement Maria Hofbauer
in Sailer Lane in Vienna at almost the same time. Did we not also have our Möhler,
Sauer, and Hirscher, and the unfortunate Döllinger, who later became friends with
you, and who reached almost the same patriarchal age? For us, they are names from

terms with this music. His brothers and friends wear the bright tailcoats and colored top hats, high collars and neckerchiefs that we know from miniatures and *genre* paintings. He travels to Rome by stagecoach. He writes with a goose quill and complains very much about the imposition that he has to use a steel pen. In the second half of his life, the smaller European revolutions, the expansion of England into an empire, the Industrial and Social Revolutions take place. As he ages, this Oratorian preaches about the atrocities of the Indian uprising, mourns the deaths of the Crimean War and the Sudan Expedition; as an old man, he exchanges countless letters regarding the [First] Vatican Council; the elderly cardinal once again campaigns for religious freedom and care for Catholic girls working in factories.

Properly translated [into German], his writings should actually be in the language of Möhler,[3] his verses in the language of Mörike or perhaps Droste, whose spiritual poetry his curiously echoes. And, strangely enough, when he was in Rome for the last time to receive his cardinal's hat, men who are today in their sixties—the generation of Romano Guardini and Theodor Haecker—were already in the world.[4]

Newman grew to such an advanced age, and he began to age so early that we see him more plainly as an old man; this is certainly also because the advent of photography comes later in his life. But

---

libraries, mentioned with awe—though rarely!—and their texts, the value of which no one doubts, gather dust on the shelves of monasteries and seminaries.

But you live and are one of us.

The Vormärz and Biedermeier periods were the time of Newman's most powerful, masculine flourishing. In England and Germany, there are the first railroads —at that time more like playful concoctions from the minds of lunatic inventors than serious means of transport; but Newman preferred and more often used the stagecoach—even in Rome in 1867. He traveled to Malta by steamboat as early as 1833, but it was only then that the technical revolution began to change the face of Europe forever. Newman's England is still the idyllic world of William Wordsworth and Oliver Goldsmith.

Ignaz von Döllinger (1799–1890), a German Catholic priest, met John Henry Newman during a trip to England in 1836; Döllinger was excommunicated in 1871.

[3] Johann Adam Möhler (1796–1838), a German Catholic historian who sought reunion between Protestants and Catholics. In the manuscript, one originally reads "Schopenhauer" instead of "Möhler", but then this is crossed out.

[4] Gerl-Falkovitz points out that based on Guardini's date of birth, 1885, this would place the date of the composition of this chapter in 1945. Haecker was born in 1879.

he can be understood only from his origin and development. It is only from the curiously crooked, broken arc of his fate that we fathom his spiritual form because Newman's life is tragic, and his Christian character—may we say: the character of a saint?—came into being through bearing this tragedy.

The subject of this drama can be roughly described as follows: an extraordinary nature, with Goethe-like faculties, that seems destined for victory and conquering in encountering and experiencing the world, is thwarted by spirit and grace; overcoming the world has to be accomplished by way of renunciation and precisely in this rupture; it is in the fate of nonfulfillment that his nature attains its distinctly human and Christian perfection.

The boy, the eldest son of an English banker and a French mother, is extremely gifted. (The legend of Jewish descent is spurious.) With distinctive modesty, in his unfortunately short "Autobiographical Memoir", he calls himself "in no respect a precocious boy"[5]—but at the same time he reports that, at the age of eleven, he wrote English and Latin verses and prose (and did this as "recreation"[6] instead of taking part in the games of his peers), also comedies and satirical plays that were performed by his siblings; at fourteen, he wrote the text and music of a comic opera. At that time, a few years later, he developed a passion for serial publications, of which he wrote dozens of episodes by himself; once, two at a time, who fought each other—a funny early sign of an innate talent for controversy![7] From age ten into his elder years, the violin is his delight and consolation; Beethoven was his great love; he liked to call him "the gigantic nightingale"[8] and still enthused the young confreres who played string quartets and trios with him in the Oratory for his violin teacher from childhood; what came after Beethoven in music left him cold.

---

[5] "Autobiographical Memoir", in Anne Mozley, ed., *Letters and Correspondence of John Henry Newman during His Life in the English Church: With a Brief Autobiography* (London: Longmans, Green, 1903), 1:23.

[6] Mozley, *Letters*, 1:35.

[7] Newman writes, "In 1815 I wrote two periodicals—that is, papers called the 'Spy' and 'Anti-Spy.'" Mozley, *Letters*, 1:16. Special thanks to Dr. David Deavel for bringing this reference to my attention.

[8] Wilfrid Philip Ward, *The Life of John Henry Cardinal Newman: Based on His Private Journals and Correspondence* (London: Longmans, Green, 1912), 2:350.

Newman wrote about childhood in poems, without attaching much importance to them, so to speak, "for use at home", in diaries and letters to friends and siblings. The classic "imperial" English of his prose is praised everywhere. Verses, which he wrote just as a leisure activity, easily and as if they wrote themselves (while writing prose was for him like the pain of giving birth), are often so beautiful in their intentional simplicity and nonchalance that one might regret again and again that he had so little space for poetry on the margin of his life. The peculiar dramatic poem "The Dream of Gerontius" is like a plumb line that gives an idea of the scope of this talent, which was never fully realized.[9] Newman's two novels, *Callista*, about the third-century martyr Church, and *Loss and Gain*, the autobiographical story of a conversion, reveal an unusual narrative talent. Only the unusual subject matter of the two prevents them from becoming more widely known.

Diverse topics captivate him as a student in Oxford: in addition to classical languages and history, there is the classical legacy of the great Oxford tradition, the emerging natural sciences, mineralogy and geology, chemistry, mathematics, composition, and, of all things, Persian. He is not a loafer in his college who nibbles at all sorts of things. Rather, from the start he applies himself to learning and is a researcher of unheard-of diligence, tough and thorough. Newman, in spite of being tender and plagued with headaches, eye pain, and dental issues throughout his long life, was healthy and productive; only his furious pace of work without rest and breaks caused him nervous breakdowns several times, such as for the first time at the age of twenty, when the young student failed his exam after working twelve to fifteen hours a day for twenty weeks. This breakdown had significant consequences: Newman gave up his secular career and turned to theology.

The young candidate for the spiritual profession threw himself into the new subjects with the same passion, but his horizon did not narrow. He was never one of those very common religious people who have no interest outside of their piety. "Newman's mind was world-wide," said Froude about the years at Oxford. "He was

---

[9] John Henry Newman, "The Dream of Gerontius", in *Verses on Various Occasions* (London: Longmans, Green, 1905), 323–70.

interested in everything which was going on in science, in politics, in literature. Nothing was too large for him, nothing too trivial, if it threw light upon the central question, what man really was, and what was his destiny. . . . He could admire enthusiastically any greatness of action and character."[10] "When he read Gurwood's 'Despatches of the Duke of Wellington,' he said to James Anthony Froude, 'They make one burn to be a soldier!' "[11] And [William Paine] Neville, his faithful companion in old age, tells almost exactly the same from his final years: "Everything interested him—literature, politics, the trade and stipulations of the merchant, the circumstances of persons and places known to him; rural life; the studies of the young men; the thoughts of the simple and the lowly, no less than the most difficult problems and controversies."[12] His friends said, "He enjoyed the conversation of professional men—of soldiers, doctors, lawyers,—all who could give an intelligent account of what interested them, and this not merely from good nature, but from the genuine interest he took in the *quidquid agunt homines* [the various affairs of men]. He always gave one the impression that he might have been great in any department of life; that he might have been a great general, a great lawyer, a great parliamentary debater."[13] His dimensions were large.

Newman, the Englishman, is no homebody. He loves animals, plants, the sea, the mountains, the countryside. His holiday letters, especially the letters from his long trip to Sicily, the most important of his life—later he went to Rome only on business—reveal the keenest observational power for things small and large and an astonishing gift of vivid descriptions: he has the eye of an illustrator and painter for shapes, colors, and lines; of a naturalist for the details of animals, trees, terrain, and buildings. Later in Newman's letters, in the midst of the most exciting intellectual battles, we find

---

[10] Ward, *The Life*, 1:62. The footnote in the German text reads "Ward II, 352", but this does not appear to be correct.

[11] Ward, *The Life*, 1:62. The footnote in the German text says this, too, is from "Ward II, 352", but this does not appear to be correct.

[12] Ward, *The Life*, 2:352. The footnote in the German text reads "Ward II, 353", but this does not appear to be correct.

[13] Ward, *The Life*, 2:353.

accounts of "Charlie, the virtuous pony"[14] and his recent friendship with a pert lamb; or about the troubles of Ambrose's favorite
book in Rednal; the needs and survival prospects of a mulberry
tree received recently as a gift, or a non-native hazel bush are not
neglected either. His friend and fellow Oratorian Neville thought
that if Newman had had no other duties, he might have devoted
more time to his garden and his love of growing plants than to his
library. Somewhere, Newman left a very revealing sketch of "the
ideal of a happy life"[15]: a vivid picture of the existence of a wealthy
bachelor in a cultivated English country house, surrounded by all
the noble delights of mind and body. Even strawberry beds and a
sunny wall for [peaches] are included.[16]

W. G. Ward remembers his friend's unusual sharpness and sub-
tlety of mind; he used to choose the wines for the college cellar,
although he himself more often drank only moderately.

He was by nature a man of such strength and talent that he had
a sense for the beautiful and the pleasant, the important and the
delightful in creation, able to feel and to grasp; he was an artist
and a scholar at the same time. For him, there were many ways to
encounter the world, whether conquering or enjoying it. But already in the fifteen-year-old, the decision had been made to use the
world to escape from the world—namely, in the earth-shattering
experience of his conversion in 1816. Newman was no young Augustine, even if, at one point, he calls himself "more like a devil
than a wicked boy".[17] To the outside world, nothing had happened,
and, in this change, nothing happened that would have been noticed
even in his intimately connected, deeply affectionate family home.
Newman came under the influence of a staunch Calvinist teacher,
Dr. Mayers. For the boy who was interested in spiritual matters and
aesthetics without clear religious notions, dogma suddenly became
real and alive: God, judgment, sin, eternity, predestination. He "realizes" what he believes: a new world opens up to him, the invisible,

---

[14] Ward, The Life, 2:322.
[15] Ward, The Life, 2:336. The footnote in the German text reads "Ward II, 33", but
this does not appear to be correct.
[16] The German text reads "apricots", but the passage Görres is referring to from Ward
reads "peaches". Ward, The Life, 2:337.
[17] Ward, The Life, 1:575.

supernatural. It is very telling for Newman that this "conversion", which in old age he considers the most important event of his life, does not entail an externally noticeable departure from the world— at most, for a time a certain puritanical rigor in the rejection of the usual pleasures that he judged very harshly, including among the students. The breadth and impartiality of his gaze as well as the abundance and liveliness of his interests remain unchanged, but his values have found their rank order: the religious center alone "really" counts; everything else is "edge". In weighty internal struggles, the young man renounces dreams that are only natural to such a talent: "How active still are the evil passions of vainglory, ambition, &c., within me! After my failure last November, I thought that they would never be unruly again. Alas! no sooner is any mention made of my standing for a fellowship than every barrier seems swept away; and they spread, and overflow, and deluge me."[18] He prays ardently to be spared from fame, distinction, and wealth—and it may well be that the failure of his fate, incomprehensible with this abundance of gifts, has a secret connection with this prayer of his youth. A great, unforgettable summer of splendor is still granted to Newman: his power to embrace the world, as we called it, reaches its peak in the power that is given to him for a while over people.

All the accounts of his Oxford years unanimously state that his impact on the environment cannot be described in words; the most glowing report would not do justice to the facts. "The influence of his singular combination of genius and devotion has had no parallel there before or since", writes Dean Lake.[19] "For hundreds of young men *Credo in Newmannum* was the genuine symbol of faith", [writes Froude].[20] "But now the character of a prophet and leader of men was added. And the movement in Oxford of which he was the life and soul aroused all the enthusiasm of the time", describes Ward,[21] who, later in the Catholic Church, which he entered [prior to][22]

---

[18] "Autobiographical Memoir", 1:59.

[19] Ward, *The Life*, 1:60.

[20] Ward, *The Life*, 1:63.

[21] Ward, *The Life*, 1:63.

[22] The German texts says William George Ward (1812–1882) entered the Catholic Church "following" Newman. W. G. Ward entered the Church in September 1845, however, before Newman did so in October 1845.

his mentor's example, stands in painful opposition to his beloved friend for decades. "The simplest word which dropped from him was treasured as if it had been an intellectual diamond."[23] Ward even confesses how his heart pounded as soon as he heard Newman's gait on the staircase.[24] And he writes to him long after those blissfully memorable years: "I will say that I have felt myself a kind of intellectual orphan", and "*The whole colour of my life has changed* . . . from the loss of your sympathy. But my gratitude for the past will ever remain intact."[25]

Newman maintained lifelong friendships and correspondence with women, but none played a special role in his life; it can be assumed that the reason was his decidedly ascetic demeanor because it can only be assumed that they, too, experienced the potent magic of his nature. His strongest impact was on young men, with whom he allowed himself to be open. He was more distant with boys, although he understood children well, as the delightful letters to his friends' little ones show. Most distant to him were those of staid middle age, whom he seldom spared or apologized to. Here, too, lies a large part of the tragedy of Newman's life: the pastoral care of students, his greatest concern, to which he seemed predestined, was granted to him only during his twelve years at Oxford; later he headed a boys' school for decades.

His exterior is also part of his magic. Contemporaries remember the strong impression of his appearance. He was somewhat tall and slim. His head was large, and some found a resemblance to Julius Caesar in his features.[26] Ryder's well-known image of Newman as a young man is almost frighteningly beautiful—we see one of those minds of the early nineteenth century (Kierkegaard and Möhler also belong among them) in which spirit, character, warmth of life, and gracefulness merge into a humanly perfected unity almost unbelievable today. Aubrey de Vere portrays Newman at an evening party in the 1830s: "singularly graceful figure in cap and gown. . . . The slight form and gracious address might have belonged either to a

---

[23] Ward, *The Life*, 1:63.
[24] Ward, *The Life*, 2:348.
[25] Appendix 2 in Ward, *The Life*, 2:566.
[26] Ward, *The Life*, 1:61.

youthful ascetic of the middle ages or to a graceful high-bred lady of our own days. He was pale and thin . . . swift of pace, but when not walking intensely still. . . . When touching on subjects which interested him much, he used gestures rapid and decisive, though not vehement."[27]

The images of his later years show him strangely withered and as if he had sunk back into himself; cruel aging manifests itself as decay and death, even more so as melancholy and unspeakable tiredness. Newman was well aware of this, and also, he knew which bitter depth of sadness this change came from. But even in his old age, visitors lovingly and wistfully describe the delicacy, gracefulness, almost fragility of his appearance—"delicate as an old lady washed in milk"[28]—the quick, silvery whisper, the wonderful magic of his voice, well known to the Oxford preaching community as well as the young students of Edgbaston. "His soul was in his voice, as a bird is in its song."[29]

Froude believes that he recognizes a kinship with the great Roman not only in Newman's face but also in his nature: "There was an original force of character which refused to be moulded by circumstances, which was to make its own way, and become a power in the world."[30] Newman has an unprecedented clarity of mind, a lively, excitable mind—plus an extremely winning gentleness, warmth, and mildness—sweetness, the "sweetness" that the Englishman can also say about a man without the word's feeling mushy and sticky like the German word *süss*. He could be ironic, never stinging and biting—that means something with this master of satire. Others emphasize the unique combination of sparkling spirit, tenderness, and refinement ("loud people, ambiguous jokes, everything vulgar and tasteless was hated by him"), of kind affability and lively piety. Yes, one dares to make the very significant remark: "His friends loved his very faults"—his sensitivity and occasionally irascible intensity, his obstinacy and his sharpness—"as one may love those of a fascinating woman."[31] By his nature, he was meant to lead people

---

[27] Ward, *The Life*, 1:66.
[28] Ward, *The Life*, 2:369.
[29] Ward, *The Life*, 2:370.
[30] Ward, *The Life*, 1:61
[31] Ward, *The Life*, 2:348.

and was gifted in arousing passionate attachment and devotion in friends and disciples. So Froude tells us.

Newman is nothing less than a "gentleman" in appearance, no less the model of a "brilliant" worldly man. He is, even in this, a real Englishman (only the crystal clarity of thought reveals his French heritage); he is shy and inhibited throughout his life. He wants to sink into the earth with embarrassment and shame in the Oriel College greetings with the newly admitted fellow, who will soon surpass his colleagues in influence and prestige; the impertinence that he should now simply speak to the others by name, without "master" and other titles, seems to him incomprehensible. Into old age, he dreads invitations and visits: "I am so dreadfully shy, that I never show to advantage, and feel it myself acutely all the time."[32] "A house full of company and I looking like a fool."[33] Wearing Catholic clerical garb causes him agony: "I look like a fool, from my own great intrinsic absurdity."[34] "Perhaps his supreme merit as a talker", says Ward [quoting Froude], "was that he never tried to be witty or to say striking things. Ironical he could be, but not ill-natured. Not a malicious anecdote was ever heard from him. Prosy he could not be. He was lightness itself—the lightness of elastic strength—and he was interesting because he never talked for talking's sake, but because he had something real to say."[35] Even so, Father Neville emphasizes in his description of the elderly cardinal how he had "nothing of the scholar about him"[36] and carefully avoided everything pedantic and academic in conversation.

Here we must not forget his genuinely English humor—terse and subdued in expression but with an unerring sense for the funny thing about people and situations in his environment. His descriptions are delightful: his seasickness on the Sicilian voyage; the cautious but spot-on depiction of the French clergymen on his first trip to Rome; the meals, ceremonies, and life in Italian seminaries and institutes; or his own inconvenient visit in an English boarding school in England, how he bursts into a school party unannounced, and

[32] Letter to Mr. Hutton, in Ward, *The Life*, 2:332.
[33] Letter to St. John, in Ward, *The Life*, 1:133.
[34] Letter to Dalgairns, July 6, 1846, in Ward, *The Life*, 1:124.
[35] Ward, *The Life*, 1:63.
[36] Ward, *The Life*, 2:352.

the embarrassed leaders of the school want to tell him that the drink on the banquet table is very harmless: "They certainly were scandalized at my detecting the punch—for they said again and again that it was made of lemon and sugar. All I can say is that *ours* at the high table was remarkably stiff, and that I was obliged to dilute it to twice or thrice its quantity with water."[37] Or he comments quite seriously in his diary on the great trouble of an unusable house at the Oratory, which causes him a lot of expenses and headaches: "There is the famous story of the man who bought an elephant, and was too poor to keep, and too merciful to kill it, and was unable to persuade anyone to accept of it."[38] The report about some adventures in "wild Ireland" is compellingly comical—especially the last one, how he strays into an Irish nunnery, is supposed to make a speech off the cuff to the pupils, does not exactly pull it off with glory, falls out of favor with the superior, and finally has to drink raspberry juice with her, "bitter-sweet as the anger of a nun", "just because he wasn't able to play the role of the holy fool for a group of girls".

Newman's modesty can be explained only by the fact that it is the visible expression of a much deeper attitude, religious humility, and at the same time a certain melancholy about himself. His mother's judgment of the twenty-one-year-old is very important: "To show you I do not think you *too old* for a mother's correction and advice, I shall not hesitate to tell you I see one great fault in your character which alarms me, as I observe it grows upon you seriously; and as all virtues may degenerate into vices, it is everyone's duty to have a strict guard over themselves to avoid extremes. Your fault is a want of self-confidence and a dissatisfaction with yourself."[39] But the son, reverent, corrigible, always with a childlike touch in relation to his mother, withstands this loving reproach calmly. No, it is by no means, as the parents hope, a temporary darkening of his disposition as a result of overly stern religious perspectives, perhaps also overexertion or weakened health: "Believe me, those sentiments

---

[37] Ward, *The Life*, 1:104.

[38] Ward, *The Life*, 1:221.

[39] Letter from Newman's mother to Newman, March 11, 1822, in Mozley, *Letters*, 1:51. In the German text, Görres has the last sentence in italics.

are neither new nor slightly founded. If they made me melancholy, morose, austere, distant, reserved, sullen, then indeed they might with justice be the subject of anxiety; but . . . take me when I am most foolish at home, and extend mirth into childishness; stop me short and ask me then what I think of myself, whether my opinions are less gloomy; no, I think I should seriously return the same answer, that 'I shuddered at myself.' "[40]

This deep humility remains Newman's characteristic throughout his life—hand in hand with very clear insight into the extraordinary and unique nature of his talent and calling. As an Anglican minister, he writes to a lady: "It is dangerous to say 'I have great powers' though it be true, and one knows it to be true. It becomes a temptation to dwell on the fact. I think it a duty for a person to turn away from the thought as a suggestion from an evil principle, and to note it down as such; nay even to mention it in confession as an approach to sin."[41]

Later he reports about the long, painful struggles over his conversion: "I have kept my conviction under, only from the notion that my sins might have brought upon me some extreme delusion, or some abuse of intellect, of which I was not conscious, might have judicially inflicted on me captivity to some sophism, which others could see through."[42]

At the time of the [First] Vatican Council, when his name shines like a star over the entire English spiritual world after a long period of darkness, he writes to an old friend regarding her serious notions that he should participate in preparation for the Council: "Really and truly I am *not* a theologian. A theologian is one who has mastered theology—who can say how many opinions there are on every point . . . who can pronounce which are safe, which allowable, which dangerous . . . this and a hundred things besides—which I am not, and never shall be."[43]

At age seventy, the acclaimed Newman writes to the certainly much younger philosopher Dr. Meynell, who reads through New-

---

[40] Letter to his mother, March 11, 1822, in Mozley, *Letters*, 1:51–52.

[41] Letter to a "lady . . . who had sought his counsel", in Mozley, *Letters*, 2:382.

[42] Letter to Henry Wilberforce, June 25, 1846, in Ward, *The Life*, 1:129.

[43] Letter to Sister Maria Pia, February 10, 1869, in Ward, *The Life*, 2:281.

man's great epistemological work *Grammar of Assent* to determine whether it is in agreement with the Scholastic school: "I am quite ashamed to think what I have cost you in paper, pens, ink, stamps and time."[44] And again: "I am also deeply conscious of my own ignorance on the whole matter, and it sometimes amazes me that I have ventured to write on a subject which is even accidentally connected with it"[45]—regarding a subject that he had carried around in his mind for three decades! And how we are moved by his complaint about his beloved friend Ambrose St. John: "This, of course, made me love him; but what has so greatly moved me and made me fear that I shall be so far below him if I ever get to Heaven that he will not notice me, is his fulness in good works. He was ever doing something good."[46]

So, when he says to Hutton that every word of praise or blame, "tear[s] off his morbidly sensitive skin",[47] we admittedly understand. He suffered bitterly from misunderstanding, emotional iciness, and injustice, especially from loved ones or those who should have been. His gratitude for every kind word of appreciation or concern is almost painful to read.

Like almost everyone whose nature is endowed with suffering, he is not "heroic" in a superficial sense. As Ward aptly said, Newman managed to put his hand in the fire when it was necessary but did not always manage to hold back cries of pain.[48] This is how we understand the passionate complaint in so many of his familiar letters. And we understand his deep inner suffering from our own thin-skinned sensitivity to pain. "O rid me of this frightful *cowardice*, for this is at the bottom of all my ills. When I was young, I was bold, because I was ignorant—now I have lost my boldness, because I have advanced in experience. I am able to count the cost, better than I did, of being brave for Thy sake, and therefore I shrink from

---

[44] Letter to Dr. [Wilfrid] Meynell, August 1870, in Ward, *The Life*, 2:261.

[45] Letter to Dr. Meynell, July 27, 1869, in Ward, *The Life*, 2:257.

[46] Letter to Reverend John Wolford, S.J., June 2, 1875, in Ward, *The Life*, 2:412–13. In the manuscript, Görres wrote that the letter was to "the faithful Dominican nuns in Stone".

[47] Letter to Mr. [Arthur Wollaston] Hutton, in Ward, *The Life*, 1:20.

[48] Ward, *The Life*, 1:21.

sacrifices. Here is a second reason, over and above the deadness of my soul, why I have so little faith or love in me."[49]

This already indicates the rare capability of the mind of this man. We know Newman as a giant of intellectual force, knowledge, and incomparable intellectual sharpness, as a philosopher and a theologian, as the psychologist of sermons, who, in relentless, implacable reflection, shines through and dissects his own soul and that of others. Today, it is commonplace to assume such a man to be a "cold intellectual" with a withered heart and far from real life. The terrifying impoverishment and barbarization of minds of the last two generations has largely distorted and reduced our standards of what is both human and male. Newman is far from such one-sidedness. In this context, he is wholly a person of the early nineteenth century, the type we know only from novels and romantic letters. Despite all the restraint and nobility of his nature, we find testimonies of such passionate, unbroken emotion that it almost hurts just to read them. Who felt departure and separation like him! A hundred years later, our hearts cramp at the confessions we find in his letters and diaries, not least in the veiled autobiography, *Loss and Gain*.

Newman had the most wonderful family life. He, the eldest, was the pride and hope of his father and mother. He had an intimate, trusting friendship with his siblings. After the early death of his father, his mother called him "my guardian angel".[50] As a grown man, he writes her five letters over twelve days of vacation; he carefully follows the education of his sisters. He makes suggestions, provides them with "tasks" in math and classics, is happy about their progress in translation and music, examines their verses[51]—and he does all this in the midst of the heaviest work pressure of his teaching at Oxford. The numerous long letters from his trip to Sicily clearly show how he hardly separates himself from his loved ones at home. He watches and observes with and for them, as it were; he collects flower seeds for his mother; he writes unreservedly, childishly: dreams, fun, poems, serious reflections. His homesickness

---

[49] Journal, December 15, 1859, in Ward, *The Life*, 1:576.
[50] Letter from Newman's mother to her eldest daughter, November 5, 1827, in Mozley, *Letters*, 1:149.
[51] See Mozley, *Letters*, 1:71.

during this one trip, a trip he longed for and enjoyed greatly, is almost astonishing. The sudden death of his youngest sister, Mary, tears him apart inside. Half a year later, he cannot stand the sight of her handwriting, and yet he is a man of more than thirty and she was barely seventeen. Friendship plays an important role in his life. All the important spiritual and religious transformations and decisions of his youth come from personal encounters, not from books. The Oxford Movement, which continues to transform the Anglican church to this day, was a joint venture of a young circle of friends and allies, headed by Newman, Pusey, and Keble; it was an attempt to reawaken and bring to the fore aspects of pre-Reformation tradition. A number of those from the Oxford Movement followed him on the way to Rome—but not those in his closest group of friends.

Only from Newman's tremendous strength of heart and depth of mind can we at least, from a distance, measure the sacrifice he made during his conversion. His mother did not live to witness this step of his, which was fortunate for both of them; this step detached him from his sisters, "part of himself; there was nothing on earth which he prized like his home"[52]; that is how he lets Charles Reding, his hero in *Loss and Gain*, articulate this. "Yes, I give up home, I give up all who have ever known me, loved me, valued me, wished me well; I know well I am making myself a by-word and an outcast."[53] " 'Oh, it is very hard to leave you all, to go to strangers. . . . I do not wish it, but I cannot help it; I am called, I am compelled'. . . . The tears flowed down his cheeks. . . . 'And scarcely any one to feel for me; black looks, bitter words.' "[54] When Reding departs from Oxford: "At the first view of that beloved place he stood still with folded arms, unable to proceed. . . . The silver Isis, the grey willows, the far-stretching plains, the dark groves . . . wood, water, stone, all so calm, so bright, they might have been his, but his they were not. . . . Whatever he was to gain higher and better, at least this and such as this he never could have again."[55] And Reding tears

---

[52] John Henry Newman, *Loss and Gain*, rev. ed. (London: Longman, Green, 1906), 346.

[53] *Loss and Gain*, 341–42.

[54] *Loss and Gain*, 372.

[55] *Loss and Gain*, 353–54.

a few withered leaves from the willows, kisses them with tears, and hides them in his heart.[56] The letter that describes his departure from Littlemore, the site of his decision, is similar: "I quite tore myself away, and could not help kissing my bed, and mantelpiece, and other parts of the house. I have been most happy there, though in a state of suspense. And there it has been that I have both been taught my way and received an answer to my prayers."[57]

Twenty-two years later [in June 1868], the Anglican canon Irvine, out for a walk in Littlemore, sees an old, very poorly dressed man leaning against the fence and crying bitterly. The collar of his old gray coat was open, his hat pulled low over his face. It was Newman, who had come to say a last goodbye to the place of his youth. When the minister addressed him deferentially and asked him to enter the church, "He . . . burst out crying and said, 'Oh no, oh no! . . . I cannot.'"[58]

At about the same time, the plan for a Catholic college in Oxford was being considered with Newman. "Personally, it would be as painful a step as I could be called upon to make. Oxford never can be to me what it was. It and I are severed. It would be like the dead visiting the dead. I should be a stranger in my dearest home. I look forward to it with great distress—and certainly would not contemplate it except under an imperative call of duty."[59]

From the age of seventy-six, and probably until his death, he kept a small piece of wood from a roof beam at Oriel College in Oxford, like a relic.

In 1864, when he wrote for the public in England his *Apologia*, his great retrospective and account of his spiritual path, all his old wounds broke open and bled as they had at the start: "I have been constantly in tears, and constantly crying out with distress."[60] "I never had such a time, and once or twice thought I was breaking down. . . . It has been nothing but the good prayers of my friends

[56] *Loss and Gain*, 376.

[57] Letter to W. J. Copeland, his curate at Littlemore, February 1846, in Ward, *The Life*, 1:117.

[58] Letter from Canon Irvine to Ward, no date, in Ward, *The Life*, 2:206.

[59] Letter to Dr. Pusey, April 29, 1866, in Ward, *The Life*, 2:122.

[60] Letter to Hope-Scott, the Oratory, Birmingham, May 2, 1864, in Ward, *The Life*, 2:25.

which has brought me through."[61] Yet it is "with so much suffering, such profuse crying, such long spells of work—sometimes sixteen hours, once twenty-two hours at once,—that it is a prodigious, awful marvel that I have got through it and that I am not simply knocked up by it."[62] At the time of his conversion, he wrote to Rosa Giberne, a loyal friend from his youth: "But alas! can you point to any one who has lost more in the way of friendship, whether by death or alienation, than I have? . . . My mother gone; my sisters nothing to me, or rather foreign to me; of my greatest friends, Froude, Wood, Bowden taken away, all of whom would now be, or be coming, on my side. . . . Of my friends of a dozen years ago whom have I now?"[63]

Newman never got over the loss of his first, most beloved community. Again, in this he is very English in that he is attached tooth and nail to the past, to tradition, to whatever had been. In addition, he has an extraordinary strength and fidelity of memory, which makes him cherish the veritable rituals of birthdays and other memorial days.

"What did I know of my present friends a dozen years ago? Why, they were at school, or they were freshmen looking up to me, if they knew my name, as some immense and unapproachable don; and now they know nothing, can know nothing of my earlier life; things which to me are as yesterday are to them as dreams of the past; . . . they have not the associations, which are part of my own world, in which I live."[64] And again: "New friends cannot love one. . . . They know nothing of one—but to one who has known another twenty years, his face and his name is a history. . . . And thus I feel that no one here [in Rome] can sympathize with me duly . . . [and their] respect [is] not for me, but for some imagination of their own which bears my name."[65]

Here the pain for the lost friends of Newman sets up something unjust against the "new ones" who accompanied him through the

---

[61] Letter to Mother Imelda Poole, Rednal, June 25, 1864, in Ward, *The Life*, 2:29.

[62] Letter to "another of the Dominican Sisters", in Ward, *The Life*, 2:30–31.

[63] "Wood" and "Bowden" were Samuel Francis Wood and John William Bowden. Letter to Miss Maria Rosina Giberne, January 28, 1846, in Ward, *The Life*, 1:112–13.

[64] Letter to Miss Maria Rosina Giberne, January 28, 1846, in Ward, *The Life*, 1:113.

[65] Letter to Henry Wilberforce, December 13, 1846, in Ward, *The Life*, 1:150.

second half of his life, who, always given to him anew, surrounded him for decades with ever-growing love, tenderness, and veneration. Newman once mentioned four people (three Oratorians: Ambrose St. John, Caswall, Joseph Gordon, and a widow: Mrs. Wootten, the housemother of his boyhood boarding school) who, "have generously thrown themselves and all they had into my hands".[66] But when he reconnected after seventeen years with some of his oldest companions, he wrote to his former curate, Copeland, his successor in the parish of Littlemore: "You must not disappoint me. I have a hundred questions to ask you, and a hundred things to show you . . . and I want you to see the place where I am to be buried." "No one knows but myself how great an infliction upon me it has been that you all have so simply treated me as *dead.*" "Except Ambrose St. John, I have not spoken to any one so near to my heart and memory as you are, for near 17 years."[67] And in February 1846, Newman wrote to Wilberforce even about Ambrose: "And that is the reason perhaps I love St. John so much because he comes from you and from your teaching. Oh that he might be a pledge to me that you are yourself to repair that breach which you sorrow over, by your doing what he has done—but I say the above whatever you resolve upon, Carissime, great indeed as must be my distress, as well as yours, while we are divided."[68]

But when Father Ambrose died thirty years later [in 1875], the aged Newman threw himself next to the body on the deathbed and spent the whole night there, wishing to be buried in his grave. He wrote [to Miss Holmes]: "This is the greatest affliction I have had in my life. . . . I do not expect ever to get over the loss I have had. It is like an open wound which in old men cannot be healed."[69] Even fourteen years later he could not mention Father Ambrose's name without crying.

---

[66] Edward Caswall. Newman, letter to Mother Imelda Poole, December 29, 1876, in Ward, *The Life*, 2:414.

[67] Various letters to Copeland, Summer 1862, in Ward, *The Life*, 1:597–600. The Copeland Görres refers to here is William John Copeland (1804–1885).

[68] Letter to Henry Wilberforce, February 26, 1846, in Ward, *The Life*, 1:118.

[69] Görres wrote that this is from a letter to "his loyal Dominican nuns"; it is from a letter to Miss Holmes. Letter to Miss Holmes, 1875, in Ward, *The Life*, 2:412.

Newman outlived almost all his friends. As an elderly patriarch, he stands like a tree from which the leaves keep falling. For many years, the old man practically lives simply from the anticipation of reunion.

Still, Newman was lonely, lonely in the very depths of his interior. His sermons are startlingly full of lament that humans are alone. It is an assertion. It is not theory but, rather, experience. In the deepest interior, in that which matters most, we are without companions—unattainable, untouchable, incomprehensible to others. God is absolutely the only One who knows us, sees through us, understands us, and shares our inner life with us. This surprises us with a person whose long life played out in ongoing interactions within a network of personal relationships almost too vast to apprehend. Newman's confession of loneliness is so haunting that Bremond sees him above all as a solitary man.[70] Bremond even goes so far as to assert that Newman's innermost secret is his painful inability to love. This is how Bremond wants to understand the "myself and my Creator"[71] of his first conversion. Along these lines is the admission of the thirty-year-old that he could not part with his old coat as his only comrade. Apart from the fact that this trait came from his trip to Sicily when Newman lay forlorn and seriously ill among strangers, Bremond, the Frenchman, with all the ingenuity of his interpretation seems to be construing something that goes beyond Newman's English behavior. How much does the shy letter to his younger fellow Oratorian Philip Gordon say: "My dearest Brother . . . many is the time I have stood over the fire at breakfast and looked at you at Recreation, hunting for something to talk about. The song says that 'love cannot live on flowers': not so, yet it requires material, if not for sustenance, at least for display—and I have fancied too

---

[70] Görres cites Henri "Bremond, 200 and 266"; Gerl-Falkovitz adds, "*Newman. Essai de biographie psychologique* (Paris, 1906)". The passages Görres cites are on pages 163–64 and 220–21 in the English edition: Henri Bremond, *The Mystery of Newman*, trans. H. C. Corrance (London: Williams and Norgate, 1907). The German word *einsam* has a range of meanings, including "lonely", "solitary", and "isolated". I have translated it here as "solitary"; the opening chapter by Bremond on Newman's emotional life is titled "L'Isloé Voluntaire" in French (25–52), which is translated as "The Solitary by Choice" in Bremond, *The Mystery of Newman*, 17–39.

[71] John Henry Newman, *Apologia pro Vita Sua*, trans. Ian Ker (London: Penguin Books, 1994), 4.

that younger and lighter minds perhaps could not, if they would, care much for one who has had so much to wear him down. All blessings come on you my dear Brother—in proportion to my waning."[72] Or, after the death of Ambrose St. John, Newman wrote to Miss Rosina Giberne (then Sister Maria Pia in Autun): "Since his death, I have been reproaching myself for not expressing to *him* how much I felt *his* love—and I write this lest I should feel the same about you, should it be God's will that I should outlive you."[73]

At one point Newman admits, "I cannot ever realise to myself that any one loves me."[74] And again: "I feel I must be a hypocrite, and taking them in, that they are so loving to me."[75] Here again his deep modesty becomes apparent, combined with the lack of self-confidence that his mother recognized as almost life-threatening.

Yet, it seems to us, this strong tension between loneliness and friendship, which so determined Newman's life, is situated far deeper than just in a natural predisposition. It is situated in the secret of his vocation, which at the same time fulfilled and overrode his nature in its innermost core. Here, it seems to us, is at the same time the secret of his power over the hearts of people. To use a term that is often sentimentalized but is fitting here: Newman is, with reverence and shyness, truly a chaste man. The encounter with God has so overwhelmed him, so captivated him, that he is henceforth surrounded by a mysterious ring that no human can cross. He who faces the world in the fullness of its glory by nature with such vivid senses and overwhelming spirit, has in reality experienced it only "in a mirror dimly" (1 Cor 13:12):

> Till Thou art seen, it seems to be
> A sort of fairy ground,
> Where suns unsetting light the sky,
> And flowers and fruits abound. . . .
> But when Thy keener, purer beam

---

[72] Letter to fellow Oratorian Philip Gordon, no date (in a passage with letters from 1848), in Ward, *The Life*, 1:204.

[73] Letter to Sister Maria Pia, no date (in a passage with letters from 1875), in Ward, *The Life*, 2:412.

[74] Letter to Reverend J. Keble, August 27, 1837, in Mozley, *Letters*, 2:216.

[75] Letter to Mrs. W. Froude, the Oratory, January 9, 1877, in Ward, *The Life*, 2:572.

Is pour'd upon our sight,
It loses all its power to charm,
And what was day is night.

His bond with God is so strong that this truly existential turning
away from creatures does not even mean struggle and sacrifice, as
the final verse of the above poem seems to say:

Poor is our sacrifice, whose eyes
Are lighted from above;
We offer what we cannot keep,
What we have ceased to love.[76]

His decision is all-inclusive, once and for all; but there remains
the quiet melancholy, the unfulfilled longing, the always alert waiting for the invisible world.

For Newman, celibacy is therefore not (as it is for so many cradle
Catholics) a tragic constraint, a hard necessity based on ecclesial-
political calculations, *the* sacrifice of life, as something certainly to
be respected as a discipline but only to the extent that the individual
definitely has the right to offset and alleviate this life-wasting un-
fulfillment through careful compensatory measures. For Newman,
rather, it is an inner necessity of authentic priesthood. It is not a
matter of puritanical narrowness and fear; Newman knew the noblest of family life, and he cultivated lifelong friendships with pious
women. But—sacred unto the Lord, reserved for God, separated
and untouchable for claims of human desire and possession, be they
passion or habit: this is how he sees the priest.

In *Loss and Gain*, he has Charles Reding say to his sister: "But
I am sure, that, did I give my heart to any creature, I should be
withdrawing it from God."[77] It worries and preoccupies the young
Anglican theologian that his church has exchanged the great Catholic tradition on this point for the lentils of the culture-preserving
rectory idyll.[78] We know from *Loss and Gain* how he was tormented
by the sight of married brothers in [the Anglican priestly] office.[79]

---

[76] "175. The Two Worlds", in *Verses*, 319–20. The full text of "The Two Worlds"
appears in chapter 9 of this volume.

[77] *Loss and Gain*, 103.

[78] Regarding "the lentils", see Genesis 25:34. Special thanks to Richard Whitekettle
for bringing this reference to my attention.

[79] See *Loss and Gain*, 189–94, 196–97, 204.

And the letters from the first half of his life reveal that the clergymen from his circle of friends kept betrothal engagements from him out of embarrassment and even with a certain fear of his disapproval.

During his vacation in the summer of 1831 on the Isle of Wight, the peculiar beauty and abundance of nature overwhelmed him and delighted him into writing letters of an exuberant, almost intoxicated enthusiasm, very different from his usual restraint. From these weeks in July come the melancholy and determined verses that give a hint of what was going on in his soul in the face of this assailing earthly glory:

> There stray'd awhile, amid the woods of Dart,
> One who could love them, but who durst not love.
> A vow had bound him, ne'er to give his heart
> To streamlet bright, or soft secluded grove.
> 'Twas a hard humbling task, onwards to move
> His easy-captured eyes from each fair spot,
> With unattach'd and lonely step to rove
> O'er happy meads, which soon its print forgot:—
> Yet kept he safe his pledge, prizing his pilgrim-lot.[80]

His sisters too, even his best friends, felt the unsurpassable ring of consecrated austerity that surrounded him. His gentleness was masculine, without a shadow of softness, writes Aubrey de Vere; "an iron hardness in J. Newman; but in him, as in Dante, there is also an exquisite and surpassing sweetness."[81] And that is why neither Newman's heart nor his life got poorer. Because he genuinely renounced all human ties for the sake of the kingdom of heaven, he received a hundred times over already in this life. Few people have been loved like him—with the awesome, devoted, infinitely grateful love with which the mirrors of God are loved on earth, a love that fills the most human powers of the heart and yet is not of this world. "A mysterious veneration had by degrees gathered round him", says Ward, "till now it was almost as though some Ambrose or Augustine of older ages had reappeared."[82] An Anglican

---

[80] "21. The Pilgrim", in *Verses*, 61.

[81] Wilfrid Philip Ward, *Aubrey de Vere: A Memoir, Based on His Unpublished Diaries and Correspondence* (London: Longmans, Green, 1904), 182.

[82] Ward, quoting [John Campbell] Shairp, in Ward, *The Life*, 1:63–64.

friend characterizes this peculiar enchantment even more clearly in the sense we mean: "Then there was the utter unworldliness, the setting aside of all the things which men most prize, the tameless-ness of soul which was ready to essay the impossible." Men felt that here was:

> One of that small transfigured band
> Which the world cannot tame.[83]

And Newman describes this himself, without knowing it, in his hero Reding: "So the strange unknown odour, pleasing to some, odious to others, went abroad from him upon the winds, and made them marvel what could be near them, and make them look curiously and anxiously at him, while he was unconscious of his own condition."[84] He never disappointed those closest to him. He remained a priest until the end, wholly and with undivided loyalty. "Yet kept he safe his pledge, prizing his pilgrim-lot."[85]

---

[83] Ward, quoting from the essay "Studies in Poetry and Philosophy", by Principal Shairp of St. Andrews, in Ward, *The Life*, 1:64. In the German edition, Görres has "utter unworldliness," and "tamelessness" emphasized with italics.

[84] *Loss and Gain*, 206–7.

[85] "The Pilgrim", 61.

4

PASSION FOR THE TRUTH

Newman bestows on others the gentle light of his kindness, the warm tenderness of his loyalty. The glow and passion that live in him, the real eros of his soul, are directed toward another goal: the *Truth*. In the same way Francis of Assisi called poverty his Lady and his Beloved,[1] Newman could have said, "My bride is the Truth."

"I have not sinned against light",[2] the thirty-year-old repeats again and again in the face of death, semiconscious in serious illness; the ninety-year-old cardinal could have said the same thing on his deathbed, with even greater justification. The drama of his fate, which is so quiet on the outside, tragically tense and moving on the inside, is played out for the sake of Truth, not for love or power. This is because Newman is one of those people, curiously a rarity, for whom Truth is the central concern of life: finding and possessing, preaching and defending the Truth. I say finding, not seeking, because in today's parlance the word "seeking" has strangely become something unserious. How much self-congratulatory posturing, how much inability for decision and resolve, how much aversion to what is final, irrevocable, binding, and submissive hides behind this! For Newman, there is only one possible attitude toward the Truth: absolute willingness to obey at any cost. Lessing's well-known remark about renouncing the Truth for the sake of seeking would not only have been meaningless to Newman but would have seemed pernicious.[3] Because for him, what confronts the human

---

[1] "Then the Saint answered . . . 'I chose Poverty for my riches, and for my Lady.'" Brother Thomas of Celano, *The Lives of Saint Francis of Assisi*, trans. A. G. Ferrers Howell (London: Methuen, 1908), 224.

[2] John Henry Newman, *Apologia pro Vita Sua*, ed. Ian Ker (London: Penguin Books, 1994), 50.

[3] "If God were to hold all truth in his right hand and in his left just the constant drive toward truth, and say to me, 'Choose!,' even with the proviso that I always and forever err, I would fall into his left hand and say, 'Father, give [me this]!' After all, pure truth is

mind in thought really is an object, not just an emanation from one-self: something larger than what is human speaks to him, and this claim authoritatively demands recognition, acceptance, and submission. Because the Truth is that which one must follow—for the one who has grasped it, there is no other response to that claim. So the question of the Truth is never just an intellectual process; it is always a religious process as well. In every thought of Truth, God bears witness.

Already Newman's first conversion is subject to this law. In this most important event of his life, from which all his following religious development grows like a tree from a seed, what happened was essentially "just" one thing: that the long-familiar religious teachings became real to the fifteen-year-old, and he accepted them as true. John Henry was no youthful Augustine but rather the well-cared-for son of a model English middle-class family. His father was "somewhat free-thoughted . . . a man of independent mind"; from his mother and grandmother he learned "sentiments of 'simple piety,' together with a great love of the Bible, and . . . 'the non-controversial points of Christianity, on which all agreed' ".[4]

This is in keeping with the Enlightenment religion of the eighteenth century in which Newman is rooted. Like all children on the threshold of an era, in his early youth he initially absorbed the spirit of the past age; in the development of the new one, he himself was involved. Thus, Christianity was a sentiment, an attitude, an ethos, an inclination of one's spirit to its prescriptions and recommendations—not creed, decision, and spiritual law. As a ten-year-old, he seemed to his sister like "a very philosophical young gentleman, always full of thought and never at a loss for an

---

for you alone." Gotthold Ephraim Lessing, "Theologische Streitschriften", in *Lessings ausgewählte Werke* (Leipzig: G. J. Göschen, 1867), 7:19.

[4] Henry Tristram, "With Newman at Prayer", in Henry Tristram, ed., *John Henry Newman: Centenary Essays* (London: Burns, Oates and Washbourne, 1945), 101. These passages appear in *Correspondence of John Henry Newman with John Keble and Others, 1839–1845* (London: Longmans, Green, 1917), 394, which Tristram cites, but I think Görres took these quotes from Tristram. Her excerpts directly parallel the excerpts in Tristram's essay, including Tristram's phrase "sentiments of"; moreover, Görres quotes from this essay by Tristram in her following paragraph.

answer, very observant and considerate".[5] Later, Newman recalled
that as a boy he thought, "I should like to be virtuous, but not
religious",[6] that being "religious"[7] was in an undefined way repugnant to him, and especially what was said about love for God was
completely incomprehensible;[8] all of this is the eighteenth century
in full bloom. Also, he recalled that as an early and eager reader, he
began, with a mixture of pleasure and unease, reading and copying
texts of the unbelieving philosophers of the recent past—Voltaire,
[H]ume,[9] and Paine—and that their mental acuity seemed to be
correct, in opposition to the pious atmosphere of his family home.
"How dreadful, but how plausible!"[10] he remarked about Voltaire's
verses against immortality.

In Ealing, "a great change of thought took place in me. I fell
under the influences of a definite Creed",[11] namely, the Calvinism of his esteemed teacher, the Reverend Walter Mayers. It may
have been similar to what he later attributes to the spiritual awakening of his hero Reding in *Loss and Gain*: "He had now come, in
the course of a year, to one or two conclusions, not very novel,
but very important:—first, that there are a great many opinions
in the world on the most momentous subjects; secondly, that all
are not equally true; thirdly, that it is a duty to hold true opinions; and, fourthly, that it is uncommonly difficult to get hold of

---

[5] Tristram, "With Newman at Prayer", 101-2. His citation is "*Family Adventures* by
H. E. Newman (Mrs Thomas Mozley) *passim*", 102n1. (Ward quotes this too. See Wilfrid Philip Ward, *The Life of John Henry Cardinal Newman: Based on His Private Journals
and Correspondence* [London: Longmans, Green, 1912], 1:28).

[6] Anne Mozley, ed., *Letters and Correspondence of John Henry Newman during His Life in
the English Church: With a Brief Autobiography* (London: Longmans, Green, 1903), 1:19.

[7] The term Görres has in quotation marks here is *Religiosität*, that is, being religious,
religiosity, or religiousness. I translated this as "being 'religious'" because I think she is
still referring to the passage in Mozley, *Letters*, where the term "religious" is used, 1:19.
Newman elsewhere, however, writes about "religiousness" and its hazards; for example,
"Sermon 22. Watching", in John Henry Newman, *Parochial and Plain Sermons* (London:
Longmans, Green, 1906), 4:329.

[8] Mozley, *Letters*, 1:19.

[9] The printed German text reads "Voltaire, Flume und Paine". Newman writes of
reading Voltaire, Hume, and Paine, however, in his *Apologia*, 25. I do not know what
appears in the handwritten text, but "Flume" and "Hume" are visually very similar.

[10] *Apologia*, 25.

[11] *Apologia*, 25.

them."[12] As Father Tristram (one of Newman's last community
members in the Birmingham Oratory [still] living [in 1945])[13] reports from the cardinal's unprinted writings, there was also an illness, a " 'keen terrible one', which . . . 'made me a Christian, with
experiences before and after, awful and known only to God' ".[14]

The deep, modest silence about his inner life, which distinguishes
Newman so refreshingly from the bustling self-disclosure of some
pious people, has forever concealed the details of that crucial process
from us. But his factual recollection in the *Apologia* testifies clearly
enough that it is not a matter of a breakthrough in "his own feelings"[15] and experiences of puberty or one of those "revivals"[16] that
were the order of the day in Methodist and Evangelical circles. He
always rejected with cool distrust this form of religious conversion,
along with its fierce emotions and excitement. I "received into my
intellect impressions of dogma, which, through God's mercy, have
never been effaced or obscured".[17] Can one express this any more
matter-of-factly? That his conversion was "a returning to, a renew-
ing of, principles . . . which I had already felt"?[18] It even seemed
to him to bring its authenticity into question from time to time,
insofar as it differed from the descriptions of similar processes in
others.

For the spiritually and aesthetically interested boy without clear
religious terminology, suddenly dogma had become real and alive:
God, judgment, sin, eternity, predestination. It is nothing new: but
now he "realizes" it. To *realize*, this word that Newman filled with

---

[12] John Henry Newman, *Loss and Gain*, rev. ed. (London: Longman, Green, 1906),
65.

[13] The manuscript indicates that Görres wrote this chapter in 1945. Tristram died in
1955.

[14] Tristram, "With Newman at Prayer", 102. Tristram notes: "From a paper dated
June 25, 1869" on 102n6. (The footnote in the German edition says this is on page 108.
The correct page is 102.)

[15] Tristram, "With Newman at Prayer", 102-3. Here Tristram cites "*M.* 1, 124"
(which corresponds to Mozley, *Letters*, 1:109 in the edition of Mozley cited in this book);
see *John Henry Newman*, 103n11.

[16] Perhaps Görres is referring to Newman's discussion of *Church History* by Joseph
Milner. See Newman, *Apologia*, 27.

[17] *Apologia*, 25.

[18] Mozley, *Letters*, 1:109.

new pathos and heft, would correspond in German to *wahrnehmen*, if the content of this German word had not been completely ground down and narrowed almost exclusively to sensory perception. *Wahrnehmen*, grasping (*nehmen*) something as true (*wahr*), becoming aware of it, taking it into one's consciousness: all of this means to *realize*, not to "accomplish" something, as is obstinately portrayed.

Thus, those teachings are no longer just external claims—"it is so"—rather, with unreserved inner affirmation: "*Yes*, that is how it is." This yes distinguishes the new attitude of this young Christian from the previous faith Newman often called "assent". The will gives its assent to what it has so far passively "been aware of". Certainty that this claim coincides with a reality emerges: this, far more than the claim "about" it, is grasped and "held to be true". Newman would certainly not have regarded this last expression, which today is so readily rejected as deficient, as a pale formula. To hold something to be true: what seriousness! On closer inspection, what passion fills every word! To hold on to something for life and death, for time and eternity, not because it is beautiful, worthy, useful, and even good but because it is true.

Thinking can deal with statements "about" something or with the reality itself "about which" one speaks. Decades later, that is how Newman distinguished "conceptual" and "actual" thinking, thinking factually. For him, the first is a logical and "non-binding", albeit self-justified and interesting, process. The second is the momentous commitment of the whole person, dealing not with what has been deduced from his own thoughts but with realities outside himself—because when something recognized is "realized", accepted, and "held", something happens. Such reception means not only an action and taking hold but also a letting go, letting go of oneself, surrendering oneself, letting oneself be seized and led. Once Truth has been recognized, there is no appeal against it, no evasion from it. The popular modern question about the living lie and dead truth would have seemed completely senseless to Newman. A person can, of course, play dead in facing a truth. But every truth is outright urgently alive as soon as one engages it.

When that is how it is, then the question of what is true is, of course, the most consequential, the most unpredictable, the most

dangerous undertaking that a person can embark on. Every recognition imposes a decision, be it recognition with approval or feeling
in resistance—because whoever has recognized Truth must from
then on "align" himself with it and "judge" himself according to it
in the terrifying double sense of the German word *richten*, meaning
"to align" as well as "to judge".

For Newman, this results in the continuous investigation, over
many decades, into how one must conduct oneself in order to be
able to recognize Truth, be worthy of the Truth, be capable of
the Truth, and able to cope with the Truth; how one is to seek,
foster, seize, and preserve it; how one endangers, diminishes, and
loses it; where, how, and when people find the security to believe
something, and with what right and heft one can allow oneself to
hold something to be true; what the relationship is between reason and faith, and what certainty even is, and the difference in
the weight of claims, views, opinions, prejudices, speculation, and
conviction. This is the subject of many sermons, countless letters,
and how many more conversations! And it is the subject of his last
great work, perhaps the most important for laypeople, on personal
reasoning, the *Grammar of Assent*. I would have preferred to translate this title [into German] as *Fibel der Zustimmung* (Primer of assent) rather than as *Philosophie des Glaubens* (Philosophy of faith), as
Haecker did.[19] It tries to show the individual Christian, specifically
one who is uneducated—not the philosopher and his audience—
why *he* believes, why *one* should believe. It is specifically not written for experts; instead, it is "written especially for those who can't
go into questions of the inspiration of Scripture, authenticity of
books, passages in the Fathers, &c. &c.—especially for such ladies
as are bullied by infidels and do not know how to answer them—
a misfortune which I fear is not rare in this day."[20] So he wrote in
a letter to a longtime friend.

Newman was a classic embodiment of education and scholarship
without any jealous constraint of the academic conceit of one who
is "learned"; as such, it is astonishing and remarkable how again

---

[19] Theodor Haecker translated Newman's book *An Essay in Aid of a Grammar of Assent*
into German as *Philosophie des Glaubens*, published in 1921.

[20] Letter to Miss Holmes, March 26, 1871, in Ward, *The Life*, 2:275.

and again he insists on the rightness and weightiness, the dignity and independence of the simple, honest thinking of the uneducated and untrained believer, how he takes it seriously and defends it. He defends himself, the Christian and the pastor in him, against the narrowing of the Christian faith to a religion for the educated, to the barrier that the "learned writer" repeatedly erects against the "poor in spirit", who are not conversant in the law, so that he can boast of his special position in religious affairs. The Christian recognizes and honors the light of Divine Truth in the "little people". The one who understands people makes no mistake about how it is only for a few that logical templates have really been the vessel and girder of their decision to believe. The thinker and explorer of human nature is attracted to pursue the barely noticed activity of the inarticulate, seemingly dark, and silent mind and to listen in on its as-yet-unknown laws, away from the rigidity-inducing institution of schools.

> Persons are sometimes taunted with having only what is called an hereditary religion; with believing what they believe, and practising what they practise, because they have been taught so to do, without any reasons of their own. Now it may very possibly happen that they have no reasons to produce, that they do not know their own reasons, that they have never analyzed what passes through their minds, and causes their impressions and convictions; but that is no proof that they have no reasons; and in truth they have always, whether they recognize them or not, very good reasons. It does not make a man more religious that he knows why and how he became so; . . . yet, for all that, it [our religion] may be much more than hereditary, when we have lived long enough to have made trial of it.[21]

Thus: "Faith cannot exist without grounds or without an object; but it does not follow that all who have faith should recognize, and be able to state what they believe, and why. . . . All men have a reason, but not all men can give a reason."[22] "Theologians (who

---

[21] John Henry Newman, "Sermon 23. Grounds for Steadfastness in Due Religious Profession", in *Sermons Bearing on Subjects of the Day* (London: Longmans, Green, 1902), 343–44.

[22] John Henry Newman, "Sermon 13. Implicit and Explicit Reason", in *Fifteen Sermons Preached before the University of Oxford between A.D. 1826 and 1843* (London: Longmans, Green, 1909), 253–54.

ought to know in *Arte sua*) all affirm that Christianity is proved by
the same rigorous scientific processes by which it is proved . . .
that the earth goes around the sun. . . . But the scientific proof
of Christianity is not the popular, practical, personal evidence on
which a given individual believes in it."[23]

What interests Newman is this actual, as it were unofficial, ra-
tionale for faith, on which the religion of the ordinary Christian
is based, and he pursues it, like the discoverers among his contemporaries pursuing the sources of a major river in distant, primeval
forests. In this way, he distinguishes sharply and crisply from the
actual, superficial habitual religion lacking authentic engagement
and conviction: "It is true of others, that good grounds they have
none for their religious profession; they may, indeed, have got together some reasons from books, and may make a show with them;
but they have none of their own. . . . They have been taught the
truths, and taught the reasons; but the reasons are their own as little
as the truths; . . . they have no root in themselves; they have nothing
within them connecting the reasons with, and grafting them upon,
the divine doctrines. And be they ever so intellectual and acute,
ever so able to investigate, and argue, and reflect upon themselves,
this will avail them nothing"; "him, who has much to say, and says
what is true, but says it not from himself, but by rote, and could say
quite as well just the reverse, did it so happen that he mistook it for
truth. His, indeed, is in the worst sense mere hereditary religion."
And with an audible sigh: "But so it is, from the circumstance that
these sensual, gross-hearted, indevout, or insincere persons are often men of education and ability, they show to advantage in the
world, talk loudly and largely, are powerful controversialists, are
considered bulwarks of the truth."[24]

"I felt then, and all along felt, that there was an intellectual cowardice in not finding a basis in reason for my belief, and a moral
cowardice in not avowing that basis. I should have felt myself less

---

[23] Letter to William Froude, January 18, 1860, in Gordon Huntington Harper, *Cardinal Newman and William Froude, F.R.S.: A Correspondence* (Baltimore: Johns Hopkins
Press, 1933), 131.

[24] "Sermon 23: Grounds for Steadfastness in Our Religious Profession", in *Subjects
of the Day*, 344–45.

than a man, if I did not bring it out, whatever it was."[25] With each line, the reader senses that what is at hand was not primarily theory but existence. Admittedly, a person is not able to recognize in an unmediated manner those realities in which he believes in this life but only through the message, which is almost as much a veiling as it is an unveiling. "So we have to learn to endure hearing that revelation is a comfort adjusted to our weakness, an 'economy' (*oikonomia*) that is inherently unequal to what it expresses."[26] At the end of a long life, *umbrae et imagines*—that is, shadows and images—are also the words and signs through which the believer learned and confessed his faith. For certain, he can primarily recognize "only" that this message should be taken seriously, perceived, held true; in a word: it is to be believed.

Sometimes, though rarely, recognition takes place in an incontrovertible flash of epiphany. More important and frequent is the slow growth of the often unconsciously received onset of a fruitful Truth, inconspicuous like the sprouting of the seeds in the field, "by day and by night, whether the person is awake or asleep".[27] That is why the slightest, apparently insignificant glimmer of knowledge must not be pushed aside, suppressed, or throttled. "He was not a person to let a truth sleep in his mind", writes Newman in his novel about Charles Reding, to whom Newman probably lent some of his own features; "though it did not vegetate very quickly, it was sure ultimately to be pursued into its consequences."[28] This does not mean that people have to battle frantically and violently with every question that comes up in order to force a solution on the spot, and it certainly does not mean uninhibited disclosure of every new impression one has. On the contrary: "A new idea was not lost on him [Reding], but it did not distress him, if it was obscure,

---

[25] *Apologia*, 75.

[26] The German edition presents this as a quote from the *Apologia*, but it could more aptly be described as a paraphrase. The original quote reads: "Holy Church in her sacraments and her hierarchical appointments, will remain, even to the end of the world, after all but a symbol of those heavenly facts which fill eternity. Her mysteries are but the expressions in human language of truths to which the human mind is unequal." *Apologia*, 44.

[27] This appears to be a paraphrase of part of Mark 4:27. Newman quotes Mark 4:26–27, for example, in "Sermon 20. Wisdom and Innocence", in *Subjects of the Day*, 303–4.

[28] *Loss and Gain*, 34.

or conflicted with his habitual view of things. He let it work its
way and find its place, and shape itself within him, by the slow
spontaneous action of the mind."[29]

This means conscientious, ant-like work, however—no, more
like the diligent work of gardening—but in the mind: searching
and gathering, comparing and differentiating, weighing and reject-
ing views, opinions, claims, observations, experiences, and questions as they surround us every day, intruding on us trying to woo
or conquer, or also waiting hidden and impenetrable to the one
truly seeking. Having reached the goal of his search, Reding will
say retrospectively: "One did not see at first sight . . . how it was
rational to maintain that so much depended on holding this or that
doctrine, or a little more or a little less, but it might be a test of the
heart."[30]

These teachings can be read as if from Newman's own life. That
was what happened to him. The young person's first conversion
"judges" (richtet) his life; it puts him on trial and also "gives him
direction". If God is real, then indeed mere human standards fall
to the wayside. This is the only explanation for the severity with
which Newman, the mild "Father of Souls",[31] the great understanding friend of youth, retrospectively condemns his own childhood
in harsh words: "When I was a boy of fifteen, and living a life
of sin, with a very dark conscience and a very profane spirit, He
mercifully touched my heart."[32] He writes this almost thirty years
later, during a great crisis of his life, to Keble, the brotherly friend
to whom he entrusted the guidance of his soul; Newman truly cannot be suspected of having engaged in either [evasive] wording or
exaggeration to him.

Later, he found it "difficult to realise or imagine the identity of
the boy before and after August 1816",[33] "when I was more like
a devil than a wicked boy."[34] A note leaves little unsaid: "Was any

---

[29] *Loss and Gain*, 65.
[30] *Loss and Gain*, 379.
[31] Tristram cites this as a label that Father Henry Coleridge, S.J., gave to Newman.
Tristram, "On Reading Newman", 223.
[32] Letter to Keble, Littlemore, June 8, 1844, in *Correspondence with Keble*, 314.
[33] Mozley, *Letters*, 1:19.
[34] Journal, December 15, 1859, in Ward, *The Life*, 1:575.

boyhood so impious as some years of mine! Did I not in fact dare Thee to do thy worst?"[35] Was the "keen and terrible illness"[36] in the year he reached his decision perhaps God's answer to that defiance? "Ah, how I struggled to get free from Thee; but Thou are stronger than I and hast prevailed."[37]

This can actually have happened only after the conversion of his intellect: a startled nature rears up when faced with a yoke that it now recognizes; an attempt to escape from the countenance that has been revealed. How closely it suits Newman's thoroughly English disposition that this drama is oriented entirely to the interior. Neither his family members nor peers are called upon as spectators or supporters. No conversion fanaticism calls for a sudden departure from previous habits. The fact that the quiet, inward-looking boy, as a young man, refrains from drinking, dancing, and other uncouth pastimes of his contemporaries is probably due to the taste and attitude toward life in his environment. Beyond that, his judgment of his peers is mild and without arrogance. Only his mother's keen eyes notice her son's peculiar melancholy about himself.[38]

He is like a man under the spell of a love that completely overwhelms him, silent, constantly aware of it, as if walking under a glass bell, still seeing the world but no longer touched by it: from now on, John Henry Newman lives in a secret, exclusive, exclusionary solitude with God, "face to face, 'solus cum solo' ",[39] "making me rest in the thought of two and two only absolute and luminously self-evident beings, myself and my Creator".[40] This is his secret, not expressed until the threshold of his seventh decade and yet somehow felt by everyone who became close to him with an open heart; "intense spirituality and therefore his utter unworldliness"[41]

---

[35] John Henry Newman, *Meditations and Devotions* (London: Longmans, Green, 1912), 552.

[36] Tristram, "With Newman at Prayer", 102. According to Tristram, this is "from a paper dated June 25, 1869", 102n6.

[37] *Meditations and Devotions*, as cited in Tristram, "With Newman at Prayer", 102.

[38] Mozley, *Letters*, 1:51. In this section of this chapter, Gerl-Falkovitz removed a quotation from the manuscript, noting that Görres has already quoted from this passage in Mozley in chapter 3 of this volume.

[39] *Apologia*, 179.

[40] *Apologia*, 25.

[41] R. D. Middleton, "The Vicar of St. Mary's", in Tristram, *John Henry Newman*, 127.

appeared to all his acquaintances as the essence of his being. From
now on, God is "enthroned . . . at the very springs of thought and
affection".[42] "It made me a Christian."[43] But that means, according
to his own famous definition: "One who looks for Christ; not who
looks for gain, or distinction, or power, or pleasure, or comfort, but
who looks 'for the Saviour, the Lord Jesus Christ'. . . . He surely
is a . . . Christian, and he only, who has no aim of this world, who
has no wish to be other in this world than he is; whose thoughts
and aims have relation to the unseen, the future world; who has
lost his taste for this world."[44]

He reminded the observer of Moses in the powerful sketch in
the letter to the Hebrews.[45] A relative wrote to her brother after a
brief visit by an elderly uncle: "One sees that Dr. Newman's great
power . . . is a certain vivid realization of the unseen, or rather that
there is an unseen that you cannot see."[46]

But let us not forget: Newman was never a person of "experiences", of religious feeling. He was even heavily burdened by the
fact that his innermost life with God in prayer very much lacked
warmth and enthusiasm. "But I cannot in a few words express to
you what the matter is with what I may call the *physical* texture
of my soul. It is not a matter of reason, nor of grace—but, just
as the body wearies under continual toil, so does the mind. . . .
Whenever I have attempted to do anything for God, I find after a
little while that my arms or my legs have a string round them—and
perhaps I sprain myself in the effort to move them in spite of it."[47]
Of course, considering Newman's astonishing range of emotions,
these and many similar passages may remind us of the saints' sighs

---

[42] Tristram, "With Newman at Prayer", 107. Tristram cites *Parochial and Plain Sermons*, 5:236.

[43] Tristram, "With Newman at Prayer", 106. In Tristram's essay, the phrase "It
made me a Christian" is in single quotation marks. Perhaps Tristram was paraphrasing Newman.

[44] "Sermon 19. The Apostolical Christian", in *Subjects of the Day*, 279.

[45] See Hebrews 11:27: "By faith he left Egypt, not being afraid of the anger of the
king; for he endured as seeing him who is invisible."

[46] Tristram, "With Newman at Prayer", 108. Tristram writes that this is from "Elizabeth Mozley . . . in a letter to her brother, J. B. Mozley, in October, 1874, after Newman had paid her and her sister a brief visit".

[47] Letter to Edward Bellasis, the Oratory, August 20, 1861, in Ward, *The Life*, 1:596.

about their lack of love. Only the one who loves keeps complaining about his lack of ability to love. But Newman, in any case, did *not experience* the tremendous intensity of his belief *as a feeling*: It unfolded as faith and in faith, that is, in its relationship to Divine Truth.

His 1816 conversion was a beginning, not a conclusion. Such faith, based on such reality, ignited by such reality, is anything but rigid; it is necessarily designed for growth; it necessarily thrives with the development of the whole person. Very characteristic is Newman's retrospective on his life, his "History of my Religious Opinions" [in his *Apologia*].[48] What it tries to present is by no means autobiography in the ordinary sense, but only this: the slow, surprising, and sequential growth from the acknowledgment of Truth and obedience to Truth and obedience in his life, step by step, from rung to rung. "To live is to change, and to be perfect is to have changed often."[49]

Of course, such development happens any way but "automatically". As with all living things, it is constantly endangered and threatened. A thousand influences from outside and from inside can, at almost every step, stop, bend, distort, displace, disfigure, and bury almost any budding knowledge; it is no different from how it is described in the Gospel passage of the sower and the seed (see Mt 13:1-23; Mk 4:1-20; Lk 8:1-15). In addition, all living things have the possibility of malformation, deformity, degeneration, tumor, crippling, and decomposition. So the growth of Truth in one's spirit requires conscientious, vigilant, careful, unwavering tending, ready for any sacrifice.

Not everyone can recognize everything. Even in the field of natural [science] research and academic study, a very specific attitude, *the philosophical temper*, is required to gain knowledge. Newman describes this state of mind in detail in one of his most beautiful university sermons: "To be dispassionate and cautious, to be fair in discussion,

---

[48] The titles of each of the first four out of five chapters in Newman's *Apologia*, covering the period from his childhood to 1845, begin with "A History of My Religious Opinions from . . . to . . .". Thus, the *Apologia* is sometimes referred to by the name "A History of My Religious Opinions".

[49] John Henry Newman, *An Essay on the Development of Christian Doctrine* (London: Longmans, Green, 1909), 40.

to give to each phenomenon which nature successively presents its due weight, candidly to admit those which militate against our own theory, to be willing to be ignorant for a time, to submit to difficulties, and patiently and meekly proceed".[50]

This applies even more to the search for spiritual Truth:

> For is not this the error, the common and fatal error, of the world, to think itself a judge of Religious Truth without preparation of heart? . . . But in the schools of the world the ways towards Truth are considered high roads open to all men, however disposed, at all times. Truth is to be approached without homage. . . . Men consider that they have as full a right to discuss religious subjects, as if they were themselves religious. They will enter upon the most sacred points of Faith at the moment, at their pleasure,—if it so happen, in a careless frame of mind, in their hours of recreation, over the wine cup.[51]

So the question of Truth turns inevitably not only to the mind, but also to the character of the seeker: The whole person is engaged; the attempt to exclude something imperceptibly spoils the rest of the effort, however honest it may be. Newman speaks at one point in blunt clarity about those "religious men" who "resign their cause into God's hands, and are well-pleased that the world should seem to triumph over them".[52]

"But a man *is* responsible for his faith, because he is responsible for his likings and dislikings, his hopes and his opinions, on all of which his faith depends. . . . But in truth, though a given evidence does not vary in force, the antecedent probability attending it does vary indefinitely, according to the temper of the mind surveying it."[53]

Already at the age of twenty-two, he wrote to a young skeptic: "The first point, then, is to press upon the conscience that we are playing with edged tools; if, instead of endeavouring perseveringly to ascertain what the truth is, we consider the subject carelessly,

---

[50] "Sermon 1. The Philosophical Temper, First Enjoined by the Gospel", in *Fifteen Sermons*, 9–10.

[51] "Sermon 10. Faith and Reason, contrasted as Habits of Mind", in *Fifteen Sermons*, 190–91.

[52] "Wisdom and Innocence", 302.

[53] "Faith and Reason", in 192–93.

captiously, or with indifference."[54] And a few years later: "The
love and pursuit of truth in the subject-matter of religion, if it be
genuine, must always be accompanied by the fear of error, of error
which may be sin."[55] Here Newman coincides with the teaching of
Saint Thomas Aquinas (with which he probably was not familiar):
"Even if one can neither earn nor gain divine grace by the resolve
of his free decision-making power, he can prevent himself from
receiving it."[56]

Searching for Truth is a matter of conscience in the strictest sense.
Seen in this light, the objection that the believer no longer needs
to "search", because as a Christian he "possesses" the Truth with
humility, thanks, and pride, is superfluous. Certainly, Newman repeatedly praised the blissful grace of this security as a particular
privilege of the Church, but it does not relieve the strict commitment to serve the Truth. For the believer, it is no longer "searching"
but "acquiring in order to own it".[57] He must acquire and preserve
what he has inherited without his effort, to overcome the danger
of erosion into mere habitual Christianity, which has already been
mentioned and which threatens every lethargic and indifferent conscience. Knowingly and sharply, Newman describes the superficial-
ity of the average "believer":

> Many a man gathers up, here and there, some fragments of religious
> knowledge. He hears one thing said in Church, he sees another thing
> in the Prayer-book. . . . In this way he gets possession of sacred words
> and statements, knowing very little about them really. He interprets
> them, as it may happen, according to the various and inconsistent

---

[54] Letter "to a young man of sceptical opinions", April 13, 1823, in Mozley, *Letters*,
1:70.

[55] John Henry Newman, *The Via Media of the Anglican Church* (London: Basil Montagu Pickering, 1877), 1:54.

[56] Thomas Aquinas writes, "But what a man merits, he infallibly receives from God,
unless hindered by subsequent sin" and "What we merit, we obtain from God, unless it
is hindered by sin". Thomas Aquinas, "Question 114. Merit", in *The Summa Theologiæ
of St. Thomas Aquinas*, trans. Fathers of the English Dominican Province, 2nd ed. (London: Burns, Oates and Washbourne, 1920), I–II, q. 114, arts. 8 and 9.

[57] See Johann Wolfgang von Goethe, *Faust*, pt. 1, lines 682–83: "All that your an-
cestors bequeathed to you. / To make it really yours, earn it anew." Johann Wolfgang
von Goethe, *Faust. A Tragedy: In a Modern Translation*, trans. Alice Raphael (New York:
Heritage Press, 1932), 24.

opinions which he has met with, or he puts his own meaning upon them, that is, the meaning, as must needs be, of an untaught, not to say a carnal and irreverent mind. How can a man expect he shall discern and apprehend the real meaning and language of Scripture, if he has never approached it as a learner, and waited on the Divine Author of it for the gift of wisdom? . . . Even when he is most orthodox in word, he has but a collection of phrases, on which he puts, not the right meaning, but his own meaning. And the least reflection must show you what a very poor and unworthy meaning, or rather how false a meaning "the natural man" will put upon "the things of the Spirit of God."[58]

Newman himself has also been tried and tested. At the age of twenty-five, shortly after his ordination to the clergy of the state church, he experienced a profound spiritual crisis—the third one that led to his conversion was of a different nature. Respected and already noticed as a rising star, he came under the influence of older colleagues from the rationalist school, to whom he owed a great deal intellectually because they loosened the somewhat narrow shells of his early, Calvinist-hued faith. The expansion of his mental awareness brought with it his own challenge: "The truth is, I was beginning to prefer intellectual excellence to moral; I was drifting in the direction of the Liberalism of the day."[59] It is easy to skim over the sober sentence as if it were a matter of course in the development of a young academic. But after what has just been said, the severity of this temptation is revealed: already in this quiet, initially uplifting, and playful attempt to seat vanity and influence above the purity of the soul, a subtle betrayal of the Truth arises. God intervenes, the way He intervenes to save His saints: "I was rudely awakened from my dream at the end of 1827 by two great blows— illness and bereavement."[60] He mentions the first in "an unpublished paper": it was "not painful, but tedious and shattering"; it "broke me off from an incipient Liberalism, and determined my

---

[58] "Sermon 12. The Humiliation of the Eternal Son", in *Parochial and Plain Sermons*, 3:160–61.

[59] *Apologia*, 33.

[60] *Apologia*, 33.

religious course".[61] The other was the sudden death of his beloved youngest sister. Shortly thereafter, Hurrell Froude crossed his path. From now on, Newman will be the fiery and persistent protagonist of what he calls the "dogmatic principle".[62] To him, "Liberalism in religion is the doctrine that there is no positive truth in religion, but that one creed is as good as another, and this is the teaching which is gaining substance and force daily. It is inconsistent with any recognition of any religion, as *true*."[63] It is clear that such an attitude struck a nerve and aroused his passionate opposition. "From the age of fifteen", one reads in his *Apologia*, "dogma has been the fundamental principle of my religion: I know no other religion; I cannot enter into the idea of any other sort of religion; religion, as a mere sentiment, is to me a dream and a mockery. As well can there be filial love without the fact of a father, as devotion without the fact of a Supreme Being."[64]

And again: "There is no such thing as abstract religion. When persons attempt to worship in this (what they call) more spiritual manner, they end, in fact, in not worshipping at all."[65] Elsewhere he mentions "so-called religion of the heart", which feeds on the reverberation of the discarded dogmas, with iron harshness: it "is but the warmth of a corpse, real for a time, but sure to fail".[66]

But such a belief is nothing less than rigid and dead, as people of today often assume with the mere mention of the word "dogmatic". The image of the foundation of rock is essential to complement the other parable of the growing seed. Dogmatic belief is alive; it is active and dynamic. It is to Newman's eternal amazement how little and at the same time how much the doctrine as presented

---

[61] Tristram, "Praying with Newman,", 108. (The German edition cites page 104, but this quote is on page 108.)

[62] Newman uses the phrase "dogmatic principle" in several works. See, for example, Newman, *Christian Doctrine*, 350, 360, 361; John Henry Newman, *Certain Difficulties Felt by Anglicans in Catholic Teaching* (London: Longmans, Green, 1901), 1:1; John Henry Newman, *The Idea of a University* (London: Longmans, Green, 1907), 395.

[63] Ward, in Ward, *The Life*, 2:4. This quotation is from Newman's "Biglietto" speech in Rome on May 12, 1879, delivered when he was elevated to being a cardinal.

[64] *Apologia*, 61.

[65] "Sermon 7. The Feast of the Circumcision of Our Lord", in *Parochial and Plain Sermons*, 2:74.

[66] "The Humiliation of the Eternal Son", 3:171.

contains. The Christian by no means has a well-rounded, complete, and satisfactory pat solution in his pocket for all the world's puzzles and life's questions. No one has described the irresolvable conflict between believing and seeing, the apparent conflict between belief and experience, in a more precise, detailed, uncompromising, and honest manner than Newman in his university sermons. Every word reveals how honestly and soberly he has experienced—that is, tasted—and examined this conflict down to its foundation. The revelation of God is such a bottomless pit of riddles and darkness. It never satisfies our sheer thirst for knowledge. It tells us not what we would like to know but what we need; nowhere are people simply dispensed from the laborious work of our own seeking. He is always startled by how little God's Word reveals to him. "The Dispensation of mercy is revealed to us in its great and blessed result, our redemption, and in one or two other momentous points. Upon all these we ought to dwell and enlarge, mindfully and thankfully, but with the constant recollection that after all, as regards the Dispensation itself, only one or two partial notices are revealed to us altogether of a great Divine Work. Enlarge upon them we ought, even because they are few and partial, not slighting what is given us, because it is not all (like the servant who buried his lord's talent), but giving it what increase we can."[67] Human thought and understanding are called upon continuously to prove themselves in this infinite task. The starting point is given to us firmly and steadfastly; we must travel the path ourselves.

"Revelation is all in all in doctrine; the Apostles its sole depository, the inferential method its sole instrument, and ecclesiastical authority its sole sanction. The Divine Voice has spoken once for all, and the only question is about its meaning."[68]

This spirit of faith is both male and female: more receptive than begetting, as well as faithful and obedient to that which has been received despite all pain and danger. The unwavering consistency that neither shies away nor looks back like soldiers in the purest sense of this fraught statement is manly: "thousands fall to your right, tens of thousands to your left" (see Ps 91:7). Anyone who

---

[67] "The Humiliation of the Eternal Son", 3:159.
[68] *The Idea of a University*, 223.

thinks like this is, of course, in for an adventure—his path is not mapped out; on the contrary, he is at the mercy of the light that guides only step by step.

Newman's proclamation strikes his contemporaries as unusual and startling; for some it is pleasing, for others alarming. The new and outrageous thing he does is nothing but this: he takes what is traditional and familiar seriously and situates it in an unprecedented reality and obligation. Thus, the young pastor of Littlemore refused to conduct a wedding because the woman belonged to a sect and was not baptized. This refusal seems entirely understandable to Catholics. At the time, it triggered a storm of indignation and bewildered incomprehension. The Anglican church of that era unquestionably included everything that was popularly called Christian. There was a real scandal. Newman wrote to his mother: "Till the last hour I have felt to be one man against a multitude. No one, apparently, to encourage me, and so many black averted faces, that unless from my youth I had been schooled to fall back upon myself, I should have been quite out of heart. . . . I seem as if I could bear anything now. I felt that I could not have done otherwise than I did. Yet it is very distressing to be alone."[69]

His famous sermons in the pulpit at St Mary's came from a similar impetus. For centuries, the university's house law required all students to receive Communion on certain days. Until now, no one had thought about it. Newman, provoking significant alarm, asked about the spiritual preparation of the communicants. His sermons stemmed from the desire to awaken young people religiously.[70] The fact that he regarded and exercised his position as a tutor not only as an academic teaching position but also as a duty to care for and guide souls created serious clashes for him with the provost of Oxford. When the provost prohibited such innovations, Newman resigned from the position, along with some like-minded friends.

In his little parish at Littlemore, his holy earnestness to evangelize drove him outside to go door-to-door among the rural cottages. The scholar-to-be found it in no way beneath his dignity to visit

---

[69] Letter to his mother, July 8, 1834, in Mozley, *Letters*, 2:49–50.

[70] Charlotte Blennerhassett, *John Henry Kardinal Newman: Ein Beitrag zur Religiösen Entwicklungsgeschichte der Gegenwart* (Berlin: Verlag Gebrüder Paetel, 1904), 27.

the small artisans, shopkeepers, and tenants in their homes to speak
to them of the Last Things in Christian life: "on our being sinful
and corrupt till death; on the necessity of sin being found a burden
always, on the fear of self-deception and of falling away even after
the most vivid feelings; and on the awful state of those who, *having* left religion for their death-bed, could give no *evidence* of their
sincerity".[71]

Newman had the most amazing gift of empathy for souls, and he
used to say that the same thought could certainly be as different in
different people as their faces. He was a master of patient, reverent
spiritual guidance. Generous as a result of deep insight into the diversity of mankind, he distrusted the "black self-will, a bitterness
of religious passion",[72] as he used to characterize the sectarians.

"I do not feel our differences", he wrote around 1870 [that is, in
1866] to the perpetually contentious [W. G.] Ward,

> to be such a trouble as you do; for such differences always have been,
> always will be, in the Church; and Christians would have ceased to
> have spiritual and intellectual life if such differences did not exist. It
> is part of their militant state. No human power can hinder it; nor, if
> it attempted it, could do more than make a solitude and call it peace.
> And thus thinking that man cannot hinder it, however much he try,
> I have no great anxiety or trouble. Man cannot, and God will not.
> He means such differences to be an exercise of charity. Of course I
> wish as much as possible to agree with all my friends; but if, in spite
> of my utmost efforts, they go beyond me or come short of me, I
> can't help it, and take it easy.[73]

This is how Newman thought about diversity *within* the faith. But
when it comes to the foundations, he comes forth with surprising
severity. He is the sworn enemy of all religious vagueness and all
tolerance that is ready to give up a single word of preaching for
the sake of peace. "In the present day . . . mistiness is the mother

---

[71] Under the heading "Some private notes . . . of Mr. Newman's visits to his sick
parishioners", in Mozley, *Letters*, 1:81.

[72] Letter to Mrs. John Mozley, Oriel, January 19, 1837, in Mozley, *Letters*, 2:200.

[73] Letter to W. G. Ward, February 18, 1866, in Edmund Sheridan Purcell, *Life of Cardinal Manning, Archbishop of Westminster* (London: Macmillan, 1896), 2:321–22. Görres
quotes this from Blennerhassett, *John Henry Newman*, 205. Blennerhassett cites Purcell's
Life of Cardinal Manning as her source: *John Henry Newman*, 206n1.

of wisdom", he writes with sharp criticism of the theology of his day. "A man who can set down a half-a-dozen general propositions, which escape from destroying one another only by being diluted into truisms, who can hold the balance between opposites so skilfully as to do without fulcrum or beam, who never enunciates a truth without guarding himself against being supposed to exclude the contradictory . . .—this is your safe man and the hope of the Church; this is what the Church is said to want, not party men, but sensible, temperate, sober, well-judging persons, to guide it through the channel of no-meaning, between the Scylla and Charybdis of Aye and No."[74] "This state of things, however, I said, could not last, if men were to read and think. . . . They cannot go on for ever standing on one leg, or sitting without a chair, or walking with their feet tied, or grazing like Tityrus's stags gazing in the air. They will take one view or another, but it will be a consistent view. It may be Liberalism, . . . or Popery, or Catholicity; but it will be real."[75]

He wished that his Church would have "some really working Court of heresy and false doctrine".[76] One would have to say that in his view, the concept of heresy is still alive, while his contemporaries saw nothing but a divergence of religious opinion, which, like every other personal view, has its rights. Newman alone appreciates the heavy and burning pathos of this statement. A Protestant woman interested in theology who referred to him in his Anglican period as a Pelagian, "without wanting to question his piety", led him to say: "I observe that it is inconsistent in her calling me a Pelagian and yet spiritually-minded. Let her be quite sure that when I think a person a heretic, I shall never call him religious. A spiritually-minded heretic may exist in the 'Protestant' world, but not in the Church."[77]

As an Anglican, he had reservations about receiving a Catholic clergyman as a guest at his table for a meal because the early Church forbade engaging with heretics. This was a reverberation of his zealous stringency that had become foreign in his day, as it has in ours,

---

[74] *Apologia*, 104.

[75] *Apologia*, 104–5.

[76] Letter to Reverend R. H. Froude, London, January 18, 1835, in Mozley, *Letters*, 2:77.

[77] Letter to Reverend S. Rickards, July 30, 1834, in Mozley, *Letters*, 2:53–54.

like the zealous austerity that led the beloved disciple John to avoid bathing with someone teaching heresy in Ephesus.[78] In his first great work, *The Arians of the Fourth Century*, Newman juxtaposed heretics and leaders of heretical groups—the main teachers of heresy—and said: "The latter should meet with no mercy; he assumes the office of the Tempter, and, so far forth as his error goes, must be dealt with by the competent authority, as if he were embodied evil. To spare him is a false and dangerous pity. It is to endanger the souls of thousands, and it is uncharitable towards himself."[79]

Sure enough, in his *Apologia*, Newman quotes that passage and then adds this point: "I cannot deny that this is a very fierce passage; but Arius was banished, not burned; and it is only fair to myself to say that neither at this, nor any other time of my life, not even when I was fiercest, could I have even cut off a Puritan's ears, and I think the sight of a Spanish *auto-da-fé* would have been the death of me."[80]

As a Catholic, Newman became much milder. Though at the age of seventy, he declined an invitation to evenings with a metaphysical society and wrote: "It is something of a wonder to me, that a mind so religious as Miss Fox's, should feel pleasure in meeting men who either disbelieved the Divine mission or had no love for the person of One she calls '*her* God and *her* Saviour.' "[81]

And there may have been a strange echo when the famous preacher in the pulpit of St Mary announced to the most exquisite and educated audience of the day: "Here I will not shrink from uttering my firm conviction, that it would be a gain to this country, were it vastly more superstitious, more bigoted, more gloomy, more fierce in its religion, than at present it shows itself to be. Not, of course, that I think the tempers of mind herein implied desirable, which would be an evident absurdity; but I think them infinitely

---

[78] Irenaeus, *Against Heresies* 3, 3, trans. Alexander Roberts and William Rambaut, in *Ante-Nicene Fathers*, vol. 1, ed. Alexander Roberts, James Donaldson, and A. Cleveland Coxe (Buffalo: Christian Literature Publishing, 1885), rev. and ed. Kevin Knight for New Advent.

[79] *Apologia*, 59–60.

[80] *Apologia*, 60.

[81] Letter to Mr. G. T. Edwards, in Ward, *The Life*, 2:333.

more desirable and more promising than a heathen obduracy, and a cold, self-sufficient, self-wise tranquillity."[82]

No wonder an opponent of the Tractarians, the famous Dr. Arnold,[83] called him a sinister fanatic and Judaizing zealot.

Throughout his life, Newman has championed the conviction that the connection between knowing the Truth and the moral state of man is inseparable: intelligence and hard work alone are not enough to grasp religious Truth. Truth is a strict master, for whose sake much, indeed everything, must be sacrificed. The inner eye must be cleansed before it can receive Truth; any clouding of conscience obscures light of conscience in us—even until it is blocked entirely. Much could be said about this. One text instead of many may suffice, set down many years later:

(9) that, as the rich man or the man in authority has his serious difficulties in going to heaven, so also has the learned. . . .

(10) that the more a man is educated, whether in theology or secular science, the holier he needs to be if he would be saved. . . .

(11) that devotion and self-rule are worth all the intellectual cultivation in the world. . . .

(12) that in the case of most men literature and science and the habits they create, so far from ensuring these highest of gifts, indispose the mind towards their acquisition.[84]

In Newman's mouth, such words are not cheap "edifying" obscurantism, but a shocking testimony to the majesty of Truth, which lays claim not only to the brain but to the whole person. This passion for the Truth makes him—what may perhaps surprise some—the opposite of a fanatic. Because Truth is that which is most interior, most important, most intimate, and inescapably compulsory, it can never be treated with too much awe, discretion, or care. People's willingness to believe must never be unduly burdened, least of all

---

[82] "Sermon 24. The Religion of the Day" in *Parochial and Plain Sermons*, 1:320–21, quoted by Görres from Blennerhassett, *John Henry Newman*, 63–64, where Blennerhassett quotes from and cites this sermon. In a citation in the German text, Gerl-Falkovitz inserted "<Apologia 62>", that is, page 62 of the German edition of the *Apologia*. In the *Apologia*, however, Newman quotes only part of this passage (in the English edition, *Apologia*, 59). The correct source for this quote is the sermon, not the *Apologia*.

[83] Dr. Thomas Arnold (1795–1842).

[84] Letter to W. G. Ward, November 8, 1860, in Ward, *The Life*, 1:516.

with violence, cunning, or cajoling. Newman's chivalrous anger, his blazing will to fight, flares up where such seriousness is lacking— where human obsession with power ousts humble service to the Truth, where one tosses around claims of faith that the Church is not behind. "I acknowledge one Pope, *jure divino*, I acknowledge no other, and that I think it a usurpation, too wicked to be comfortably dwelt upon, when individuals use their own private judgment, in the discussion of religious questions . . . for the purpose of anathematizing the private judgment of others."[85]

When a few fiery Ultramontanes want to push through the advocacy of the secular power of the papacy as an obligation of faith, Newman speaks, outraged, about flogging, terror, insolence, and moral homicide. It is well known how much he had doubts about the Vatican Council's declaration of infallibility, though not because he did not believe in the infallibility of the pope but since he was convinced that it was too much for many souls to profess a belief with absolute conscience now: "What call have we to shock and frighten away the weak brothers for whom Christ died?"[86] "As to myself personally, please God, I do not expect any trial at all, but I cannot help suffering with the various souls that are suffering."[87]

Indeed, he calls such an approach "aggressive and insolent" and laments, "What have we done to be treated as the Faithful never were treated before?"—namely, that a dogma is defined not to save the Church from grave danger or to settle a longstanding dispute but because a handful of fanatics want "a luxury of devotion"![88]

His attitude is very clear: "If it be God's will that some definition in favour of the Pope's infallibility is passed, I then should at once submit—but up to that very moment I shall pray most heartily and earnestly against it."[89] It is precisely in this attitude that he knows he is "ecclesial" because "what the genius of the Church cannot bear . . . is changes in thought being hurried, abrupt, violent—out

---

[85] "A Letter Addressed to the Duke of Norfolk", in *Certain Difficulties*, 2:346.

[86] Letter to Miss Holmes, Easter Day, 1870, in Ward, *The Life*, 2:554.

[87] Letter to Bishop Ullathorne, January 28, 1870, in Ward, *The Life*, 2:288.

[88] And Newman writes, "No impending danger is to be averted, but a great difficulty is to be created." Newman, Letter to Bishop Ullathorne, January 28, 1870, in Ward, *The Life*, 2:288.

[89] Letter to Dr. Moriarty, bishop of Kerry, March 20, 1870, in Ward, *The Life*, 2:289.

of tenderness to souls, for unlearned and narrow-minded men get
unsettled and miserable."[90]

> Every consideration and the fullest time should be given to those
> who have to make up their minds to hold an article of faith which
> is new to them. To take up at once such an article, may be the act
> of a vigorous faith, but it may also be the act of a man who will
> believe anything because he believes nothing, and is ready to profess
> whatever his ecclesiastical, that is his political, party requires of him.
> There are too many high ecclesiastics in Italy and England, who think
> that to believe is as easy as to obey—that is, they talk as if they did
> not know what an act of faith is. A German who hesitates may have
> more of the real spirit of faith than an Italian who swallows. I have
> never myself had a difficulty about the Pope's Infallibility, but that is
> no reason why I should forget Luke xvii. 1.[91]

(But this Scripture passage is a headache for those who generate the
outrages.)

Newman's struggle in the Church, which will soon be discussed,
is essentially about this justice. It has nothing to do with "tolerance"
in the liberal sense—for example, with a dogma- or authority-shy
Christianity "of the heart". Newman hated every sort of bigotry,
"a fierce and intolerant temper . . . which scorns and virtually tram-
ples on the little ones of Christ."[92] And he hated all religious fanaticism, which [as Frédéric Ozanam wrote] "does not propose to
bring back unbelievers, but to stir up the passions of believers"[93]
because this narrows the Truth, makes the Truth hated, blocks the
way for honest seekers through completely unnecessary obstacles.
Because Newman knows what Truth is, he is tremendously cautious and circumspect in formulating and reaching conclusions; he
does this relentlessly against all hasty, cheap, superficial, not entirely honest "evidence" and defensive artifices. This is why he
takes his opponents so seriously. That is why Newman, when there
are differences within orthodoxy, at the first approach to a serious

[90] Letter to Mr. Hutton, in Ward, *The Life*, 2:335.
[91] Letter to Canon McColl, in Ward, *The Life*, 2:332. Luke 17:1: "And he said to his
disciples, 'Temptations to sin are sure to come; but woe to him by whom they come!'"
[92] "Duke of Norfolk", 2:139.
[93] Ward, *The Life*, 1:465.

departure from true doctrine, shows such a sensitive, protective ability of "clairaudience", to hear with all due breadth, freedom, and generosity almost more than what is said; this includes when the participants themselves do not yet have any idea of the consequences. This unerring nose, this incorruptible consistency, had once taken him from the Oxford Movement to Rome; now it often sets him in opposition to the leading men of the Catholic Church, even to his brothers within the Oratory. His great heartache at conversion is only the first and most difficult of the many separations and farewells. Again and again, by way of a thousand pains, the passion for Truth must defeat the allegiance of the heart.

"To live is to change, and to be perfect is to have changed often"[94]: what a statement for someone who, with such fervor, is attached to everything he has grasped! How much farewell this statement commands, how much loneliness: because, again and again, the illumination of new knowledge guides away from the path of the grand parade route, namely, the path of public prestige. Who can demand that all his companions simply keep accompanying himself? Their time has not yet come. With each change, one outgrows the companions of the earlier stage, who "can't go along". Newman was touched deeply by this. He was never beholden to a "loyalty" that does not allow one to outperform friends from one's youth; he was never a vassal who would prefer to mutilate his own soul rather than to break free from a familiar circle. So his heart is covered with scars of repeated renunciation, like the trunk of an old tree, from the traces of torn branches. But nothing can surpass the tender loyalty, the insurmountable gratitude that he preserves. Nothing is further from him than burning with lightness of heart what he once worshipped; *Loss and Gain* is a unique testimony to this. "Catholics did not make us Catholics; Oxford made us Catholics."[95] And seventeen years later, he wrote to Copeland, "You could not be kinder to me than you are in telling me that persons whom I love have not forgotten me."[96]

---

[94] *Christian Doctrine*, 40.
[95] Letter to Canon Estcourt, June 2, 1860, in Ward, *The Life*, 2:57.
[96] Letter to Copeland, in Ward, *The Life*, 1:598.

5

TAKING CHRISTIANITY SERIOUSLY

The Tracts and Sermons

The Whigs were at the helm—progressive, liberal, and hostile to tradition.[1] For the first time, the question of the separation of church and state was in the air; although the 120 years since then have still not brought this about, it seemed very close at the time.

For us, this phrase has long since lost any horror. On the contrary, to the generations who do not know anything other than the Church's being on the side of an un-Christian or even anti-Christian state, it seems that having an actual separation, that is, an authentic and respected independence, such as that of the Catholic Church in the United States, is a far better solution than the always precarious, often dangerous, often unworthy dependence of the Church on an often hostile, usually unpredictable partner.

But the English church, the established church, was born of the state; they shared the same existence. Separation, disestablishment, would have meant dissolution of the church and thus that of Christianity in England—at least in the minds of contemporaries.

As a Catholic, Newman later pointed out in various ways how much English kingship felt and acted in the spiritual realm as the heir to the papacy. It was far more papal than the pope in Rome. Because of this merging of offices, every religious offense actually bore the stamp of being against the Crown itself and resulted in immediate punishment: exclusion from public office, loss of essential civil rights, even dungeon and deportation. Nobody who had been elected to an administrative or governmental office in a city or township was allowed to take up his office until he had demonstrated reception of the sacrament according to the rite of the state church

---

[1] The Whig Party in the UK came back into power in 1830 and held power on and off until 1859.

during the past year. Failure to attend Sunday service was punished in Newman's youth by fines "to the King", as in the days of Elizabeth, when this law was used as one of the most important tools for the gradual confiscation of Catholics' property. The influence of the church within the state was so strong that participation in any form of governance through such a structure constituted a pure monopoly over church believers. In turn, the church was equally subject to royal guardianship. From the moment of the church's birth, the king and Parliament had determined what its believers should profess in order to be faithful children of this church. The king and Parliament still kept this right, and who should prevent them from making use of it again in stormy times, notwithstanding that their opinion regarding the content of "Christianity" has changed considerably since then? Significant proposals were already under consideration: abolition of the Book of Common Prayer, that is, the time-honored liturgical book that included the pre-Reformation tradition; equality of the independent churches, which deviated enormously from the official teaching; even bishops, it was said, voted for the abandonment of "outdated" dogmas such as the Trinity and forgiveness of sins. Rationalism seemed to be headed for triumph by means of political power.

The small circle of young theologians in Oxford—Pusey, Keble, Newman, and their friends—discerned from the beginning too deeply and too clearly to be content with a political defense of the "rights of the church" or a "worthy cause". "I had rather the Church were levelled to the ground by a nation, really, honestly, and seriously, thinking they did God service in doing so (fearful indeed as the sin would be), than that it should be upheld by a nation on the *mere* ground of maintaining property, for I think this a much greater sin", said Newman with characteristic earnestness.[2]

For them, the church was not just the bulwark against anarchy, dissolution, and atheism, as it was for the other conservatives. If it was the only power against moral negation and moral anarchy, it was so as the guardian of divine revelation. Faith had to be strengthened so that the faithful could face the onslaught coming from outside. Strengthened? It had to be rediscovered altogether.

---

[2] John Henry Newman, "Sermon 15. Contest between Truth and Falsehood in the Church", in *Parochial and Plain Sermons* (London: Longmans, Green, 1906), 3:213.

The young clergymen, who enthusiastically threw themselves into the breach, had no illusions about the internal condition of their church. The Enlightenment had done its job. Theology and religious life diverged widely and almost irreconcilably. The universities still maintained the teachings of the seventeenth century, the classic scholarship of theology since the split in the church; the *Prayerbook* retained Catholic rites and rubrics. But the faithful, the clergy right on up to the bishops, actually ranged from predominantly Protestant in increasingly pale hues to pure deist. The lower classes, almost completely neglected by pastoral care, clung to the zealous, missionary independent churches, especially Methodism.

Dean Church, who, as prelate of the state church, would attest without suspicion, said the Anglican clergy, "anxiously avoided professing certain principles". The parsonages were models of educated noble family life; the clergy at best, "amiable and respectable gentlemen who were satisfied to read morning and afternoon services on a Sunday and to dislike Dissenters".[3]

The great and heartfelt piety that was widespread in families was nourished from the Bible without asking much about the teachings that were confirmed or justified by it. Now that an external upheaval was imminent, it was pleasing and encouraging that petitions with the signatures of 7,000 clergymen "to maintain the doctrine [or teaching], the constitution, and the prayerbook", one with 230,000 lay signatures, were sent to the archbishop of Canterbury; but while it said a lot from a religious point of view, from a political perspective it meant much less. For the Englishman as the most traditional Westerner, these things meant far more as "customs" and a national patrimony than as creed.

The Oxford friends set out to awaken the slumbering and unformed consciousness of faith. With deliberate brusqueness and intensity, the tracts presented the tenets of faith and doctrines of the tradition, especially those forgotten from the old, Catholic, pre-Reformation faith. The selection of topics unfolded of its own accord. The imperative question was: If the state should no longer

---

[3] Sidney Dark, *Great Lives*, vol. 36, *Newman* (London: Duckworth, 1934), 16. Dark quotes this from Canon Sidney Ollard. This does not, however, appear to be from Sidney Leslie Ollard, *A Short History of the Oxford Movement*. (This citation in the German text reads "Dark, 17"; however, in the edition I had access to, this appears on page 16.)

support the church, then what was the basis of the church's reputation and dignity? It rested on the authority of the apostles, on the ordination of the bishops. But who knew anything about the principle of apostolic succession, who distinguished a consecration by the bishops from a simple, albeit solemn and ceremonial, appointment to office? Forgotten dogmatic terminology emerged, pressing for an explanation. What was baptism, what was rebirth, what was the difference between priests and laity? These are the topics the tracts addressed. These were no devotional books. They posed challenges that forced readers to make decisions and take sides. Again, Dean Church: "They were clear, brief, stern appeals to conscience and reason. They were like the short, sharp, rapid utterances of men in pain and danger and pressing emergency."[4] And, "Isaac, we must make a row in the world",[5] Hurrell Froude, the wonderful, ingenious, knightly figure of the bond of friendship, is reported to have said to Isaac Williams. And make a row they did.

Regarding the bishops, right on the first page of the *Tracts*: "And, black event as it would be for the country, yet, (as far as they are concerned,) we could not wish them a more blessed termination of their course, than the spoiling of their goods, and martyrdom."[6]

One after the other, forty-six of them were issued. In addition to the topics mentioned, they also contained extracts from the works of classical English theologians of the seventeenth century and from the early Church Fathers. They appeared anonymously, not out of cowardice but to emphasize the nonindividualistic nature of this ministry—the voice of the church should speak, not a few young clergymen, who were as of yet not well known, except Pusey. Newman wrote most of the pieces, which were printed in various formats, from actual leaflets to book-length brochures. The circle of friends covered the costs themselves. There was still neither railroad nor organized postal service. The first postal stamp was printed in 1840. During his long vacations, Newman roamed the countryside

---

[4] Sidney Leslie Ollard, *A Short History of the Oxford Movement* (London: Mowbray, 1983), 44.

[5] Ollard, *A Short History*, 43.

[6] John Henry Newman, Tract 1, "Thoughts on the Ministerial Commission Respectfully Addressed to the Clergy", in *Tracts for the Times*, ed. James Tolhurst, vol. 10 of *The Works of Cardinal Newman: Birmingham Oratory Millennium Edition* (Leominster, Herefordshire, UK: Gracewing, 2013), 1–2.

on horseback and tirelessly distributed parcels to the remotest parsonages.

But the tracts were not the only tool of the movement, and when they were discontinued because of the bishops' objection, the movement only increased. Its ideas were carried more powerfully by the sermons that Newman gave weekly from the pulpit at St Mary's. "None but those who remember them can adequately estimate the effect of Mr. Newman's four o'clock sermons at St. Mary's", wrote Dean Church. "The world . . . hardly realises that without those sermons the movement . . . would never have been what it was. . . . While men were reading and talking about the Tracts, they were hearing the sermons; and in the sermons they heard the living meaning, and reason, and bearing of the Tracts. . . . The sermons created a moral atmosphere in which men judged the questions in debate."[7]

What does this mean? Newman the preacher conveyed the problems hovering in the air from the mind to the conscience. The listeners began to understand what had already been forgotten in the eighteenth century and what enveloped the new era with a thousand other concerns: namely, that religion had something to do with life. Queen Victoria—a reflection of average English consciousness— whose reign began soon after, maintained throughout her life that "religion was not a thing to be mixed up with life", said E. F. Benson.[8] And Lytton Strachey, the agnostic, whose portrayal of the Victorian era was not at all church-friendly, hits the heart of the Oxford Movement with his ironic remark: "The original and remarkable characteristic of these three men was that they took the Christian Religion *au pied de la lettre*" (literally, seriously); this delighted serious minds, but it also frightened them—"they meant it. When they repeated the Athanasian Creed, they meant it."[9] How wonderful!

---

[7] Richard W. Church, *The Oxford Movement: Twelve Years, 1833–1845* (London: Macmillan, 1891), 113–14.

[8] Edward Frederic Benson, *As We Were: A Victorian Peep Show* (London: Longmans, Green, 1930), 103. Queen Victoria reigned from 1837 to 1901.

[9] Lytton Strachey, *Eminent Victorians* (New York: Modern Library, 1918), 17–18. The German text presents the entire passage, from "The original and remarkable" through "How wonderful!", as one quote from Strachey, but only the two sections of this text presented here in quotation marks appear in Strachey's book.

This, precisely, is what Newman wanted. And he stood before his listeners as the living witness who "meant every word". Before then, who "gave it a second thought"? Newman compelled his listeners to relive his own direct relationship to Truth: "When this is true, well, then . . . !" Then the Christian who "perceives" this, takes it to be true, right down to his innermost conception of himself, to the root of his decisions and in each of his actions, different from those who do not know the Truth he knows or who deny it.

Christian behavior, then, is the touchstone for the authenticity of the creed. Newman was never an "idealist". His familiarity with human nature—anything but "psychology"—always has something unnerving about it; it seems to stem from the inscrutable humility of a man who actually dared to contemplate himself unwaveringly and bluntly in the light of Holy God.

Newman had turned away from the Calvinist system only when he realized that "it has no answer to the phenomenon of human nature."[10] He knew well that Christian behavior is anything but something to be taken for granted. It is, rather, although "to the saints . . . easy and comforting", nonetheless "to the natural man . . . difficult, embarrassing, almost impossible without the assistance of grace".[11] His sermons are above all a call to repentance, to a true, perfect conversion of life. They talk about seriousness and responsibility, about fear and trembling, about patience and practice, about humility, corrigibility, readiness to listen to God's Word, singleness of heart in the search for the Truth. "Holiness Necessary for Future Blessedness", "Self-Denial the Test of Religious Earnestness", "Obedience the Remedy for Religious Perplexity", "Dangers to

---

[10] This quotation appears to be from a secondary source, but I do not know which. Mozley observes something similar and remarks that Newman "notes down in memoranda made at the time, his conviction, gained by personal experience, that the religion which he had received from John Newton and Thomas Scott would not work in a parish; that it was unreal; that this he had actually found as a fact, as Mr. Hawkins had told him beforehand; that Calvinism was not a key to the phenomena of human nature, as they occur in the world". Anne Mozley, ed., *Letters and Correspondence of John Henry Newman during His Life in the English Church: With a Brief Autobiography* (London: Longmans, Green, 1903), 1:107.

[11] Charlotte Blennerhassett, *John Henry Kardinal Newman: Ein Beitrag zur Religiösen Entwicklungsgeschichte der Gegenwart* (Berlin: Verlag Gebrüder Paetel, 1904), 63.

the Penitent", "Saintliness not Forfeited by the Penitent", "Secret Faults", "Human Responsibility, as Independent of Circumstances"[12]—these are only some of the titles in the later printed editions. Many listeners found in these hours the turning point of their lives. But the preacher fared like the sorcerer's apprentice: he had set something in motion, and now it was moving, more and more violently and stormily, and soon he recognized the current that was drifting elsewhere than he had wanted.[13]

A powerful sense of mission had urged him to take on this matter. "I have a work to do in England"[14]—he had repeated these words, which were puzzling even to himself, over and over again in feverish fantasies on that almost fatal excursion to Sicily, lying sick in a foreign country. Perhaps the force of this mission, which was still veiled to him, had strengthened in this man in great peril the flickering will to recover. Now he felt he was consecrated and prepared to be sent onto a battlefield. Too modest to see himself as a founder of a religion or even just as the founder of a church, he understood his mission as a restoration of the "old Truth": "It is no slight thing to be made the instrument of handing down the principles of Laud [the great seventeenth-century bishop] till the time comes", he wrote in 1833.[15] He did not strive for anything for himself, neither the experience of victory nor even posthumous fame. This integrity radiates gloriously from the following sentences of this letter: "It is well to fall if you kill your adversary. Nor can I wish anyone a happier lot than to be himself unfortunate, yet to

---

[12] "Holiness Necessary for Future Blessedness", "Self-Denial the Test of Religious Earnestness", "Obedience the Remedy for Religious Perplexity", "Secret Faults", in *Parochial and Plain Sermons*, vol. 1; "Dangers to the Penitent", "Saintliness not Forfeited by the Penitent", in *Sermons on the Subjects of the Day* (London: Longmans, Green, 1902); "Human Responsibility, as Independent of Circumstances", in *Fifteen Sermons Preached before the University of Oxford between A.D. 1826 and 1843* (London: Longmans, Green, 1909).

[13] See Johann Wolfgang von Goethe, "The Sorcerer's Apprentice", in *103 Great Poems: A Dual-Language Book = 103 Meistergedichte*, trans. and ed. Stanley Applebaum (Mineola, N.Y.: Dover Publications).

[14] John Henry Newman, *Apologia pro Vita Sua*, ed. Ian Ker (London: Penguin Books, 1994), 50.

[15] Letter to R. F. Wilson, Esq., Oriel College, September 8, 1833, in Mozley, *Letters*, 1:400. William Laud (1573–1645), Anglican bishop.

urge on a triumphant cause; like Laud and Ken in their day, who left a name which after ages censure or pity, but whose works do follow them. Let it be the lot of those I love to live in the heart of one or two in each succeeding generation, or to be altogether forgotten, while they have helped forward the truth."[16]

With the same high-spirited masculinity, the friends knew themselves and each other to be dedicated to this work: when Newman fell ill, Hurrell Froude advised him not to go easy on himself. "No matter whether one perished: in the eyes of one who was fated to an early death, the cause is what counted, not life."[17]

But they were like men who had discovered the buried layout of a city long buried and rebuilt in an entirely different manner: some towers and gates are still standing as landmarks; ramparts and ditches stand out under the lawns and promenades of the layout; street names, bridgeheads, forsaken memorial stones reveal the location of former buildings. But the new era no longer pays attention to any of this. The new plan overlaps with and covers the former cityscape; the remains of the old city layout are considered by the residents as venerable but incomprehensible, useless, and often annoying rubble; people think about clearing them away soon and thoroughly to ease the flow of traffic. Who could expect the municipal authority and his architects simply to tear down the city as it exists at present, which has stood for almost three centuries, in order to rebuild it according to the long-forgotten layout, just because a few enthusiasts unearthed it in the old city library and find it more beautiful or more functional?

Walter Scott's historical novels had created a strong wave of Romantic enthusiasm for the Middle Ages. The fad of neo-Gothic buildings filled the country with artificial knightly castles and churches, the fantastic creations of [Ewell] and Pugin.[18] Many

---

[16] Letter to Reverend S. Rickards, Oriel College, November 22, 1833, in Mozley, *Letters*, 1:429. Thomas Ken (1637–1711), Anglican bishop.

[17] Blennerhassett, *John Henry Newman*, 66.

[18] The German text reads "Wewells"; this may be an error by Görres, or perhaps her handwriting was unclear. Görres is more likely referring here to Ewell Castle, a Gothic Revival–style castle built in the nineteenth century. Augustus Welby Northmore Pugin (1812–1852) was a pioneer of neo-Gothic architecture in England; several of his sons became architects.

were likely to put the new religious excitement emanating from Oxford in the same category and see nothing more than the echo of Romanticism in the suddenly awakened advocacy for the stylistically appropriate restoration of old village churches, for altar candles, liturgical vestments, stained-glass windows, and monastic traditions' spiritual realm, an understandable pushback against the long predominance of Puritan coldness and sobriety. Newman defends himself vigorously and decisively against such mistaken notions, even if he frankly admits the connection. As someone who was independent in taste as well as thought, who did not go along with Gothic trends and preferred the Greek—namely, classical—style, for him it was really not about aesthetic dalliances:

> Much curiosity is directed towards the science of ecclesiastical architecture, and much appreciation shown of architectural proprieties. Attention, too, is paid to the internal arrangement and embellishment of sacred buildings. Devotional books also of an imaginative cast, religious music, painting, poetry, and the like are in request. Churches are more frequently attended on weekdays, and continual service is felt to be a privilege, not a task. . . . Many a man, and especially many a woman, may abandon themselves to the real delight, as it will prove, of passing hours in repeating the Psalms, or in saying Litanies and Hymns, and in frequenting those Cathedrals and Churches where the old Catholic ideas are especially impressed upon their minds. . . . O my brethren, be jealous of these things, excellent as they are in themselves, lest they be not accompanied with godly fear. I grieve to say, that the spirit of penitence does not keep pace with the spirit of joy. With all this outward promise of piety, we are suspicious of that which alone is its inward soul and life; we are very jealous indeed of personal strictness and austerity. . . . We like to be told of the excellence of our institutions, we do not like to hear of their defects; we like to abandon ourselves to the satisfactions of religion, we do not like to hear of its severities. . . . Alas! . . . Surely we are pretending allegiance to the Church to no purpose, or rather to our own serious injury, if we select her doctrines and precepts at our pleasure; choose this, reject that; take what is beautiful and attractive, shrink from what is stern and painful. I fear a number of persons, a growing number, in various parts of the country, are likely to abandon themselves to what may be called the luxuries of religion—nay, I will even

call them the luxuries of devotion; and the consequence of this it is very distressing to contemplate. . . . Let us not keep festivals without keeping vigils; let us not keep Eastertide without observing Lent; let us not approach the Sunday feast without keeping the Friday abstinence; let us not adorn churches without studying personal simplicity and austereness; let us not cultivate the accomplishments of taste and literature without the corrective of personal discomfort; let us not attempt to advance the power of the Church, to enthrone her rulers, to rear her palaces, and to ennoble her name, without recollecting that she must be mortified within while she is in honour in the world, and must wear the Baptist's hair-shirt and leathern girdle under the purple ephod and the jewelled breastplate.[19]

The serious, the discerning, and those truly taking heed in his growing community had already advanced to other depths. The truth he was preaching had moved and roused them. Who had taken a fast day seriously up to now, regardless of whether it was still on old calendars? "This Lent", wrote Newman to Dalgairns in April 1843, "the University authorities were obliged to put up a notice ordering the men to attend dinner in Hall on Fridays." He adds, "It is quite impossible such persons can stop where they are, i.e., unless they marry, which reconciles one to any amount of intellectual inconsistency."[20] But Pusey and Keble, who were both married and whose wives walked the same path with joy and understanding, practiced fasting and austerity, poverty and charity. Newman built himself a home in Littlemore, where he used to retreat for weeks at a time with some of his disciples during Lent for silence, prayer, and study. The fasting there was so strict that Newman was amazed at his mental efficiency during such asceticism. While Pusey was busy founding a kind of Sisters of Mercy, Newman had in mind something like the attempt at a kind of monastic life.

The "Catholic tendencies" of this circle were already beginning to arouse suspicion and unease. "I fully sympathize in what you say about the temper of some younger men", writes Newman already in February 1839 to some of the concerned men in his circle.

---

[19] "Sermon 9. Indulgence in Religious Privileges", in *Subjects of the Day*, 115–16, 118, 116, 117, 122–23.

[20] Letter to J. B. Dalgairns, April 26, 1843, in *Correspondence of John Henry Newman with John Keble and Others, 1839–1845* (London: Longmans, Green, 1917), 214–15.

"I suppose the case is simply this, that we have raised desires, of which our Church does not supply the objects, and that they have not the patience, or humility, or discretion to keep from seeking those objects where they are supplied. I have from the first thought that nothing but a *quasi* miracle, would carry us through the trial with no proselytes whatever to Rome."[21]

> The age is moving towards something, and most unhappily the one religious communion among us which has of late years been in possession of this something, is the Church of Rome. She alone, amid all the errors and evils of her practical system, has given free scope to the feelings of awe, mystery, tenderness, reverence, devotedness, and other feelings which may be especially called Catholic. The question then is, whether we shall give them up to the Roman Church or claim them for ourselves, as we well may, by reverting to that older system, which has of late years indeed been superseded, but which has been and is, quite congenial . . . to our Church.[22]

It was certainly no longer a question of political positions in the church. Not out of modesty but with the strict objectivity of a witness, Newman defended himself then and later against being misunderstood as a head of a party or even as the leader of a movement. Something bigger was underway here. No prior plan, no long-term calculation had organized the so-very-different minds for any purpose. "What head of a sect is there? What march of opinions can be traced from mind to mind among preachers such as these? They are one and all in their degree the organs of one Sentiment, which has risen up simultaneously in many places very mysteriously."[23]

It was like this at the beginning of our [twentieth] century with the awakening of the German Youth Movement, when a peculiar unrest fermented under the solid blanket of bourgeois convention, which had seemed to prevail unchallenged. There was a new attitude toward life that did not yet know what its goals were and yet, feeling its way blind and dumb, came together with unanimous

---

[21] Letter to Reverend W. Dodsworth, November 19, 1839, in *Correspondence with Keble*, 41–42.

[22] *Correspondence with Keble*, 82n2, quoting from John Henry Newman, *The Via Media of the Anglican Church* (London: Basil Montagu Pickering, 1877), 2:386.

[23] *Apologia*, 101.

agreement, and they recognized each other clearly when the conference in the Hoher Meissner hills proclaimed its well-known slogan into the land.[24]

~

That is how it was back then [in Newman's time]: "It was not so much a movement as a 'spirit afloat'; it was within us, 'rising up in hearts where it was least suspected, and working itself, though not in secret, yet so subtly and impalpably, as hardly to admit of precaution or encounter on any ordinary human rules of opposition. It is,' I continued, 'an adversary in the air, a something one and entire, a whole wherever it is, unapproachable and incapable of being grasped, as being the result of causes far deeper than political or other visible agencies, the spiritual awakening of spiritual wants.' "[25]

Newman's preaching gave them terminology and awareness. He proclaimed the tentative religious longing, the receptiveness that was waiting in anticipation at his feet; he proclaimed not vague feelings and intoxicating words but the reality of grace and revelation, of God's kingdom and conscience, of responsibility and longing for holiness. And those who were touched, who were seized, wanted in response expression, form, and principles for this life that had been awakened; they wanted liturgy and sacrament, a rule of faith and guidance of the soul, tried and tested Christian experience in penance and prayer. His sermon from Easter 1842 on "Dangers to the Penitent" clearly shows what kind of fire was kindled and how difficult it was to tame the rising embers:

> I observe, then, that repentant sinners are often impatient to put themselves upon some new line of action, or to adopt some particular rule of life. . . . And their heart yearns towards humiliation, and burns with a godly indignation against themselves, as if nothing were too

---

[24] Gerl-Falkovitz explains, "The slogan 'The free German youth want to shape their lives with inner truthfulness on their own initiative, out of their own responsibility' was formulated in 1913, on the occasion of the centenary of the Battle of Leipzig (the Battle of the Nations) at a gathering of two thousand young people."

[25] *Apologia*, 100–101. In the German edition, Görres emphasizes the phrase "the spiritual awakening of spiritual wants" with italics.

bad for them. . . . Persons do not know what they can bear, and what they cannot, till they have tried it. They think almost they can live without food, without rest, without the conveniences of life to which they are accustomed. Then when they find they cannot, they despond and are miserable, or fall back, and a reaction ensues. . . . Moreover, if penitents are bent on lading themselves heavily, let them know that the greatest of burdens, as well as the most appropriate, is what is lasting, what is continual. . . . When persons are in acute distress about their sins, they are sometimes tempted to make rash promises, and to take on them professions without counting the cost. . . . They do not know whether [a vow they have made] is binding or not—they cannot recollect the mode in which, or the feelings under which, they took it; or any of the minute circumstances on which its validity turns. Now all this on the very first view of the case shows thus much, how very wrong it is to make private vows. . . . The Church should hear them, and the Church should bless them. In the early Church even the highest ecclesiastical authorities were appealed to as their witnesses and imposers. But unless in some sense or form the Church is present, it seems rash to make vows. . . . What was said just now naturally leads to . . . that when men are in the first fervour of penitence, they should be careful not to act on their own private judgment, and without proper advice . . . and as no one would ever dream of being his own lawyer or his own physician, however great exposures, whatever sacrifice of feeling may be the consequence, so we must take it for granted, if we would serve God comfortably, that we cannot be our own divines, and our own casuists.[26]

Who could doubt where this was going? Soon it was clear to every discerning person, every savvy and even every suspicious observer where the journey was going. "It is quite impossible such persons can stop where they are", said Newman himself.[27] Already the talk begins, which will not fall silent for many years, that Newman is a traitor to his church who, living on her bread, wearing her official attire, abusing her authority and his position, as a secret papist, imperceptibly turns the youth entrusted to him into apostates to lead them into Rome's arms. What he intended was not the renewal of his own church but its undermining and dissolution from

---

[26] "Sermon 4. Dangers to the Penitent", in *Subjects of the Day*, 42, 44, 45, 46, 48, 50.
[27] Letter to J. B. Dalgairns, April 26, 1843, in *Correspondence with Keble*, 214.

within—today, one would call it partisan work, as if the Tractarians were a fifth column of the pope. Newman repeatedly accuses himself of this charge in his letters.

So it was questionable whether he could keep his ministry under these circumstances: "that my sermons are calculated to undermine things established".

> I cannot disguise from myself that they are. No one will deny that most of my sermons are on moral subjects, not doctrinal; still I am leading my hearers to the Primitive Church, if you will, but not to the Church of England. Now, ought one to be disgusting the minds of young men with the received religion, in the exercise of a sacred office, yet without a commission, and against the wish of their guides and governors? . . . I fear I must allow that, whether I will or no, I am disposing them towards Rome. First, because Rome is the only representative of the Primitive Church besides ourselves; in proportion then as they are loosened from the one, they will go to the other.[28]

For "we have raised desires, of which our church does not supply the objects", and in the long run one cannot demand that the young men who have awakened to this new spiritual life have "the patience, or humility, or discretion to keep from seeking those objects where they are supplied".[29]

In other words: Newman, the lonely voice crying in the desert, had awakened souls and at the same time showed the leaders of his church the wellsprings. It was up to them, and not him, whether they would give the expected answer or disappoint those who were waiting, always impetuously demanding. With fervent hope, with tireless fervor, with unrelenting urgency, Newman strives year after year to show the people of the church and the bishops this necessity and the way. He knows with consuming tension that it is an attempt and a risk. Here lies, it seems to us, the razor-thin but dreadful gap that starts from the beginning between him and his close-knit brothers-in-arms Keble and Pusey. For these two, the English church is already indisputably a fully valid branch of the

---

[28] Letter to Keble, October 1840, in *Apologia*, 129. Görres cites "Corr. Keble 150", but this passage does not appear on page 150 of *Correspondence with Keble*.

[29] Letter to Reverend W. Dodsworth, November 19, 1839, in *Correspondence with Keble*, 41–42.

Catholic Church, which needs "only" to be refreshed and cleansed in order to exist alongside the Roman and the Greek churches as the heir to the singular Primitive Church. For Newman, it was not yet this; it could, should, had to become this. It is true that he drafted the broad theory of the *Via Media*, the middle way between Protestantism and papism, in an important work. But his honest, fair-and-square sober look soon enough saw that his Anglicanism was only a "paper religion", a blueprint, a dream, a goal, while Protestant and Roman beliefs are "real religions".[30] "Anglicanism has never yet been put to the test whether it will bear life; it may break to pieces in the rush and transport of existence, and die of joy."[31]

Still, "I trusted that some day it"—the *Via Media*—"would prove to be a substantive religion."[32] With ever more unease, the realization dawns on him that the concept he is constructing will not find its way into reality. The new city is too firmly established, too densely populated; its residents like it much too much for any serious renovation to be expected. A decisive attempt still had to be made: the Thirty-Nine Articles, which every Oxford student had to sign upon admission and which every clergyman had to swear to recognize as the official compilation of Anglican doctrine since the days of Edward [VI].[33] Long study had led Newman to the conviction that they should be viewed purely as a creation out of compromise. They came from a time when the old Catholic faith was still alive among many in England, in too many to be able to do without their cooperation entirely. The creators of the Articles were Protestants; they had no intention of spreading Catholic doctrines. Nevertheless, intentionally and deliberately, they had

---

[30] *Apologia*, 77.

[31] Letter to S. F. Wood, March 10, 1840, in *Correspondence with Keble*, 62.

[32] *Apologia*, 77.

[33] The Thirty-Nine Articles, also known as the Thirty-Nine Articles of Religion, were Anglican doctrinal statements that developed after King Henry VIII was excommunicated from the Catholic Church in 1533. The German edition of this book states that the Articles were first issued under Edward IV. This is an error, however. Under King Edward IV (r. 1461–1470), England was still Catholic. It was, rather, under King Edward VI (r. 1547–1553), that Archbishop of Canterbury Thomas Cranmer issued the Forty-Two Articles. These were later revised and promulgated in 1571 as the Thirty-Nine Articles. Until 1865, Anglican bishops and clergy were required to assent to them.

worded the document in such a way that people with Catholic in-
clinations could sign it without violating their consciences but also
without violating the literal meaning of the Articles. The Articles
could bear a Catholic interpretation; they did not strive for it—
this is how Newman later formulated his thesis. Why should the
Catholic-minded Anglicans of the day not be able to invoke this
possibility? Who should be allowed to deny them recourse to the
inheritance of the [Church] Fathers, as long as they did not deny
the real meaning of the Articles—namely, the rejection of Rome?
Certainly, the Articles were aimed against "Popery"—but "Popery" in Elizabeth's day, meant "not any religious doctrine at all, but
a political principle", as Newman explains his undertaking in retrospect in the *Apologia*. "The Supremacy of the Pope was the essence
of the 'Popery.' "[34] "Well, one would distance oneself sharply and
clearly from the 'Roman corruption' and the papal presumptions:
Then one would be free to profess the ancient creeds"; Newman
published these thoughts in the famous Tract 90.[35]

"Man had done his worst to disfigure, to mutilate, the old Catholic Truth; but there it was, in spite of them, in the Articles still.
It was there,—but this must be shown. It was a matter of life and
death to us to show it. And I believed that it could be shown . . .
and therefore I set about showing it at once. This was in March,
1840, when I went up to Littlemore. . . . I had in mind to remove
all such obstacles as lay in the way of holding the Apostolic and
Catholic character of the Anglican teaching; to assert the right of

---

[34] *Apologia*, 87.

[35] This passage does not appear as such in Tract 90. In the German edition, the two
sentences from "The Supremacy of the Pope" to "the ancient creeds" appear together
in double quotation marks, and Görres' citation for this is Tract 90. As noted in the
previous citation, however, the sentence "The Supremacy of the Pope was the essence
of the 'Popery'" appears in *Apologia*, 87. It follows and is in the same paragraph as the
quote directly preceding here, "Not any religious doctrine at all, but a political principle". The idea expressed in the sentence "Well, one would . . . the ancient creeds"
(here as my translation from the German text) does not appear as such in any of the
passages where Newman uses the phrase "Roman corruption", namely, *Apologia*, 107,
and "Roman corruptions" in *Apologia*, 142; Wilfrid Philip Ward, *The Life of John Henry
Cardinal Newman: Based on His Private Journals and Correspondence* (London: Longmans,
Green, 1912), 1:87, 186, 238; and John Henry Newman, *Certain Difficulties Felt by Anglicans in Catholic Teaching* (London: Longmans, Green, 1901), 1:395.

all who chose, to say in the face of day, 'Our Church teaches the Primitive Ancient faith.' "[36] "I have no doubt that then I acknowledged to myself that it would be a trial of the Anglican Church, which it had never undergone before."[37]

It was a gamble, and it failed. Newman later confessed that he never expected such a stormy response. Recent researchers have demonstrated that what he postulated was not even entirely new. Perhaps the same material from a different pen would have been read and discussed in academic circles without causing any particular stir. Tract 90 set off a wild thunderstorm. Bishops and universities were in an uproar. The bishop of Chester called the whole movement a work of Satan; Archbishop Whately of Dublin, Newman's one-time friend and leader, called it a "pestilence".[38] A senior clergyman declared that he would regret it if he had entrusted even his purse to the author.[39] Newman's name was attacked in the universities: "Like that of a pastry chef who had fallen into disrepute. . . . From pulpits, at dining tables, in coffee shops, and in railroad cars, [he] was exposed as a traitor who had laid his fuse and had been caught in the act of lighting it. At the same time, there was an ugly suspicion in Roman Catholic circles that the author and his friends had long been Catholic at heart, but—unwilling to give up their good salaries—that they tried to justify staying in the state church with logical sleight of hand."[40] Obedient to his

---

[36] *Apologia*, 126–27.

[37] *Apologia*, 126.

[38] Blennerhassett, *John Henry Newman*, 85. Blennerhassett cites Church, *The Oxford Movement*, 132, 219. Reverend Richard Whately was bishop and later archbishop of the Church of Ireland (a province of the Anglican Communion) from 1831 to 1863.

[39] See Ollard, *A Short History*, 71.

[40] Görres has this passage, from "Like that of a pastry chef" to "sleight of hand", in double quotation marks, and she cites "C.E. 26", namely, Henry Tristram, ed., *John Henry Newman: Centenary Essays* (London: Burns, Oates and Washbourne, 1945), 26. This is not a quotation, however, but only a loose paraphrase of the following passage from an essay by Denis Gwynn in Tristram's book:

> Newman was near forty-five, and for almost thirty years his life had been centred in Oxford. His official status in the Church of England had never been more than that of a Fellow of Oriel and Vicar of St. Mary's. The leadership of the Tractarian movement had fallen to him only for his intellectual and spiritual gifts, and he had in later years avoided all public responsibilities. As a convert to the Catholic

bishop, in whom he saw the vicar of God and "his pope" despite all differences of opinion, Newman discontinued the tracts without being ordered or coerced. But, achingly, he wrote to a friend: "I am startled myself in turn, that persons, who have in years past and present borne patiently disclaimers of the Athanasian Creed, or of the doctrine of Baptismal Regeneration, or of belief in many of the Scripture miracles, should now be alarmed so much, when a private Member of the University, without his name, makes statements in an opposite direction".[41]

In the autumn of that year, when one pastoral letter after another was directed against Newman—"It was a formal, determinate movement"—he wrote agonizingly but firmly to a friend, "If the view [in this tract] were silenced, I could not remain in the Church, nor could many others." And further: "If our rulers speak either against the Tracts, or not at all, if any number of them, not only do not favour, but even do not suffer the principles contained in them, it is plain that our members may easily be persuaded either to give up those principles, or to give up the Church. If this state of

Church, he had to join a communion of which he knew practically nothing, and he had every reason to expect that he would feel isolated and be regarded with suspicion. Wiseman had been almost alone in treating the Tractarians as men of absolute sincerity, and he had often been attacked for showing sympathy to Anglican theologians who were admittedly trying to prevent waverers from becoming Catholics. They were widely accused among Catholics of twisting their consciences so that they might retain their livings as Anglicans although secretly convinced that the Catholic Church alone possessed the true faith. Newman himself had been the most subtle and the most learned exponent of the Anglo-Catholic compromise, and it was years before the older Catholics overcame their suspicions of his integrity.

Denis Gwynn, "John Henry Newman, 1801–1890", in Tristram, *John Henry Newman*, 25–26. Related to this, on the topic of attacks on Newman's reputation, Gwynn writes, "Wiseman died in February, 1865, and during his last years Newman's reputation was becoming seriously clouded by the attacks of Manning and of Ward, whose extravagant Papalism made Newman decline his invitation to contribute to the *Dublin Review* when he became its editor. His status had shrunk sadly since that brief period of enthusiasm when he was the hero of an unjust trial, rector of a Catholic University which seemed to fulfil the hopes of years, and Superior of the Oratory. Now the London Oratory under Faber had become more prominent than his own at Edgbaston; the University had collapsed in failure; and Newman himself was becoming suspect by authority." "John Henry Newman", 33.

[41] Letter to Dr. Jelf, March 13, 1841, in *Correspondence with Keble*, 86.

things goes on, I mournfully prophesy, not one or two, but many secessions to the Church of Rome."[42]

In other words: Newman realized that his church did not pose the question of tracts at all—only questions of public opinion, opportunism, and the maintenance of power. A political event also shone a light on this: the envoy of the Prussian king Frederick William IV, [Karl Josias] von Bunsen, negotiated with the archbishop of Canterbury about the establishment of an Anglo-Prussian bishopric in Jerusalem. It was about the balance of powers in the Near East: France acted there as the patron of the Catholics and Russia as that of the Orthodox, and now England was to take over the patronage of the Protestant Christians. In fact, there was not a single Anglican on the spot, only German Lutherans and Reformed, as well as oriental sects—Nestorians, Jacobites, and Monophysites. The English archbishopric thus publicly associated itself with the Protestant community.

Newman alone understood the religious implications of this step. He alone raised his voice in solemn, if useless, protest in a letter to his bishop:

Whereas the Church of England has a claim on the allegiance of Catholic believers only on the ground of her own claim to be considered a branch of the Catholic Church:

And whereas the recognition of heresy, indirect as well as direct, goes far to destroy such claim in the case of any religious body:

And whereas to admit maintainers of heresy to communion, without formal renunciation of their errors, goes far towards recognizing the same:

And whereas Lutheranism and Calvinism are heresies, repugnant to Scripture, springing up three centuries since, and anathematized by East as well as West:

And whereas it is reported that the Most Reverend Primate and other Right Reverend Rulers of our Church have consecrated a Bishop with a view to exercising spiritual jurisdiction over Protestant, that is, Lutheran and Calvinist congregations in the East . . . , dispensing at the same time, not in particular cases and accidentally, but as if on principle and universally, with any abjuration of error on the part of

---

[42] *Apologia*, 134–35.

such congregations, and with any reconciliation to the Church . . . ;
thereby giving some sort of formal recognition to the doctrines which
such congregations maintain . . .

On these grounds, I in my place, being a priest of the English
Church and Vicar of St. Mary the Virgin's, Oxford, by way of reliev-
ing my conscience, do hereby solemnly protest against the measure
aforesaid, and disown it, as removing our Church from her present
ground and tending to her disorganization.

JOHN HENRY NEWMAN.

November 11, 1841.[43]

The letter went unanswered, of course. In severe bitterness, perplexed and hopeless, Newman wrote to a friend: "I have been for
a long while assuring persons that the English Church was a branch
of the Catholic Church. If, then a measure in progress which in my
judgment tends to cut from under me the very ground on which I
have been writing and talking, and to prove all I hold a mere theory
and illusion . . . who will not excuse me if I am deeply pained at
such proceedings? When friends who rely on my word come to
me and say, 'You *told* us the English Church was *Catholic*,' what
am I to say to this reproach?"[44] The question became more and
more acute: "Can a church belong to Christ if it does not have a
faith? What if it contradicts itself in its documents and its history,
in its documents and theologians, and in the theologians and other
members against each other?" When personal taste and one's origin, party affiliation, school, and, ultimately, the will of the Crown
decide what one believes and rejects—one has to ask: "Is there any
belief in the English church at all?" Or are the Thirty-Nine Articles, their foundational doctrine, just "the views of persons in the
16th century; and, again, it is not clear how far they are, or are not,
modified by the unauthoritative views of the 19th"? as Newman
lets Charles Reding ask; "my judgment", says Reding, "is unequal
to so great a task."[45]

---

[43] *Apologia*, 138–39.

[44] Letter to Hope, November 24, 1841, in *Correspondence with Keble*, 157.

[45] *Loss and Gain*, 222.

6

ROME

A Mix of Hatred and Love

But if the English church refuses to align its claim that it is "a branch"[1] of Catholicity, if it actually proves to be "Protestant", that is, if it relinquishes the private judgment of its children, the degree of their theological education, and, finally, the law to Parliament and to what parliamentarians imagine Christianity to be: *Where* then is the continuation of that original foundation of Christ, the Church of Augustine and Athanasius? Is there a living and inhabited city somewhere over and above the foundation that the former English theologians invoked? There is one, there is only one: it is the City on the Hill that cannot remain hidden, and its name is Rome.

Yet this response is not so easy to offer. Perhaps only a few separated Christians today are able to feel the pathos with which Newman was convinced of this: that Rome was the Antichrist.

Ever since the boy convert devoured Milner's church history[2] with passion, the belief that the pope was the Antichrist was a "stain upon my imagination".[3] This was not an empty catchphrase, nor was it a mere archaic horror figure that was becoming less of a reality for the critical young scholar of the Oriel Common Room. For certain, he was far too clear-minded and clever simply to cling to a youthful

---

[1] See for example, Newman's "Protest" that he sent to the bishop of Oxford in November 1841: "Whereas the Church of England has a claim on the allegiance of Catholic believers only on the ground of her own claim to be considered a branch of the Catholic Church", in Anne Mozley, ed., *Letters and Correspondence of John Henry Newman during His Life in the English Church: With a Brief Autobiography* (London: Longmans, Green, 1903), 2:324.

[2] This was a five-volume series called *The History of the Church of Christ*, started by Joseph Milner and completed by others after his death. See John Henry Newman, *Apologia pro Vita Sua*, ed. Ian Ker (London: Penguin Books, 1994), 27.

[3] *Apologia*, 119.

prejudice. Engaging with the Church Fathers expanded his image
of faith to a catholic breadth and fullness and taught him to recognize and grasp the depth and richness of the original teaching, far
beyond the meager Calvinist paradigm of his religious beginning.
Hurrell Froude corrected his judgment on the Reformation and
the Reformers, laughed at the grim seriousness of his anti-Roman
affect, which he never liked to take seriously, and even rebuked
him sternly and sorrowfully for his "cursing and swearing" against
"Popery".[4] Gradually, Newman moved away from interpreting the
person of the pope as the adversary of God; he called the Roman
Church "only" in league with the cause of the Antichrist—one of
many anti-Christian phenomena that Saint John had foretold—or
"as being influenced by 'the *spirit* of Antichrist' ".[5] But still in 1838,
he was convinced that it was "not the Church of Rome, but the
spirit of the old pagan city, the fourth monster of Daniel which was
still alive, and which had corrupted the Church which was planted
there".[6]

But that was more than enough for it "to be a duty to protest
against the Church of Rome",[7] that is, a matter of conscience. For
what else did it mean but that the spirit of lies and darkness had over-
powered the former seat of Truth itself and made it subservient?
As an alien will dwells in someone who is possessed, making use
of his voice, his senses, and his limbs, so an evil rule reigned in
the glorious inheritance of the early Church, and all its treasures
and works were left to his discretion, now just being organs that
have been seduced. Rome was the embodiment of betraying Divine Truth. And the more strongly Newman leaned toward Catholic *doctrine*, the more his loathing grew, his loathing of the "Roman
system",[8] which misused, falsified, and degraded this holy temple
as an instrument of its hubris and lust for power.

Gazing at the Catholic Church fills him again and again with an
agonizing mix of hatred and love. "Considering the high gifts and
the strong claims of the Church of Rome and its dependencies on

---

[4] *Apologia*, 120–21.
[5] *Apologia*, 64.
[6] *Apologia*, 119.
[7] *Apologia*, 66.
[8] *Apologia*, 129.

our admiration, reverence, love, and gratitude; how could we with-
stand it, as we do, how could we refrain from being melted into
tenderness, and rushing into communion with it, but for the words
of Truth itself, which bid us prefer It to the whole world?"[9] That
was how it might have been for him when he looked at the picture
of that which is Catholic in the documents of the Fathers. But the
spectacle of the Church's living reality made resistance easy and
objective praise almost impossible.

Newman hardly knew a single Catholic personally. In England,
there were a few quiet, almost publicity-shy loners and eccentrics
from the old Catholic families, and there was the flood of Irish
workers that poured unceasingly into the new industrial cities, re-
pulsive, incredibly neglected hordes, who were shaken by the stun-
ning depth of their misery to a level below even the lowest levels
of the English proletariat: that is who the Catholics were.

Then there were Catholic politicians such as O'Connell, entirely
abhorrent to Newman, "because . . . he associated himself with
men of all religions and no religion against the Anglican Church,
and advanced Catholicism by violence and intrigue".[10] His tactics
seemed to prove that Rome's attitude, which apparently protected
and sustained this champion, was purely secular and political.

During the trip to Italy in 1833, Newman and his friends had
deliberately avoided any encounter with Catholics. The brief visit
to the young rector of the English College in Rome, Dr. Wiseman,
made a deep impression on Dr. Wiseman, but not on the travelers
from Oxford. The Eternal City plunged Newman altogether into a
deep melancholy that colors many of his poems from those weeks.
A God-favored beauty in the claws of the Evil One, glorious and
desecrated, still shimmering from the splendor of its origin, but
with the mark of Satan on the forehead; that is how Rome appears
to him.

"You are in the place of martyrdom and burial of apostles and
saints . . . you are in the city to which England owes the blessing of
the Gospel. But then, on the other hand, the superstitions, or rather,

---

[9] *Apologia*, 65.
[10] *Apologia*, 121. Daniel O'Connell (1775–1847) was an Irish politician who advocated for the interests of Catholics.

what is far worse, the solemn reception of them as an essential part
of Christianity. But then, again, the extreme beauty and costliness
of the churches . . . was built (in part) by the sale of indulgences.
Really this is a cruel place."[11] "I fear I must look upon Rome, as
a city, still under a curse."[12] "Oh that Rome were not Rome!"[13]
"Thus these countries have the evils of Protestantism without its
advantages. . . . But here, too, they have infidelity and profaneness,
as if the whole world (Western) were tending towards some dreadful crisis."[14] This is his impression of the moral and religious depravity of the Italian people. The young painters and poets who
flocked to Rome and Florence from all over the world at that time,
Berlioz and Liszt, Kopisch, Overbeck, Andersen, Thorvaldsen, saw
the colors and ruins, the traditional costumes and folk festivals, got
intoxicated by the picturesque and regarded the natives only as ele-
ments of the landscape and models, even if not all of them dared to
speak like the aesthete Gautier:[15] "What do I care about this population, whether they are pigs or criminals, so long as I am not killed
while looking at the buildings?" But Newman traced the footsteps
of the early Church with a bleeding heart.

This judgment is certainly not harsh if one compares it with the
descriptions of Catholic researchers about the conditions in the
Papal States at that time. Under the pontificate of Pope Leo XII,
which filled Newman's youth, there was, according to Schmidlin's
history of the popes, "an increasing plague of robbers and beg-
gars. . . . Sometimes imprisoned or deported, sometimes amnestied
and thus proud, protected by the population and reinforced by general fear, the brigands of the countryside and the Volsci Region
saw themselves . . . as a great power; they sent their delegations to
the cities, where they imposed their laws and took hostages. . . .
The fight that Leo XII proclaimed against the secret societies and
conspiracies on the part of the Carbonari", to which students,
artists, and craftsmen belonged, "was similar in severity, but also in

---

[11] Letter to J. F. Christie, Esq., Rome, March 7, 1833, in Mozley, *Letters*, 1:325.
[12] Letter to his sister Jemima, Rome, March 20, 1833, in Mozley, *Letters*, 1:331.
[13] Letter to his sister Jemima, Naples, April 11, 1833, in Mozley, *Letters*, 1:338.
[14] Mozley, *Letters*, 1:310.
[15] Namely, Hector Berlioz, Franz Liszt, August Kopisch, Johann Friedrich Overbeck,
Hans Christian Andersen, Bertel Thorvaldsen, and Lucien Marcelin Gautier.

outcome."[16] The violent clerical Sanfedisti group fought back with
formal complaints and acts of revenge.[17] The papal legate sentenced
those caught, by the hundreds, to death, life or multiyear imprison-
ment, or exile. One of the gentler punishments was constant police supervision: those convicted of this, punished for three years
of forced labor, had to report to the police every fourteen days,
and every four weeks they had to present a certificate that they had
gone to confession. The jails were overcrowded, monasteries were
reduced to prisons, and the bodies of those executed were on display for twelve hours.[18]

In the face of the "Roman corruptions",[20] the image of the distant home rose to the young traveler proud and comforting like an

Even under Pius VII, after the restoration of the Papal States, street
lighting, smallpox vaccinations, and measures against begging were
abolished as Bonapartist innovations, and an Inquisition, though
without torture, was reintroduced; under Pope Leo XII, the Jews
were confined in the ghetto again, their property was taken, and
they were forced to listen to conversion sermons.[19] Things did not
get any better under Gregory XVI, who came to the throne [of the
Papal States] in 1831. Inconsistent and arbitrary administration of
justice, hasty arrests, detention with postponement of interrogation
for weeks, abuse of office against unpopular citizens, book censorship, and the Inquisition for harmless matters—Newman was certainly sober enough to ascribe much of what he saw and heard to
political more than to ecclesiastical conditions. Besides, the English
judiciary was no more lenient with its victims. It was only during
these years that the sensational charity work of the Quaker Elizabeth
Fry had uncovered the outrageous conditions in English women's
prisons. Nevertheless, these things, which in other countries might
be taken for granted, are given a special tinge under the spotlight
of "priestly rule".

In the face of the "Roman corruptions",[20] the image of the distant home rose to the young traveler proud and comforting like an

---

[16] Josef Schmidlin, *Papstgeschichte der neuesten Zeit: Papsttum und Päpste im Zeitalter der Restauration (1800—1846)* (Munich: Josef Kösel and Friedrich Pustet, 1933), 1:383–84.

[17] Sanfedisti were those active in the Sanfedismo movement, an anti-Jacobin popular movement, including many peasants, in Southern Italy in the late eighteenth century.

[18] Schmidlin, *Papstgeschichte*, 1:384–85.

[19] Schmidlin, *Papstgeschichte*, 1:383.

[20] See note 35 on page 134 of this volume.

island of freedom, morality, and integrity: "I begin to hope that England after all is to be the 'Land of Saints' in this dark hour, and her Church the salt of the earth."[21] Ignorant as he was about Catholic reality, so that he did not even comprehend the celebration of Mass, he saw with astonishment the rush of the poor and coarse people to the early services, even in the Sicilian mountains, and the happy and innocent faces of the "little monks",[22] as he called the seminarians, touched his heart; he saw poor and zealous priests. All in all, "as to the *Roman* Catholic system, I have ever detested it so much that I cannot detest it more by seeing it; but to the Catholic system I am more attached than ever."[23]

That was ten years before. But conditions in Rome had not become more welcoming. England was teeming with Italian emigrants, refugees, and exiles. Newman does not mention this element in either the *Apologia* or in letters, as far as I know, yet it can hardly have escaped his attention entirely. It may be that when he alluded to "ghastliness", he had some of their reports in mind. They brought news of continued fighting, insurrections, bloody coups, and raids conjured up through new military commands and Austrian aid; of military commissions, house searches, traveling military tribunals; of the strictest rendition of judgment; and of the pope's request for Austrian warships for his protection. One heard of the increasing ignorance among the clergy and the people, of poor pedagogy in the schools, of the bestowing of offices to the highest bidders and schemers, of special courts, of legal confusion, of poor pay for lay officials, and of blocking career tracks for all nonclerics. The English press, always hostile to Catholics, was certainly not suffering from any lack of juicy news. And the pious Italians, among whom there were enough on the side of the *Rinascimento*,[24] knew about noble Rosmini's complaint *Of the Five Wounds of the Church*: "the Division between the People and the Clergy in Public Worship, the Insufficient Education of the Clergy, the Disunion of the Bishops, the Servitude . . . of Ecclesial

---

[21] Letter to his mother, February 28, 1833, in Mozley, *Letters*, 1:310.
[22] Letter to his mother, Rome, Good Friday, April 5, 1833, in Mozley, *Letters* 1:332.
[23] Letter to his mother, Rome, Good Friday, April 5, 1833, in Mozley, *Letters*, 1:332.
[24] That is, the nineteenth-century Neo-Renaissance movement.

Property".[25] And can it be that the attitude of Gregory XVI, averting any internal Church reform suspiciously and with hostility, was completely unknown to Newman? "The universal Church is affected by any and every novelty . . . nothing of the things appointed ought to be . . . changed", he proclaimed in an encyclical at the beginning of his pontificate. "To use the words of the fathers of Trent, it is certain that the Church 'was instructed by Jesus Christ . . .' Therefore, it is obviously absurd and injurious to propose a certain 'restoration and regeneration' for her as though necessary for her . . . growth, as if she could be considered subject to defect or obscuration or other misfortune."[26] Later, in his Catholic years, Newman wrote with great wisdom and discretion about the proper understanding of curial statements—as an Anglican, such declarations must have undoubtedly reinforced all his prejudices.

In the midst of the spectacle of the physical and moral distress of the Italians, he was deeply touched by the insight that the Catholic Church saw her main concern in pastoral care—unlike the English church, which essentially tended to the "respectable" circles and individuals interested in religion but which left the masses to the Methodist sects almost unopposed.

He knew nothing of the strong currents of rebirth, filled with hope, stirring in France and Germany. He certainly never heard the names of the German Romantics, of Schlegel, Brentano, or Stolberg, the circle around Princess Gallitzin or Clement Maria Hofbauer, any more than he heard of the reform of the French orders, the Benedictines of Solesmes, or the Carthusians and Trappists in those years. Lacordaire came into his view only after his conversion.

He prayed for a union of the English and Roman churches and asked for prayers for this, but with the proviso that it should not

---

[25] Antonio Rosmini, *Of the Five Wounds of the Holy Church*, ed. Henry Parry Liddon (London: Rivingtons, 1883), xxxv–xxxvi. Görres lists "wounds" one, two, three, and five. Rosmini's fourth "wound" was "that the Nomination of Bishops is Given up to Lay Power", xxxv.

[26] Pope Gregory XVI, encyclical letter *Mirari vos* (August 15, 1843), nos. 7 and 10, https://www.papalencyclicals.net/greg16/g16mirar.htm. (The German edition of Görres' book cites these passages from Schmidlin, *Papstgeschichte*, 677.)

be seriously considered until "until Rome showed positive signs of sanctity which he had hitherto been unable to discover".[27]

There is also a hint of spiritual arrogance—though not this alone—in the conscious cordoning off from any contact with English Catholics; he also strongly advised his young followers against such contact, as if it were a matter of infectious illness. But this defense stems more from the integrity of his loyalty to the English church, more intensely so the more deeply he felt his loyalty was being challenged: "And another consideration weighs with such Protestants as are in a responsible situation in their own communion, or are its ministers and functionaries. These persons feel that while they hold office in a body which is at war with Catholics, they are as little at liberty to hold friendly intercourse with them, even with the open avowal of their differing from them in serious matters, as an English officer or a member of Parliament may lawfully correspond with the French Government during a time of hostilities."[28] In addition, he himself must have had some unpleasant experiences: "By their fruits ye shall know them. . . . We see it [Rome] attempting to gain converts among us by unreal representations of its doctrines, plausible statements, bold assertions, appeals to the weaknesses of human nature, to our fancies, our eccentricities, our fears, our frivolities, our false philosophies. We see its agents, smiling and nodding and ducking to attract attention, as gipsies [sic] make up to truant boys. . . . Who can but feel shame when the religion of Ximenes, Borromeo, and Pascal, is so overlaid?"[29]

The louder and more resolutely he presents himself as the champion of catholic tradition in the high church, the sharper his tone against "Roman corruption"[30] becomes. He had to proclaim what he saw as Christian Truth, "views and principles for their own

---

[27] Denis Gwynn, "John Henry Newman, 1801–1890)", in Henry Tristram, ed., *John Henry Newman: Centenary Essays* (London: Burns, Oates and Washbourne, 1945), 22.

[28] John Henry Newman, "Lecture 8: Ignorance concerning Catholics the Protection of the Protestant View", in *Lectures on the Present Position of Catholics in England: Addressed to the Brothers of the Oratory in the Summer of 1851* (London: Longmans, Green, 1908), 342.

[29] *Apologia*, 123. "Ximenes" refers to Francisco Jiménez de Cisneros.

[30] See note 35 on page 134 of this volume.

sake, because they were true"[31] and for no other reason, but he made clear that the path he indicated need not lead to Rome. "I felt such confidence in the substantial justice of the charges which I advanced against her, that I considered them to be a safeguard and an assurance that no harm could ever arise from the freest exposition of what I used to call Anglican principles. . . . 'True, we seem to be making straight for it' ", that is, for popery, " 'but go on awhile, and you will come to a deep chasm across the path, which makes real approximation impossible.' "[32]

He regarded the converts from his band of young followers who had made their way to Rome before him with deep reservation, with grief and distrust. He did everything to stop them. "Where individuals have left us, the step has commonly been taken in a moment of excitement, or of weakness, or in a time of sickness, or under misapprehension, or with manifest eccentricity of conduct, or in deliberate disobedience to the feeling in question . . . a nameless feeling within them, forbidding and stopping them . . . as if that feeling were a human charm, or spell of earth, which it was a duty to break at all risks. . . . Angels are our guardians; Angels surely stand in our way, in mercy, not in wrath; Angels warn us back."[33] Why should one separate oneself from a community that is experiencing its moment in history?

"One thing, however, I feel very strongly", he writes to Faber, who is about to make the leap,

> that a very great experiment, if the word may be used, is going on in our Church—going on, not over. . . . Is it not our happiness to follow God's Hand? if He did not act, we should be forced to act for ourselves: but if He is working, if He is trying and testing the English Church, if He is proving whether it admits or not of being Catholicized, let us not anticipate His decision: let us not be impatient, but look on and follow. . . . Is it not the ordinary way of Providence, both as a precept and a mercy, that men should not make great changes by themselves, or on private judgement, but should

---

[31] *Apologia*, 83.

[32] *Apologia*, 66.

[33] John Henry Newman, "Sermon 22. Outward and Inward Notes of the Church", in *Sermons Bearing on the Subjects of the Day* (London: Longmans, Green, 1902), 339–41.

change with the body in which they find themselves, or at least in company?[34]

Here, shortly before his own conversion, the realization, ripened in consuming pain, resounds again that these struggles are no longer about the individual and his "religious needs" but about the Church. For himself, the question had already been decided—but if there was still the slightest uncertainty in his younger friend, still an un-acknowledged selfishness of intention that was looking for his own spiritual gain, for a spark of hope still for a possible change in his church, he should be cautioned and held back. Newman knows very well that even in conversion one can remain deeply "Protes-tant" if one believes that one can choose freely and at one's own estimation what suits oneself most among the forms and systems of personal piety on offer. If it is so, man is still at the center of religion, critical and choosy, demanding that *his* right to spiritual fulfillment be given to him, that *his* expectations not be curtailed, instead of seeking God first and above everything, listening to and obeying His message, seeking and submitting to His law.

Forty-five years later, Newman, as a cardinal of the Roman Church, will write to a seeker:

> Dear Sir,—In answer to your question, I would observe that there is a great temptation, (as it is to some people) without believing that the Catholic Church is the One Authoritative Oracle of God, and the One Ark of Salvation, to join it merely because they can pray better in it, or have more fervency than in the Anglican Church, and in consequence conceive a *"hope"* of becoming more religious in it than they are at present, whereas the demand which the Church of God makes on them is to *believe her teaching* as the teaching of God. We will say, perhaps they become Catholics; their fervour after a while dies away, their faith is demanded for some doctrine which as yet they have not heard of or considered—and they stumble at it and fall away. They have had no root in themselves—they never have been Catholics in heart, because they never have had faith.[35]

---

[34] Letter to Rev. F. W. Faber, Littlemore, September 2, 1843, in *Correspondence of John Henry Newman with John Keble and Others* (London: Longmans, Green, 1917), 253.
[35] Letter from the Oratory, October 11, 1879, in *Correspondence with Keble*, 31n3.

Faith is something other than piety. Newman already knows this in the darkest years of his agony as an Anglican Christian, as he would identify piety in retrospect when he has newly bleeding wounds in his heart. While he is shuddering at the stark edge of insight that threatens to cut him off from the roots of his life, for a while even he tries to evade the ultimate question about the true Church and to shelter himself in the security of focusing solely inward.

Is holiness not the defining characteristic of Christ's Church? Is it not missing in the rich adornments of the Roman Church, and does it not shine, from afar and unmistakably, on the brow of the English church? "Were there 'sanctity' among the Roman Catholics", he once said to a friend, "they would indeed be formidable."[36]

And he needs only to look around to see holiness—for him this means to see it lived out and carried through, not just the Truth of Christ "on paper".[37] That is where the friends of a holy way of life are, for whom the renewal of the Church was not an empty slogan. They built churches, held church services daily, founded women's religious orders, missionary organizations (especially in industrial cities), and planned the establishment of a college of celibate clergy in Oxford for such tasks. There, one found Keble and Pusey, who had once strengthened his simple piety during the critical years of his burgeoning liberalism and led him to a deeper life of faith. Both, although married, lived only for the service of God, limited themselves to the bare minimum, and set an example of pure and generous renunciation and devotion to the kingdom of Christ. Pusey, from a distinguished family, for whom every secular and ecclesiastical opportunity for advancement was open, lived poor and secretly donated small fortunes for ecclesiastical purposes. Keble, childless in those days of numerous descendants, consecrated himself, his marriage, his strength, and his possessions to serve God, as Holy Roman Emperor Henry II once did. "His existence was completely cut off from the world and immersed in God."[38] In spite of his great

---

[36] Letter to J. W. Bowden, Esq., Oriel, November 6, 1840, in Mozley, *Letters*, 2:282.

[37] See John Henry Newman, "Sermon 5. Personal Influence, the Means of Propagating the Truth", in *Fifteen Sermons Preached before the University of Oxford between A.D. 1826 and 1843* (London: Longmans, Green, 1909), 91.

[38] Charlotte Blennerhassett, *John Henry Kardinal Newman: Ein Beitrag zur Religiösen Entwicklungsgeschichte der Gegenwart* (Berlin: Verlag Gebrüder Paetel, 1904), 113.

talents, which seemed to predestine him for a brilliant university
career, he renounced this as well as any other ambition and lived for
thirty years as a country pastor. He was great in prayer and fasting,
stricter in asceticism than Newman, and even wore a hair shirt of
penance.[39]

When Bowden, his first, much-loved childhood friend, died a
holy death, Newman wrote with a broken heart to Ambrose St.
John, "Of course when one sees so blessed an end, and that at the
termination of so blameless a life, of one who really fed on our
ordinances and got strength from them—and see[s] the same continued in a whole family, the little children finding quite a solace
of their pain in the Daily Prayer, it is impossible not to feel more at
ease in our Church."[40] And did he not experience abundantly the
nearness of the Lord himself? What more could he ask for? The
sermons of those years are a single longing, affectionate clinging to
the mother church in the humbly grateful confession of the greatness that the Lord has done and is doing in her: "And we will cling
to the Church in which we are, not for its own sake, but because
we humbly trust that Christ is in it; and while He is in it, we will
abide in it. He shall leave before we do. He shall lead, and we will
but follow; we will not go before Him; we will not turn away from
Him, we will ever turn towards Him. We will but ask ourselves
this single question, '*Is* He here?' for 'with Him is the well of life,'
and justifying grace, and Divine favour."[41]

In Advent, he wrote to a friend who was privy to his struggle:
"I think you will give me credit, Carissime, of not undervaluing
the strength of the feelings which draw one that way and yet I am
(I trust) quite clear about my duty to remain where I am. Indeed
much clearer than I was some time since. If it is not presumptuous to say, I trust I have been favoured with a much more definite
view of the (promised) inward evidence of the Presence of Christ
with us in the Sacraments, now that the outward notes of it are being removed. And I am content to be with Moses in the desert or

---

[39] Blennerhassett, *John Henry Newman*, 113 and 84.

[40] Letter to Ambrose St. John, London, September 16, 1844, in *Correspondence with Keble*, 334.

[41] "Sermon 21. Invisible Presence of Christ", in *Subjects of the Day*, 322–23.

with Elijah excommunicated from the Temple."[42] Newman does not approach the Catholic Church like a homeless person who is looking in her for warmth, security, and everything that has been missing in his life. Rather, for him it is much more like a man who, happy in the lap of love, experiences in silence but ever more and more intensely the dreadful doubt about the validity of his marriage creeping up. All the forces of his past and of his character—loyalty, attachment, reliability and gratitude, friendship and family ties, pastoral responsibility—stand in his way. And with marvelous honesty he faces every objection, ready to be vanquished by the matter at hand.

Never has a person been less driven by needing to be unique, by an addiction to validation or originality. Not for a moment does he attribute the strange inner situation in which he finds himself to any superiority; for example, to wisdom, erudition, or being chosen over and above friends who can no longer understand him. He never feels he has an extraordinary calling as a misunderstood genius or as a martyr. It is quite the contrary. His humility rattles and confuses him, precisely because he finds himself "different from the others" in this regard. How should, how could, he be right against Pusey, against Keble, who is guided by his conscience, against Bowden's holy death? Still in 1844, after he had resigned his pastoral office and given up preaching, living as a layman in seclusion, he was able to write to a confidant: "To have kept silence for five years, is giving oneself a long probation. If my confidence in myself bore any proportion to the strength of my persuasion, I should not be where I am, but I know that, the more free I may be (if so) from the influence of ordinary wrong motives, so I may be warped without knowing it by some more subtle bias."[43]

At one point, when the crisis was looming, he had decided never to take such a step unless Pusey and Keble agreed with him. Another time, he wondered "whether such a step would be justifiable if a hundred of us saw it to be their duty to take it with me?"[44] That

---

[42] Letter to S. F. Wood, Esq., Oriel, December 13, 1841, in *Correspondence with Keble*, 161.

[43] Letter to J. R. Hope, Oriel, May 14, 1844, in *Correspondence with Keble*, 312.

[44] Quoted in the introductory chapter in *Correspondence with Keble*, 14.

means everything but an aversion to individual responsibility—it is only humility's deep concern of being fooled by some delusion of haughty specialness.

"It is no pleasure to me to differ from friends—no comfort to be estranged from them—no satisfaction or boast to have said things which I must unsay. Surely I will remain where I am as long as I can. I think it right to do so. If my misgivings are from above, I shall be carried on in spite of my resistance. I cannot regret in time to come having struggled to remain where I found myself placed. And believe me, the circumstance of such men as yourself being contented to remain is the strongest argument in favour of my own remaining. It is my constant prayer, that if others are right I may be drawn back that nothing may part us",[45] wrote Newman at Christmas 1843 to Manning, who was racked by similar struggles and who would later play such a peculiar role in Newman's life in the Catholic Church.

Just as other saints resisted the voices they heard and their visions until they were overwhelmed so as not to fall victim to any deception, so Newman resists his journey to Rome like the worst temptations as long as possible: if they are of God, they will return.

When his decision was finally ripe and the news got around in close quarters, he did not escape the suspicion that seems to attach to every conversion to the Catholic faith, because it corresponds to the popular image of this Church in the minds of the crowd: that it is for personal promotion, or one has fallen victim to a tendency to overexcitement.

His response to the accusation that he is giving in to a "preference" for all things Catholic is a cry of indignation and pain at the same time: "I hardly ever, even abroad, was at any of their services. I was scarcely ever for an hour in the same room with a Roman Catholic in my life. I have had no correspondence with anyone. I know absolutely nothing of them except that external aspect that is so uninviting. . . . My habits, tastes, feelings are as different as can well be conceived from theirs, as they show outwardly. No—as far as I know myself the one single over-powering feel-

---

[45] Letter to Archdeacon Manning, December 24, 1843, in *Correspondence with Keble*, 293.

ing is that our Church is in schism—and that there is no salvation in it."[46]

And to his sister Jemima: "I cannot make out that I have any motive but a sense of indefinite risk to my soul in remaining where I am. A clear conviction of the substantial identity of Christianity and the Roman system has now been on my mind for a full three years. It is more than five years since the conviction first came on me, though I struggled against it and overcame it. I believe all my feelings and wishes are against change. I have nothing to draw me elsewhere. I hardly ever was at a Roman service; even abroad I knew no Roman Catholics. I have no sympathies with them as a party. I am giving up everything. I am not conscious of any resentment, disgust, or the like to repel me from my present position; and I have no dreams whatever—far from it indeed. I seem to be throwing myself away."[47] And to Keble: "I am setting my face absolutely towards the wilderness."[48]

This is so serious, so dead serious, that he can write to Faber: "I have sometimes thought that, were I tempted to go to Rome, I should for three years pray, and get my friends to pray, that I might die rather than go."[49]

We can probably also consider this passage in *Loss and Gain* as autobiographical, since Reding confesses to his brother-in-law: "Let me tell you in confidence—lately I have been quite afraid to ride, or to bathe, or to do anything out of the way, lest something should happen, and I might be taken away with a great duty unaccomplished."[50] But finally the great hour comes when he can say: "Certainty, in its highest sense, is the reward of those who, by an act of the will, and at the dictate of reason and prudence, embrace the truth, when nature, like a coward, shrinks."[51] The path is an agony, an actual

---

[46] Letter to Reverend E. Coleridge, Littlemore, November 16, 1844, in *Correspondence with Keble*, 345.

[47] Letter to Mrs. J. Mozley, November 24, 1844, in Mozley, *Letters*, 2:398.

[48] Letter to Reverend J. Keble, Littlemore, November 11, 1844, in *Correspondence with Keble*, 351.

[49] Letter to Reverend F. W. Faber, Littlemore, September 2, 1843, in *Correspondence with Keble*, 253.

[50] John Henry Newman, *Loss and Gain*, rev. ed. (London: Longman, Green, 1906), 343.

[51] *Loss and Gain*, 385.

death, but it is worth the effort. With unspeakable patience and awe, Newman grants space for the growth of knowledge in his own soul. It takes a full five years until the first light of the Truth about the decision to convert has reached maturity: he does not preempt anything, he does not force anything in order to shorten the unbearable aspects of tension, indecision, interior homelessness, and conflict. Everything must be carried through, step by step.

> Lead, kindly Light, amid the encircling gloom
> Lead Thou me on!
> The night is dark, and I am far from home—
> Lead Thou me on!
> Keep Thou my feet; I do not ask to see
> The distant scene—one step enough for me.[52]

This, Newman's most popular poem, was written twelve years earlier, but it almost prophetically anticipates his interior path in the years of his decision. And thus, everything is accepted: his farewell to Oxford, from the pulpit of St Mary's, from the huge congregation at his sermons: "The utter confusion and perplexity, the astounding prostration of heart and mind, into which so many would be thrown, were their guide and comforter to forsake them all at once, in the very act, as it would seem to them, of giving them directions which they most needed. I really suppose that it would be to thousands quite an indescribable shock, a trial almost too hard to be borne, making them sceptical about everything and everybody",[53] writes Keble to Newman.

"There is a divine life among us, clearly manifested, in spite of all our disorders, which is as great a note of the Church, as any can be. Why should we seek our Lord's presence elsewhere, when He vouchsafes it to us where we are?"[54]

This question nears the boiling point with ever greater intensity. For when such closeness to God is experienced, it is not quibbling, pedantry, and self-torment to disrupt, even abandon, everything one

---

[52] John Henry Newman, "The Pillar of the Cloud", in *Verses on Various Occasions* (London: Longmans, Green, 1905), 156–57.

[53] Letter from Reverend J. Keble to J. H. Newman, January 22, 1844, in Newman, *Correspondence with Keble*, 298.

[54] *Apologia*, 178.

has been given for the sake of a historical dispute; but would that not be valuing the frame over the picture, the Church over faith?

Anyone who asks this question does not yet know what Newman means by "Church". Faith encompasses two things: what someone believes and from whom he believes it.[55] In religious matters, man is not simply creative; he does not build and deduce from inside, after the manner of a spider, which releases its web from itself; rather he "perceives"—"takes" to "be true" (*nimmt . . . wahr*)— something that pushes back and is objective. Faith comes from hearing, from hearing the message. "Faith simply accepts testimony."[56] "The Word of Life is offered to a man; and, on its being offered, he has Faith in it. Why? On these two grounds,—the word of its human messenger, and the likelihood of the message."[57] So the messenger must identify himself. But it is not the case that, as elsewhere, he just delivers the message and then, having become indifferent, disappears. For a while, Newman tried to deepen the view that Christian Truth could be detached and grasped "in and of itself", as it were. He expresses this idea by contrasting the images of Christ from Bethlehem and Calvary: Newman said, "The peculiarity of the Anglican theology was this,—that it 'supposed the Truth to be entirely objective and detached, not' (as in the theology of Rome) 'lying hid in the bosom of the Church as if one with her, clinging to and (as it were) lost in her embrace, but as being sole and unapproachable, as on the Cross or at the Resurrection, with the Church close by, but in the background."[58] From there it is, of course, not far to the thought, to which he was "almost obliged to take refuge". "After all . . . the Church is ever invisible in its day, and faith only apprehends it."[59]

---

[55] Görres develops this concept of dually sourced faith, "what someone believes and from whom he believes it", in chapter 3, "Why We Believe", in Ida Friederike Görres, *The Church in the Flesh*, trans. Jennifer S. Bryson (Providence: Cluny Media, 2023), 53–105.

[56] Preface, to *Fifteen Sermons*, xvi. This statement in the preface is a paraphrase of a point from "Sermon 10. Faith and Reason, contrasted as Habits of Mind", in *Fifteen Sermons*, 176–201.

[57] "Sermon 11. The Nature of Faith in Relation to Reason", in Newman, *Fifteen Sermons*, 202–203.

[58] *Apologia*, 112.

[59] *Apologia*, 113.

But Newman is a historian, and his teacher is "antiquity". The witnesses know differently. A living Church has always been the seat, shrine, and guarantor of the Truth. Without a living bearer, the teachings, which he accepts without doubt, would never have reached us. There was always a riverbed in which the rich stream of tradition flowed instead of seeping into a thousand rivulets. Of course, there have always been ancillary churches that, for whatever reason, claimed both independence and orthodoxy. So it was with the Arians and with the Monophysites and the Donatists.

It was not as if Newman had consulted Church history to resolve these doubts of his. The uncanny and compelling thing was that equating these things forced itself on him out of the blue, so to speak, like a flash of lightning. "I have no reason to suppose that the thoughts of Rome came across my mind at all",[60] he says, when, during the long vacation of 1839, tired of pamphlets, he returned to Church history, in order to retreat from the stormy present and its problems into the impersonal coolness and distance of history.

Now here, in the middle of the fifth century, I found, as it seemed to me, Christendom of the sixteenth and the nineteenth centuries reflected. I saw my face in that mirror, and I was a Monophysite. The Church of the *Via Media* was in the position of the Oriental communion . . . and the Protestants were the Eutychians. . . . The drama of religion, and the combat of truth and error, were ever one and the same. The principles and proceedings of the Church now, were those of the Church then; the principles and proceedings of heretics then, were those of Protestants now. . . . The shadow of the fifth century was on the sixteenth. It was like a spirit rising from the troubled waters of the old world, with the shape and lineaments of the new. The Church then, as now, might be called peremptory and stern, resolute, overbearing, and relentless; and heretics were shifting, changeable, reserved, and deceitful, ever courting civil power, and never agreeing together, except by its aid; and the civil power was ever aiming at comprehensions, trying to put the invisible out of view, and substituting expediency for faith.[61]

---

[60] *Apologia*, 113.
[61] *Apologia*, 114.

And:

I found it so,—almost fearfully; there was an awful similitude, more awful, because so silent and unimpassioned, between the dead records of the past and the feverish chronicle of the present.[62]

And even the "overbearing" and "stern" aspects of the Roman Church is gradually taking on a different face: "The Church of Rome has this *prima facie* mark of a prophet, that, like a prophet in Scripture, it admits no rival, and anathematizes all doctrine counter to its own. There's another thing: a prophet of God is of course at home with his message; he is not helpless and do-nothing in the midst of errors and in the war of opinions. He knows what has been given him to declare, how far it extends; he can act as an umpire; he is equal to emergencies. This again tells in favour of the Church of Rome."[63] It has always been like that. What changed was the contradiction; sects came and went, leaving a deep trace in history here, hardly a half-forgotten name there. "Rome was where she now is."[64]

Surely, the struggling Newman, like the young Reding in his novel, had to have asked himself: "This too has struck me; that either there is no prophet of the truth on earth, or the Church of Rome is that prophet. That there is a prophet still . . . seems evident by our believing in a visible Church."[65]

An apparently very insignificant phrase from Augustine's work against the Donatists hits him like the blow of a hammer—no, like contact with a magnet that yanks scattered iron fragments together in a flash into a clear shape: *Securus iudicat orbis terrarum* (the verdict of the world is clear).[66] The carefully considered judgment, in which the whole Church finally agrees and settles down, represents the "final sentence against such portions of it as protest and secede"— even when they preserve a greater or lesser part of the overall

---

[62] *Apologia*, 114.

[63] *Loss and Gain*, 225.

[64] *Apologia*, 114.

[65] *Loss and Gain*, 225–26.

[66] This Latin phrase is from Saint Augustine against the Donatists and is quoted by Newman in *Apologia*, 116.

heritage. "What a light was hereby thrown upon every controversy in the Church! . . . Who can account for the impressions which are made on him? . . . By those great words of the ancient Father, interpreting and summing up the long and varied course of ecclesiastical history, the theory of the *Via Media* was absolutely pulverized."[67]

Back then, in the summer of 1839, it was only "the shadow of a hand upon the wall", like a fleeting ghostly apparition. "The heavens had opened and closed again. The thought for the moment had been, 'The Church of Rome will be found right after all'; and then it had vanished. My old convictions remained as before."[68]

But the seed had fallen into his mind, and it continued to germinate there in silence.

It was around this time that Newman was writing the sermon on "Divine Calls": "O that we could take that simple view of things, as to feel that the one thing which lies before us is to please God! What gain is it to please the world, to please the great, nay even to please those whom we love, compared with this? What gain is it to be applauded, admired, courted, followed,—compared with this one aim, of not being disobedient to a heavenly vision? . . . Let us beg and pray Him day by day to reveal Himself to our souls more fully . . . so to work within us, that we may sincerely say, 'Thou shalt guide me with Thy counsel.' "[69]

Now that old feeling, almost forgotten during the seven years of "the happiest time of my life"[70] that are irrevocably behind him, is stirring again: "My mind had not found its ultimate rest, and that in some sense or other I was on journey"[71]—the feeling that the unforgettable verses of "Lead, Kindly Light" had breathed into the mind of the young Newman, when he, returning home from Sicily, lay on a sailing ship in the windless Strait of Bonifacio.

"But, whatever this presentiment be worth, it was no protection against the dismay and disgust, which I felt, in consequence of the

---

[67] *Apologia*, 115–16.
[68] *Apologia*, 116.
[69] *Apologia*, 116–17.
[70] *Apologia*, 82.
[71] *Apologia*, 117.

dreadful misgiving, of which I have been relating the history."[72] Take note, word for word. Here speaks a nature that, by its very essence, is oriented toward abiding and persevering, toward loyalty and steadfastness. This nature already feels the yank that will dislodge it and all its roots from the topsoil, a parting so harsh that it is like a foretaste of death. It is by no means a mere figure of speech when, in the next chapter of his great account, Newman compares the following years to a long agony and, in retrospect, considers with a torn heart the torment that he was not allowed just to die in peace back then.

And as is so often the case with death, not only is dying terrible, but above all the step into the dark unknown—because at first Newman sees himself in a situation with no way out. "I could not go to Rome, while she suffered honours to be paid to the Blessed Virgin and the Saints which I thought in my conscience to be incompatible with the Supreme, Incommunicable Glory of the One Infinite and Eternal."[73] How could he leave his church before this point? Newman being "nondenominational"—what an incomprehensible idea!

Newman withdraws to Littlemore, to his quiet country house, accompanied by some of his most loyal disciples, and there leads a life of monastic hardship with fasting, vigil, study, and prayer—a life of asceticism, which, according to the testimony of a contemporary, was unheard of even in the strict monasteries of the mainland: everything in order to prepare himself for the knowledge of the Truth, in order to remove every obstacle, the most hidden, the most unconscious, that by its nature might be opposed to insight. "How can I be sure I have not committed sins which bring this unsettled state of mind on me as a judgment? This is what is so very harassing, as you may suppose."[74] For a long time he kept a spiritual diary, which he presented to Keble so that his friend might judge whether hidden pride, obstinacy, or the like might lie at the root of Newman's spiritual change: even now subject to

---

[72] *Apologia*, 117.
[73] *Apologia*, 142.
[74] Letter to Henry Wilberforce, Littlemore, April 27, 1845, in Ward, *The Life*, 1:81.

the priestly commitment, not just the fraternal one, with moving humility.

Even in the interim, after he resigned from his office and was a lay member of the Church of England, "attending its services as usual, and abstaining altogether from intercourse with Catholics, from their places of worship, and from those religious rites and usages, such as the Invocation of Saints, which are characteristics of their creed. I did all this on principle; for I never could understand how a man could be of two religions at once."[75]

This strict sense of the orderliness of spiritual boundaries is peculiar to Newman. He does not want to be "Catholic" as a Protestant, and he does not like it when his friends tie apples from elsewhere to their pear trees. "Really I have a great repugnance at mixing religions or worships together, it is like sowing the field with mingled seed. A system is a whole; one cannot tell the effect of one part disjoined from the rest. All this you know better than I can state it. Observances which may be very right in Saints, or in a Church which creates saints, in a communion in which the aids of grace are such and such, may be dangerous in a communion which has them not. I do not like decanting Rome into England; the bottles may break."[76]

And once more: "Again, I am not sure there is not danger of presumption in taking what belongs to another system at will. Private judgement comes in, and eclecticism. There is an absence of submission to religion as a rule."[77]

The last sentence reveals his demeanor. From his first conversion, Newman understood that the essence of religion is submission: acknowledging the rule of God, being bound to a will other than one's own. A worshipping obedience: anyone who becomes aware of the Divine Counterpart loses his own authority, at least in this realm. "Led on by God's hand. . . . The one question was, what was I to do?"[78]

It is not the person who determines what is "sufficient" for him

---

[75] *Apologia*, 195.

[76] Letter to Reverend F. W. Faber, Littlemore, December 1, 1844, in *Correspondence with Keble*, 356.

[77] Letter to Reverend F. W. Faber, Littlemore, December 1, 1844, in *Correspondence with Keble*, 357.

[78] *Apologia*, 117.

in terms of religious needs; it is not his "need" that specifies the measure. Christianity consists neither of principles nor of knowledge, neither purely of commandments nor of doctrines: everything has its place in the whole, which is a living body, and each piece taken by itself is only a limb that has been torn off.

"This I am sure of, that nothing but a simple, direct call of duty is a warrant for any one leaving our Church; no preference of another Church, no delight in its services, no hope of greater religious advancement in it, no indignation, no disgust, at the persons and things, among which we may find ourselves in the Church of England. The simple question is, Can *I* (it is personal, not whether another, but can *I*) be saved in the English Church? am *I* in safety, were I to die to-night? Is it a mortal sin in *me*, not joining another communion?"[79]

He can only wait to see whether and how the insights change in this slow, almost imperceptible growth. The one thing he is *not* allowed to do is to force or anticipate the decision. How much easier it would have been to cast himself headlong and senseless into the lap of the great Mother! But "I determined to be guided, not by my imagination"—this also includes what a German calls mind (*Gemüt*) or emotional needs (*seelische Bedürfnisse*)—but only "by my reason",[80] that is, the compelling knowledge of Truth. "Had it not been for this severe resolve, I should have been a Catholic sooner than I was."[81]

He had long resisted this side of himself—and we know how strong it was!—with all his might: "In spite of my ingrained fears of Rome, and the decision of my reason and conscience against her usages, in spite of my affection for Oxford and Oriel, yet I had a secret longing love of Rome the Mother of English Christianity, and I had a true devotion to the Blessed Virgin, in whose College I lived, whose Altar I served. . . . And it was the consciousness of this bias in myself, if it is so to be called, which made me preach so earnestly against the danger of being swayed in religious inquiry by our sympathy rather than by our reason."[82]

---

[79] *Apologia*, 208.
[80] *Apologia*, 117.
[81] *Apologia*, 118.
[82] *Apologia*, 115.

In this stance, the affair with the diocese of Jerusalem hit him like a fatal blow: "The Anglican Church might have the Apostolical succession, as had the Monophysites; but such acts as were in progress led me to the gravest suspicion, not that it would soon cease to be a Church, but that, since the 16th century, it had never been a Church all along."[83] From now on, he might have realized the insight that he later expressed in his lectures on the current situation of Catholics in England: that the Tractarians were only about to exchange one form of Protestantism that they had found and which they did not like for another, more or less home-brewed one.

Finally, he confesses to his friend [Robert] Wilberforce the terrible suspicion, "Perhaps we were both out of the Church."[84] Nevertheless, he still needs a full two years to master the "one final step", "one more advance of mind", and to take the decisive last step. This final step was "to be able honestly to say that I was *certain* of the conclusions at which I had already arrived. That further step, imperative when such certitude was attained, was my *submission* to the Catholic Church . . . nor could I have made it at an earlier day, without doubt and apprehension, that is, with any true conviction of mind or certitude."[85]

This distinction between conviction and certainty is just as much a characteristic of Newman as his other distinctions, as a letter from that time, to Rosina Giberne, reveals to us: "My own convictions are as strong, as I suppose they can become: only it is so difficult to know whether it is a call of *reason* or of conscience. I cannot make out, if I am impelled by what seems *clear*, or by a sense of *duty*. You can understand how painful this doubt is; so I have waited, hoping for light, and using the words of the Psalmist, 'Show some token upon me.' But I suppose I have no right to wait for ever for this."[86]

What does this mean? That Newman later made a choice between "conceptual" and "real" insights that arose from such inner experiences. Logic alone—the cold admission that these or those

---

[83] *Apologia*, 137.
[84] *Apologia*, 153. The editor of the German edition inserted "<Henry>" before Wilberforce; however, Newman actually wrote this to Robert, not Henry, Wilberforce.
[85] *Apologia*, 195.
[86] *Apologia*, 208.

propositions are "correct"—is not enough. There is a vast expanse between such a conclusion, which takes place "in the brain alone", so to speak, and "Yes, that is it!" that an entire person declares once he is overcome. "And then I felt altogether the force of the maxim of St. Ambrose, 'Non in dialecticâ complacuit Deo salvum facere populum suum'" ("It is not by logic that it has pleased God to save his people"—suggested by Newman as the motto for his *Grammar of Assent*!).[87] "I had a great dislike of paper logic. For myself, it was not logic that carried me on; as well might one say that the quick-silver in the barometer changes the weather. It is the concrete being that reasons; pass a number of years, and I find my mind in a new place; how? the whole man moves; paper logic is but the record of it. All the logic in the world would not have made me move faster towards Rome than I did; as well might you say that I have arrived at the end of my journey, because I see the village church before me, as venture to assert that the miles, over which my soul had to pass before it got to Rome, could be annihilated."[88] It testifies to his great honesty as well as the almost chaste reverence for the faith of those entrusted to him: "But, at that date, as soon as I turned my face Romeward, I gave up, as far as ever was possible, the thought of in any respect and in any shape acting upon others."[89] Precisely because he knew his influence and his leadership over so many, which he never sought but actually achieved, it did not even occur to him to carry them off with him on his new path. "To mention it on set purpose to any one, unless indeed I was asking advice, I should have felt to be a crime."[90]

How could I in any sense direct others, who had to be guided in so momentous a matter myself? How could I be considered in a position, even to say a word to them one way or the other? How could I presume to unsettle them, as I was unsettled, when I had no means of bringing them out of such unsettlement? And, if they were unsettled already, how could I point to them a place of refuge, which I was not

---

[87] *Apologia*, 158. The translation of the Latin quotation is by editor Ian Ker in New-man, *Apologia*, 552n31.
[88] *Apologia*, 158–59.
[89] *Apologia*, 197.
[90] *Apologia*, 195.

sure that I should choose for myself? My only line, my only duty, was to keep simply to my own case. I recollected Pascal's words, "Je mourrai seul" [I will die alone]. I deliberately put out of my thoughts all other works and claims, and said nothing to any one, unless I was obliged.[91]

For his disciples and, even more so, toward friends, this conduct brought bitter misery, which sounds heartbreaking from the report thirty years later. Newman was so much in the spotlight of celebrity that he could not observe such silence without confusing and unsettling people even more. "In the newspapers there were continual reports about my intentions; I did not answer them; presently strangers or friends wrote, begging to be allowed to answer them; and, if I still kept to my resolution and said nothing, then I was thought to be mysterious, and a prejudice was excited against me."[92] How much it must have cost him not to say a word about his torments to Bowden, the beloved friend of his youth, who at the time was ailing his way toward death! "Why should I unsettle that sweet calm tranquillity, when I had nothing to offer him instead? I could not say, 'Go to Rome'; else I should have shown him the way." At one point, there was something said out loud: "But, rightly or wrongly, I could not respond. My reason was, 'I have no certainty on the matter myself. To say "I think" is to tease and to distress, not to persuade.'" Having doubt was far removed from Bowden's nature: "He used to look at me with anxiety, and wonder what had come over me." And regarding this devoted one, Newman felt, "With my opinions, to the full of which I dare not confess, I feel like a guilty person with others, though I trust I am not so."

"He was in simple good faith. He died in September the same year. I had expected that his last illness would have brought light to my mind, as to what I ought to do. It brought none. I made a note, which runs thus: 'I sobbed bitterly over his coffin, to think that he left me still dark as to what the way of truth was, and what I ought to do in order to please God and fulfil His will.'"[93]

---

[91] *Apologia*, 197–98.
[92] *Apologia*, 198.
[93] *Apologia*, 203–5.

One often has the impression that nowhere is the authentic concern of the skeptic, the incorruptible knowledge of the limits and the sources of error in human thought, taken seriously and carried through more honestly than with Newman, but also nowhere else is there the serious confidence in the power of the human spirit to recognize and grasp Truth.

7

NEWMAN BROUGHT LOW

With that, we are already in the middle of the tragedy of this fate: in the second act of the drama.

Newman had given up everything for the treasure buried in the field—but the most precious thing he had to give up was his impact on the spirit of the times, primarily among the youth. One would think that he should have found this again a hundred of times over in the Catholic Church. The prelates of England, with Cardinal Wiseman at their head,[1] who had seen Newman's splendor at Oxford, had to know what talent, what character, what promise they had now accepted into their ranks. In gratitude and joy for this unlikely gift of Providence, they should have had to put a light in the lampstand so that it would be a "light to all" (Mt 5:15). At first sight, it is almost incomprehensible that the opposite happened: that, for a generation, the English Catholics seem to have had no more pressing concern than to put this bright and splendid lamp under a bushel with diligence, cunning, and force. This is how the "law" Newman came up against is fulfilled. He who Froude once believed should be viewed as someone who, like Caesar, was destined to "become a power in the world",[2] he who seemed born and endowed to be a man of triumph for the cause of God: he has to endure his peculiar election through to the end to renounce the "world", in this, its noblest, finest, most spiritual, and godly form. He had asked God at a young age never to allow him to attain dignity, honor, and status, not even in the service of God: with such a brilliant genius, with such a winning character, this could not be achieved other than by way of injustice and misconception. The

---

[1] The German text says that Cardinal Wiseman was "a convert himself". This is incorrect, however. He was not a convert to Catholicism. Dr. David Deavel brought this to my attention.

[2] Wilfrid Philip Ward, *The Life of John Henry Cardinal Newman: Based on His Private Journals and Correspondence* (London: Longmans, Green, 1912), 1:61.

ardent youth hardly considered that at the time. But it seems that God also takes such offers seriously and accepts them when they are meant sincerely and seriously. And what He chooses to accept as a sacrifice is burned—it is never given back. Newman, too, experienced this.

Those of us living today manage, to a certain extent, to overlook the external context of the historical contours out of which his innermost—and perhaps mystical—fate was woven together.

The "old" Catholics of England were the product of a centuries-old ghetto—the word was understood with a severity that no talk of a "Catholic ghetto" in Germany had ever known. Three hundred years of oppression and restriction, with isolation from the intellectual, political, and social life of the nation, had really left a mark on their features. What does the mere fact that the sons of Catholics were excluded from studying at the great universities of Oxford and Cambridge—the source and focal point of the entire educational tradition—mean? They lived in their own closest circle, without any claim to the culture on the whole, often brought up abroad, content with a small heritage, with Italian and French practices imported for their piety. It is as if Newman comes from another world. From his childhood on, he had a peculiar, very clear sense of mission: *God has a work for me to do.*[3] This thought once carried along his will to live through a serious, lonely illness in Sicily: I cannot die yet; God has something else in mind for me. At first, the renewal of the Anglican church seemed like this task. Now it is different, bigger, and yet growing from the same root. Newman foresaw an unprecedented outbreak of disbelief around the world, and it was his special mission to counter and contain this attack. It was not that he arrogantly viewed this as the task of one man: "Truth is wrought out by many minds working together freely."[4] It could only happen if the church prepared for this tremendous onslaught; for, humanly speaking, she was not ready for this fight. At the age of twenty-five, Newman had already warned his mother

---

[3] Görres is paraphrasing Newman's statement from his *Apologia*, which she quotes in chapter 5: "I have a work to do in England." John Henry Newman, *Apologia pro Vita Sua*, ed. Ian Ker (London: Penguin Books, 1994), 50.

[4] Letter to Mr. Ornsby, 1863, in Ward, *The Life*, 2:49.

with foreboding that it was the hallmark of the time that the rising talent was outside the church—that was just as true of the Catholic Church. A new, comprehensive, deep, and genuine education and training of the minds was necessary, especially among the clergy: a huge task for the long term. But the educated laypeople also had to be called upon and instructed to take in their religious heritage in order to own it; yes, Newman wrote, "and I am sure they may be made in this day the strength of the Church."[5] But who understands the voice in the desert? What he, with a sharp eye, had already written after his first trip to Italy about the alienation between the clergy and the upper class in the Papal States was just as true for his homeland: "As far as I can make out, not instruction, but repression is the rule. I don't mean that they do not know their catechism, but their intellect is left to grow wild; in consequence it rebels; and is not met with counter and stronger intellect, but by authority."[6] "What is the province of the laity? To hunt, to shoot, to entertain. These matters they understand";[7] but they should keep their hands off spiritual questions—dealing with them was presumptuous and undue interference: that was the view that Monsignor Talbot, Newman's greatest opponent, expressed openly in Rome. This approach knows only conserving and patronizing, only prohibitions and limitations, only condemning errors already in full bloom, without attempting an argument, without asking about the roots of the errors or even about the real concern that may be behind an attack, without attempting to seek the answers that the Church has desperately been looking for.

There was also a small "modern" group identified with the name Lord Acton; here, young, rebellious intellects rallied provocatively around magazines, first the *Rambler*, then the *Home and Foreign Review*, but they represented the great cause in a hasty, tactless, and unruly manner that discredited the matter even more with the bishops. All too soon, they came into conflict with Church authorities.

---

[5] Letter to Mr. Capes, 1850, in Ward, *The Life*, 1:259.

[6] Letter to Miss Holmes, the Oratory, January 10, 1861, in Ward, *The Life*, 1:605.

[7] Letter from Geo. Talbot to Archbishop Manning, Vatican, April 25, 1867, in Edmund Sheridan Purcell, *Life of Cardinal Manning, Archbishop of Westminster* (London: Macmillan, 1896), 2:318.

With all his modesty, with all his almost saintly humility, Newman knew very well that he was the only person in England who
saw the matter in all its fullness and complexity, that he understood
it and was up to the task. He, the gentleman and Oxford scholar,
embodied the best national tradition, the epitome of the university
man; he knew the mentality of the educated, inside and out, their
presuppositions, their questions and difficulties. He knew exactly
where to reach them; he spoke their language; he had a variety of
relationships from before.

And he never gets a chance. Every attempt, every approach fails:
the university in Ireland, the great Catholic magazine,[8] the Bible
translation, the student chaplaincy at Oxford. Fails? These are carefully and cruelly *destroyed* by his confrères, by the bishops, with de-
liberation from Rome. And not just out of ignorance or indifference—that would have been bad enough. There are murky personal
motives at play. Who can entirely see inside them? The sources are
still intentionally silent about the real conflict between the convert
and Oratorian F. W. Faber with his spiritual director and supervisor,
Newman. Was it just the eternal fear by the inferior mind of the superior mind? Was it the fear of the small but weighty and dominant
"leaders" in their circle of having to hand over their little thrones
to the greatest, if they had given him the status he deserved? Was it
the deep, never-admitted envy by the mediocre against the genius
that drove them to suspect him of heresy and make him out to be
a heretic in order to eliminate him? "And Catholics in England,
from their very blindness, cannot see that they are blind. To aim,
then, at improving the condition, the status, of the Catholic body,
by a careful survey of their argumentative basis, of their position
relatively to the philosophy and the character of the day, by giving
them juster views, by enlarging and refining their minds, in one
word, by education, is (in their view) more than a superfluity or a
hobby, it is an insult. It implies that they are deficient in material
points."[9]

In any case, those who should have been Newman's natural allies

---

[8] Görres is probably referring here to the journal the *Rambler*.
[9] Journal, 163, in Ward, *The Life*, 1:584.

turn out to be his bitterest opponents: Faber, Ward, Wiseman,[10] Manning. They, too, are converts, partly brought over by Newman's example; they, too, are full of zeal and talent. They are more Catholic than the pope; they want to see quick successes, count converts, flaunt illustrious names—"scalps . . . by the hundred",[11] says Newman bitterly. They use propaganda, tactical maneuvers, and diplomacy; they compete in sounding enthusiastic; they take up the fashions of French and Italian exaggeration without criticism and present them to their compatriots as the "real" and only way to be Catholic. And they forget gratitude, awe, and objectivity toward the Anglican church, from which they come. No wonder, then, their distrust, yes their suspicion, hounds Newman, the loner, the independent one, for decades: "the most dangerous man in England", writes Talbot.[12] Newman lives out his best years for productivity "under a cloud".[13] And if they had only suspected his "direction"! But they suspect his Catholic Christianity, his loyalty to the priesthood. He is regarded as a striver and someone who is dissatisfied, as a liberal, as a secret supporter of Garibaldi and all revolutionaries; rumors are spread that he wants to leave the Oratory, even the Church, and return to the Anglicans. People wound his honor and, even more: his love for the Church.

One example of many may suffice. After endless negotiations and effort, the Church authorities succeeded in obtaining the establishment of a student chaplaincy for Catholics at Oxford in 1867. The land for the church and a house had been bought, considerable funds raised for construction and maintenance, and all this was done by those involved on the obvious assumption that Newman would take charge of the project. With fear and anxiety, but unspeakable

---

[10] As noted previously, Cardinal Wiseman was not a convert.

[11] Letter to Miss E. Bowles, May 19, 1963, in Ward, *The Life*, 1:586.

[12] Letter from Geo. Talbot to Archbishop Manning, 2:318.

[13] Ward, *The Life*, 2:151, 152. Also, Talbot writes to Manning in 1867, "It is perfectly true that a cloud has been hanging over Dr. Newman in Rome ever since the Bishop of Newport delated him to Rome for heresy in his article in the *Rambler* on consulting the laity on matters of faith. None of his writings since have removed that cloud." Purcell, *Life of Manning*, 2:317. The bishop of the Dioceses of Newport and Menevia (in Wales) at the time was Thomas Joseph Brown, O.S.B.

hope, Newman himself watched the ripening of the plan, which, it seemed would give him back his life once more. Ward recounts how William Neville was to travel ahead and take Newman for a walk the night before, pondering the future.

> Newman, sunshine on his face, talked of the prospect. "Earlier failures do not matter now," he said; "I see that I have been reserved by God for this. There are signs of a religious reaction in Oxford against the Liberalism and indifferentism of ten years ago. It is evidently a moment when a strong and persuasive assertion of Christian and Catholic principles will be invaluable. Such men as Mark Pattison may conceivably be won over. Although I am not young, I feel as full of life and thought as ever I did. . . . It may prove to be the inauguration of a second Oxford Movement." . . . Thus happily talking they returned to the Oratory. The servant, who opened the door to admit them, at once gave Newman a long, blue envelope [from the bishop].
>
> Newman opened and read the letter, and turned to William Neville: "All is over. I am not allowed to go." . . . [Newman] covered his face with his hands, and left his friend, who went to his room and unpacked his portmanteau.[14]

The Roman instruction is even labeled, " 'blandly and suavely' (*blande suaviterque*)"; this is how the bishop should prevent "the most dangerous man in England" from taking up ministry with the youth! And a Catholic newspaper can dare the temerity of publicizing this process and expressing its approval that Dr. Newman had been sidelined in time because of his "known principles" regarding the welfare of the youth.

Years in which every word he publishes meets with malevolent, malicious evaluations—sad years, since he must always fear burdening his followers. Catholic papers attack him backhandedly and maliciously; a rally of protest and confidence by English Catholics from his circle stirs up a lot of dust in Rome. Newman has to tread quietly and avoid causing a stir. Newman, the one who had written to Dalgairns twenty years earlier from his first stay in Rome, looking forward to the future: "You see I am *determined* to make a noise, if I can. It shan't be my fault if people think small-beer of

---

[14] Ward, *The Life*, 2:138–39.

me."[15] "Persons who would naturally look towards me, converts who would naturally come to me, inquirers who would naturally consult me, are stopped by some light or unkind word said against me. I am *passé* in decay, I am untrustworthy; I am strange; odd; I have my own ways and cannot get on with others; something or other is said in disparagement."[16]

Now a boundless, paralyzing melancholy descends over him: "Whenever I have attempted to do anything for God, I find after a little while that my arms or my legs have a string round them— and perhaps I sprain myself in the effort to move them in spite of it."[17] "For twenty years, I have said my work was that of raising the dead!"[18]

In response to a sympathetic letter from a distant person, his distressed heart discharges in moving words:

> It is a great relief to know that there are others, who, though they ordinarily say nothing, are aware of it, and give me their sympathy in their hearts. . . . Yet it is a burden to my feelings, which others relieve by such kind words as yours are, to reflect that I busy myself from morning to night with so little thanks from anyone. Now for thirteen years I have been in many true senses a servant; like Jacob, *die noctuque œstu urebar et gelu;*[19] with no object or will of my own; yet never was a time when apparently I am more likely than now to be visited with those suspicions and jealousies which in one shape or other have been my portion through life. Well I am used to it.[20]

Bitterly, he sees himself as "some wild incomprehensible beast, a spectacle for Dr. Wiseman to exhibit to strangers, as himself being the hunter who captured it".[21] "Of course it is discouraging to be out of joint with the time, and to be snubbed and stopped as soon as I begin to act."[22]

---

[15] Letter to J. D. Dalgairns, January 1847, Ward, *The Life*, 1:173.

[16] Journal, 1863, in Ward, *The Life*, 1:583.

[17] Letter to Edward Bellasis, August 20, 1861, in Ward, *The Life*, 1:596.

[18] Letter to Ambrose St. John from Ireland, 1854, in Ward, *The Life*, 1:336.

[19] "By day the heat consumed me, and the cold by night" (Gen 31:40).

[20] Letter to John Pollen, Epiphany 1859, in Ward, *The Life*, 1:633.

[21] Journal, in Ward, *The Life*, 1:569.

[22] Letter to Henry Wilberforce, July 17, 1859, in Ward, *The Life*, 1:500.

He feels as if he is being buried alive: "To the rising generation, to the sons of those who knew me, or read what I wrote 15 or 20 years ago, I am a mere page of history. I do not live to them; they know nothing of me; they have heard my name but they have no associations with it. . . . It was at Oxford, and by my Parochial Sermons, that I had influence,—all that is past.' "[23]

It is certainly a piece of autobiography when, in *Loss and Gain*, he has a friend try to persuade the convert Willis to return to the Anglicans after all: " 'I can't tell what keeps you; you are doing nothing; you are flung into a corner; you are wasting life. *What* keeps you?' Willis looked odd; then he simply answered, 'Grace.' "[24]

The letters and chronicles from those years are heartbreaking. Not just the laments—almost more so the gallant consolation he gives himself and others. For example, to Miss Bowles in 1863: "And when I came here, where I have been for 14 years, I deliberately gave myself to a life of obscurity, which in my heart I love best. . . . I have no leisure. I have had to superintend the successive enlargements of our Church, to get the Library in order, to devote a good deal of pains to our music, and a great deal more to our accounts . . . and now there is the school. Just now too I am Sacristan, so hard up are we for hands."[25]

But he is too honest to fool himself and others, and, in the end, the lament breaks through very quietly and cautiously: "For then I say: 'Perhaps I am hiding my talent in a napkin' . . . and then, since I think I could do a great deal if I were let to it, I become uneasy."[26] Even the many considerable successes of the Oratory he presides over do not change this deepest consciousness: "This is another matter altogether. They are works of my name; what I am speaking of is what belongs to my own person;—things, which I ought to have been especially suited to do, and have not done, not done any one of them."[27] "The feeling that I have not yet been done justice to—but I must leave all this to Him who knows what to do with me. . . . Yet sometimes it is marvellous to me how my

[23] Letter to Ambrose St. John in 1857, in Ward, *The Life*, 1:387.
[24] *Loss and Gain*, 326.
[25] Letter to Miss Bowles, May 29, 1863, in Ward, *The Life*, 1:589–90.
[26] Letter to Miss Bowles, May 29, 1863, in Ward, *The Life*, 1:590.
[27] Journal, 1863, in Ward, *The Life*, 1:583.

life is going, and I have never been brought out prominently—and now I am likely less than ever."[28] But one of the saddest letters, to Father Ambrose St. John, closes with a sigh: "Well, I suppose it is all intended to keep me from being too happy. How happy should I be if let alone—how fond of living!"[29] And, in the end, he is of the perspective that he feels like the souls in purgatory, who enjoy high privileges and special graces but also suffer more pain than we know: "It is good for me to have trials and I am in a state of chronic trial which those only who come very close to me know. This has been the way with me for many years, the clouds of one kind or another returning after the rain. . . . I might almost say that a pleasant event has not happened to me for more years than I can count."[30] This is the deep sadness of one who is spurned; despised by those who need him and whom he needs; pushed aside and given the cold shoulder, when he indicated he was fully ready to be available; excluded from the community, without which he can never fulfill his mission. Those to whom he belongs by right are no exception.

And he knows that the years are passing by, and he feels how his strength is weakening, he who has experienced aging consciously like no other. And he understands like no one else that a cutoff date is passing, that every work has its historical hour, which can be missed and will not return. This sadness affects his life; it drains his health; from age forty-five onward, he believes in an imminent death; the sadness marks his face with the indelible marks of melancholy. "The sorrows (for though not great ones, they have been various and continual) of thirty years have at last told upon my nerves. . . . In truth, though I have lived in the midst of blessings and comforts of all kinds, I have had, all through my life, nothing but disappointments, and '*gutta cavat lapidem*'" (a steady waterdrop carves a stone).[31]

"But how am I changed even in look! . . . And from that time onwards my mouth has been closed and contracted, and the

---

[28] Letter to J. D. Dalgairns, 1847, in Ward, *The Life*, 1:173.

[29] Letter to Ambrose St. John, 1862, in Ward, *The Life*, 1:546.

[30] Letter to Mr. W. Froude, Birmingham, February 28, 1860, in Ward, *The Life*, 1:602.

[31] Letter to Mr. Serjeant Bellasis, Brighton, August 5, 1861, in Ward, *The Life*, 1:594.

muscles are so set now, that I cannot but look grave and forbidding. . . . Now, I am so conscious of my own stern look that I hardly like to see people. It began when I set my face towards Rome; and since I made the great sacrifice, to which God called me, He has rewarded me in a thousand ways,—O how many! but he has marked my course with almost unintermittent mortification."[32] "This morning, when I woke, the feeling that I was cumbering the ground came on me so strongly, that I could not get myself to go to my shower-bath. I said, what is the good of trying to preserve or increase strength, when nothing comes of it? what is the good of living for nothing?"[33]

And his mind is wounded even more deeply: "And now, alas, I fear that in one sense the iron has entered into my soul. I mean that confidence in any superiors whatever never can blossom again within me. I never shall feel easy with them. I shall, I feel, always think they will be taking some advantage of me,—that at length their way will lie across mine, and that my efforts will be displeasing to them. I shall ever be suspicious that they or theirs have secret unkind thoughts of me, and that they deal with me with some *arrière-pensée*. And, as it [sic] my happiness so to be placed as not to have much intercourse with them, therefore, while I hope ever loyally to fulfil their orders, it is my highest gain and most earnest request to them, that they would let me alone."[34]

"For twenty years I have honestly and sensitively done my best to fulfil the letter and spirit of the directions of the Holy See and Propaganda, and I never have obtained the confidence of anyone at Rome. . . . I have lost my desire to gain the good will of those who thus look on me. I have abundant consolation in the unanimous sympathy of those around me. I trust I shall ever give a hearty obedience to Rome, but I never expect in my lifetime any recognition of it."[35]

---

[32] Journal, January 21, 1863, in Ward, *The Life*, 1:582–83.

[33] Journal, January 21, 1863, in Ward, *The Life*, 1:582.

[34] Journal, October 30, 1867, in Ward, *The Life*, 2:201. Arrière-pensée: an afterthought.

[35] Letter to Father Coleridge, Birmingham, April 26, 1867, in Ward, *The Life*, 2:142. The term "Propaganda" comes from the Latin name Sacra Congregatio de Propaganda Fide, namely, what was subsequently called the Sacred Congregation for the Propagation of the Faith, later renamed Congregation for the Evangelization of Peoples.

Slowly, very slowly, inexpressibly painfully, the realization emerges that this fate also means divine guidance and that the hidden torment of so many years was not in vain: "I am sure a lighter cross could not be, nor would I change it nor be without it."[36] "I take this long penance of slander and unpopularity, which has been on me for thirty years, nay rather I have taken it almost from the time when that thirty years began . . . as the price I pay for the victory, or at least the great extension, of those principles which are so near my heart;—and, I think, while I live, I shall go on paying it, because I trust, that, soon after my life, those principles will extend."[37]

At last, he reaches a grateful and cheerful agreement with his life as it is. For example, from the painful year of disappointment at Oxford comes the little hymn of thanks in his journal after the publication of the *Apologia* had restored his reputation, at least in Anglican circles:

> Nor does anything that has happened to me interfere with . . . my inward happiness. I never was in such simply happy circumstances as now, and I do not know how I can fancy I shall continue without some or other real cross. I am my own master,—I have my time my own—I am surrounded with comforts and conveniences—I am in easy circumstances, I have no cares, I have good health—I have no pain of mind or body. I enjoy life only too well. The weight of years falls on me as snow, gently though surely, but I do not feel it yet. I am surrounded with dear friends. . . . What can I want but greater gratitude and love towards the Giver of all these good things? . . . I have nothing to ask for but pardon and grace, and a happy death.[38]

"I have abundant consolation in the unanimous sympathy of those around me"[39]—yes. But it is also part of the tragedy of his life that, among those who are loyal and devoted, there is not a single mind of equal quality who would have elicited a creative spark from him in an exchange. Almost shocked, Newman once discovered that until 1859 he had written a book almost every year: thirty and a

---

[36] Letter to Mr. John Pollen, Epiphany 1859, in Ward, *The Life*, 1:643.
[37] Letter to Father Thomas Harper, S.J., February 2, 1864, in Ward, *The Life*, 1:593.
[38] Journal, October 30, 1867, in Ward, *The Life*, 2:202.
[39] Letter to Father Coleridge, Birmingham, April 26, 1867, in Ward, *The Life*, 2:142.

half volumes in thirty-three years—and only three in the last fifteen
years. For five years he did not write at all: "though such powers
of writing as I may have are not less, to say the least, than they
were. . . . But *cui bono* [for whose benefit]?"[40]

His last significant work, *An Essay in Aid of a Grammar of Assent*, is
actually the summary and conclusion of the almost lifelong spiritual
struggle for the soul of his dear [William] Froude, the brother of
his childhood friend Hurrell. [William] Froude's wife and four of
his children were received into the Church by Newman; he was
unable to win the friend himself.

The compensation for his, let us be honest, stunted intellectual activity was his Sunday sermons and the extraordinarily extensive correspondence to which Newman devoted several hours a day, and
which in itself is a life's work—who knows?—perhaps far more
valuable in our estimation for posterity than a few more volumes
of theological or historical treatises would have been. Here, too,
the divine art of arithmetic goes its own way. This treasure has
been only partially, even fragmentarily, made accessible; the editor of the correspondence with Froude, [G.] H. Harper, mentions
the scarcely believable number of seventy thousand letters in the
archives of the Oratory at Edgbaston: letters from pastoral care and
spiritual guidance, written instruction for converts, dealing with all
the spiritual, religious, and ecclesiastical issues of the time.[41] Not
least of all of these large and weighty documents are the flowers
along the side of the road among the "purely human" letters: to
children, to strangers, thanks for birthday presents, best wishes for
family gatherings, letters of comfort and holiday greetings. A few
humble examples follow.

To [William] Froude's little daughter: "I am very glad to have
your present. A penwiper is always useful. It lies on the table, and
one can't help looking at it. I have one in use, made for me by a
dear aunt, now dead, whom I knew from a little child, as I was

---

[40] Journal, October 14, 1874, in Ward, *The Life*, 2:400.
[41] The German text reads, "C. H. Harper". This is incorrect. Görres is referring to
G. H. Harper, who wrote, "Of the seventy thousand letters on file at the Oratory in
Edgbaston". Gordon Huntington Harper, *Cardinal Newman and William Froude, F.R.S.:
A Correspondence* (Baltimore: Johns Hopkins Press, 1933), 182.

once. When I take it up, I always think of her, and I assure you I shall think of you, when I see yours."[42]

To a domestic servant: "Though my intention was engaged on the 26th and I could not say Mass as you wished, I have not forgotten, and I hope to say Mass for you tomorrow, the 10th. There is always a throng of intentions to be kept at this time. . . . I am sorry that you should still be so far from well, but God will bless and keep you in His own good way. We never can trust Him too much. All things turn to good to them who trust Him. I too know what it is to lose a sister. I lost her 49 years ago, and, though so many years have past [sic], I still feel the pain."[43]

To Father Ambrose on his birthday: "My poor old man,—Yes, I congratulate you on being between, what is it, 50 or 60? No, only 40 or 50. My best congratulations that life is now so mature. May your shadow never be less, and your pocket never so empty! But why are you always born on days when my Mass is engaged? I shall say Mass for you tomorrow and Monday."[44]

To a seriously ill Dominican nun:

My dear Child . . . I do not know how to be sorry, for you are going to what is far better than anything here below, better far even than the peaceful company of a holy sisterhood. God's Angel will be with you every step you take—and I will try to help you with my best remembrances and sacred wishes as you descend into the valley—but you are to be envied not lamented over, because you are going to your own Lord and God, your Light, your Treasure, and your Life. Only pray for me in your place of peace and rest, for I at most can be but a little time behind you. Yet a little and a very little while, and He that is to come will come, and will not tarry. Ever yours affectionately in Xt., JOHN H. NEWMAN.[45]

Newman fiercely resisted having a reputation for holiness:

I have nothing of a saint about me as every one knows, and it is a severe (and salutary) mortification to be thought next door to one.

[42] Letter to Isy Froude, Dublin, July 9, 1855, in Ward, *The Life*, 2:317.
[43] Letter to a domestic servant, January 9, 1877, in Ward, *The Life*, 2:324.
[44] Letter to Ambrose St. John, July 3, 1856, in Ward, *The Life*, 2:320.
[45] Letter to a Dominican sister, 1876, in Ward, *The Life*, 2:325.

I may have a high view of many things, but it is the consequence of
education and a peculiar cast of intellect—but this is very different
from *being* what I admire. I have no tendency to be a saint—it is a
sad thing to say so. Saints are not literary men, they do not love the
classics, they do not write Tales. I may be well enough in my way, but
it is not the "high line." People ought to feel this, most people do.
But those who are at a distance have exalted notions about one. It is
enough for me to black the saints' shoes—if St. Philip uses blacking
in heaven.[46]

Thus wrote Newman in February 1850. Thérèse of Lisieux was
not yet born, she who after a long time should direct the gaze of
Christianity to that quieter holiness that does not embody the "high
line" of the striking and the exceptional. Since then, perhaps our
eyes have sharpened to recognize the sign of the face of Christ,
which is holiness, not only in the prophet, martyr, or miracle-
worker. And is this mysterious radiance not also compellingly revealed in the life of this great misunderstood and tested man—in
the way that he faces his prolonged, burdensome cross and matures
and perfects himself through this?

It seems like a miracle, a miracle of grace, that Newman did not
succumb to bitterness. Well into old age, all the witnesses acclaim,
all the letters reveal, that *sweetness*, the mildness and tenderness that
were not embittered, that no one can maintain with more difficulty
than one who is disappointed, exiled, and aggrieved. The way he
bears himself and perseveres with declared enemies may already
cross the line into "elevated" holiness. So it is when he finds the
words for Archbishop Cullen, who wrenched the founding of the
university in Dublin out of his hands and thwarted his ordination to
bishop: "I ever had the greatest, the truest reverence for the good
Cardinal Cullen. I used to say that his countenance had a light
upon it which made me feel as if, during his many years at Rome,
all the saints of the Holy City had been looking into it and he into
theirs"[47]—this of the man about whom Newman once had to write

---

[46] Letter, 1850, in Ward, *The Life*, 1:329–30. "Xt." is an abbreviation for "Christ".
[47] Letter, 1879, in Ward, *The Life*, 1:384. Cardinal Paul Cullen (1803–1878), archbishop of Dublin.

with bitter pain: "He has treated me from the first like a scrub, and you will see he will never do otherwise."[48]

Or his last letter to Monsignor Talbot, who, for years, blocked him at every turn in Rome, tarnished his reputation, aroused and stoked the mistrust of even the pope against him, and constantly caused him annoyance, hardship, and difficulties: "I am now an old man [1867], perhaps within a few years of my death, and you can now neither do me good nor harm. I have never been otherwise than well-disposed towards you. When you first entered the Holy Father's immediate service, I used to say Mass for you the first day of every month . . . and now I shall say Mass for you seven times . . . when we are keeping the Feast of St. Philip, begging him at the same time to gain for you a more equitable judgment of us and a kinder feeling towards us on the part of our friends, than we have of late years experienced."[49]

His empathy for the suffering of others, including those who were most distant, never waned, in spite of the grievances in his heart. When the press brought news during the Crimean War that a heavily loaded ship with charitable donations had foundered in a storm just off Balaklava, "he most completely broke down in tears of sorrow for the disappointment to those for whom such a cargo as that had been sent"; "the sufferings of the soldiers, which he described, seemed to be as pain to himself."[50]

The fact that his heart neither hardened nor became cold in the unspeakable little torture that was mentioned earlier is thanks in part to the never-failing loyalty and warmth of the friends who surrounded him protectively and as a remedy. But even more must he have been deeply rooted in humility and, last but not least, in invincible, unswerving love for the Church.

Given his fate with the Church, nothing suggests itself more so than proud resistance, relentless criticism, merely outward submission full of inward bitterness, contempt, and impatience. There was nothing of the sort; *sentire cum Ecclesia* (to think with the Church): this is something we could all learn from Newman. He saw the

---

[48] Letter to Mr. Ornsby, October 10, 1858, in Ward, *The Life*, 1:448.
[49] Letter to Monsignor Talbot, May 26, 1867, in Ward, *The Life*, 2:177.
[50] Father Neville, quoted in Ward, *The Life*, 2:513.

weaknesses, the blunders, the debacles of the Church like perhaps none of his contemporaries, not even Döllinger. He saw her from the vantage of a historian, an Englishman, a convert, a hindered reformer—and he saw with the sharpest, deepest penetrating gaze of imploring, rejected, wounded love. He saw the entanglements and the whole ball of wax of consequence and effect; he noticed irresponsibility because he knew what responsibility and the duties of office are. One could fill a whole volume just with critical ob-servations, insights, and judgments. And yet no one who is dissat-isfied can invoke Newman. His love and loyalty never wavered—never, and what is more, nor did his trust, his reverence, his lim-itless, unconditional devotion to this, the real Church, which he experienced so severely. He never made it easy for himself with a cheap distinction between an invisible ideal church, "which one can affirm", and a caricatured, failing church that one rebukes and fights.

There is only one real historical Church that, so as she is, is the refuge of Truth and the dispenser of mysteries. For her sake, Newman distances himself from the *Rambler* and the zealous circle around Lord Acton—he is considered to be timid, unreliable, and reactionary by these stormy youth, the only people who roughly share and defend his cause—but does not abide their tone of cold and irreverent criticism, just as he would not have endured it against his mother. Wiseman had rightly written of him once: "The Church had never received a convert who had joined her 'in more docility and simplicity of faith than Newman.' "[51]

The astonishing range of his nature unites the clearest objectivity, an incorruptible gaze, the highest, most unfaltering self-command, and the most painfully burning indignation with perfect, truly filial piety: "If the necessity of criticism lies plump in our way and can-not be turned, then we do it, but not with glee."[52] Even as an An-glican clergyman, he by no means feels like a hero in his necessary and fruitful protest against problems—on the contrary: "a position which of all others is to me most odious—that of a teacher setting

---

[51] Dark quotes Cardinal Wiseman. Sidney Dark, *Great Life*, vol. 36, *Newman* of (London: Duckworth, 1934), 56. Dark provides no citation for this quote.

[52] Letter to Sir John Acton, July 16, 1861, in Ward, *The Life*, 1:534.

up for himself against authority".[53] And in the same spirit, he takes a stand against the activities of the *Rambler*, which advocates for his own concerns: "It does not seem to me courage to run counter to constituted superiors,—they have the responsibility and to them we must leave it."[54] "I never have resisted, nor can resist, the voice of a lawful Superior speaking in his own province."[55]

"God keep us, what I trust we are", he wrote to [W. G.] Ward shortly after his conversion, "averse from every opinion, not only which may not be held, but which only *may* be held in matters of doctrine; that, in spite of the cruel suspicions of those who think there is heresy at the bottom of us, we may submit ourselves, as our conscience tells us to do, to the mind of the Church as well as to her voice."[56]

Only in this sense does he receive the cardinal's hat from the hands of the new Pope Leo XIII at the end of his days. He dares to accept it: not with the satisfaction of long-owed, now finally granted justification, not in triumph over defeated opponents—only in the deepest humble joy: finally, I am allowed to serve the Church successfully again, finally my voice is made legitimate for her again.

He believed that "the initial sin of heresy was impatience— impatience to do God's work otherwise than He would have it done and so ineffectually".[57] His belief in the Church is made complete through patience: "I am of opinion that the Bishops only see one side of things, and I have a mission, as far as my own internal feelings go, against evils which I see. On the other hand, I have always preached that things which are *really* useful, still are done, according to God's Will, *at one time, not at another*; and that, if you attempt at a *wrong* time, what in *itself* is *right*, you perhaps become a heretic or schismatic. What I may aim at may be real and good, but it may be God's Will it should be done a hundred years later. . . . When I am gone it will be seen perhaps that persons stopped

[53] Letter to Mr. Richards, Oriel College, December 1, 1841, in Anne Mozley, ed., *Letters and Correspondence of John Henry Newman during His Life in the English Church: With a Brief Autobiography* (Longmans, Green, 1903), 2:333.

[54] Letter to Sir John Acton, 1861, in Ward, *The Life*, 1: 524.

[55] Letter to Mr. Healy Thompson, May 29, 1859, in Ward, *The Life*, 1:498.

[56] Letter to Ward, 1846, in Ward, *The Life*, 1:134.

[57] Ward, *The Life*, 2:354.

me from doing a *work* which I *might* have done. God overrules all things."[58]

Regarding the letter of Pius IX to the Munich Congress [in 1863], which caused a lot of uproar, he wrote: "It is simply a providential intimation to every religious man, that, at this moment, we are simply to be silent, while scientific investigation proceeds—and say not a word on questions of interpretation of scripture &c. &c., when perplexed persons ask us—and I am not sure that it will not prove to be the best way."[59]

With what effort in kindness, long-suffering, understanding, and humor does he defend, does he apologize again and again, in his own ranks as well as against outsiders—and where he can no longer justify, he at least makes it understandable—the difficulties he endured and the wounds to his heart to the point of bleeding to death caused by Roman tactics, mistakes, subterfuge, and injustices from Church authorities. But his answer to everything is great trust in the Lord of the Church, who is with her until the end of the world: "All this will be over-ruled; it may lead to much temporary mischief, but it will be over-ruled. And we do not make things better by disobedience. We may be able indeed to complicate matters, and to delay the necessary reforms; but our part is obedience. . . . I leave it to God. The logic of facts will be the best and most thorough teacher."[60] "We are in a transition time and must wait patiently, though of course the tempest will last through our day."[61]

Newman's relationship to the Church is finally embodied once again, as in a great symbol, in the poignant scene of his farewell to his Bishop Ullathorne. The bishop, who came to visit the aged cardinal, now the most celebrated man in English Christianity, and to congratulate him on his crimson [cardinal vestments], relates:

> As I was rising to leave . . . he said in low and humble accents, "My dear Lord, will you do me a great favour?" "What is it?" I asked. He glided down on his knees, bent down his venerable head, and said, "Give me your blessing." What could I do with him before

---

[58] Letter to Henry Wilberforce, July 17, 1859, in Ward, *The Life*, 1:499–500.
[59] Letter, 1864, in Ward, *The Life*, 1:567.
[60] Letter, in Ward, *The Life*, 1:560–61.
[61] Letter to Miss Bowles, March 31, 1865, in Ward, *The Life*, 2:69.

me in such a posture? I could not refuse without giving him great embarrassment. So I laid my hand on his head and said: "My dear Lord Cardinal, notwithstanding all laws to the contrary, I pray God to bless you, and that His Holy Spirit may be full in your heart." As I walked to the door, refusing to put on his biretta as he went with me, he said: "I have been indoors all my life, whilst you have battled for the Church in the world." [62]

That the official Church fights God's battles in an evil world: this was one of Newman's reasons throughout his life to endure with patience and tender awe the flaws, the distortions, and the terrible resemblance to the world that she has come to bear in this struggle.

---

[62] Bishop Ullathorne, letter to a friend, August 18, 1887, in Ward, *The Life*, 2:531.

8

NEWMAN'S PIETY

A word should be said about Newman's piety. Some of his beautiful meditations and devotions are even well known among us [in German-speaking lands];[1] there are already Newman prayer books. Usually, the emphasis is placed on the theme of God and the soul, "myself and my Creator",[2] on the great simplicity and solitude of this juxtaposition. Less well known is how much Newman's inner life beyond this "evangelical" trait (in the literal, not the denominational sense) is also determined by Catholic abundance and breadth.

Nobody knows as well as he that there is a hierarchy in the worship services and pious exercises of the Church: historical as well as religious, original and derived, central and marginal. But in practical terms, I think he would not have gone through the polemical division into essential and nonessential, which is so popular with us. Loving and generous, with the historian's joy in diversity and development, with the joy of a person who knows what culture is in the richness and depth of its forms, with a religious person's grateful joy in the riches of God, he simply embraces everything that belongs to the living soul of the Church and that has been made concrete in text and symbol.

He made profound observations not only about the Holy Mass and as a result of living based on the Eucharist as well as the Holy Scriptures—"the lamp and the table", as Thomas à Kempis calls them. Newman's devotion to Mary, expressed in many sermons, reflections, and devotions, continues to grow into old age, blossoming from deep immersion in faith, love, genuine speculation, and reverent tradition. He loved the saints, "the glad and complete specimens of the new creation which our Lord brought into the

---

[1] The German translation of Newman's *Meditations and Devotions* was published in 1924 as John Henry Newman, *Betrachtungen und Gebete*.

[2] John Henry Newman, *Apologia pro Vita Sua*, ed. Ian Ker (London: Penguin Books, 1994), 25.

moral world"[3]—first of all, the Fathers of the early Church, among them, once more, Athanasius, his patron saint; and his priestly patron Saint Philip Neri, with whom he is connected by the most lively, peculiar filial love, which expresses itself in an almost unruly manner in lament, plea, trust; the wonderful little book about this saint,[4] which deserves much greater circulation, is a monument to Newman's love for Saint Philip. Newman loved the angels, who were so "real"[5] to him from childhood, especially his guardian angel—"The dearest and the best"—whose hand he gratefully recognizes as guarding in small and large ways.[6] The Rosary was "the most beautiful of all devotions and . . . contained all in itself," and when, in the last years of his life, he had to do without the beloved breviary due to dwindling eyesight, he found the Rosary "more than made up for it". Those who last knew him, remember him, when not reading or writing, as always with the rosary in hand.[7] He wrote a simple Way of the Cross and many litanies: the Litany of Penance, of the Passion, of the Resurrection, of the Immaculate Heart of Mary, of the Holy Name of Mary, of the Seven Dolours, of Saint Philip—wonderful, deep prayers, true fountains of meditation and spiritual joy.[8] The veneration of the Sacred Heart of Jesus was very important to him, and his disciples never forgot that he confided that no other devotion had moved him so powerfully.

"In early years, after the Oratory had settled down at Edgbaston, he built the Chapel of the Sacred Heart . . . and he covered its walls with tiling at a considerable cost. Having a preference for somewhat retired places for prayer, he meant this Chapel to be cut off from the Church by a screen."[9]

He could be very displeased when the floral decorations of the

---

[3] Newman quoted in Wilfrid Philip Ward, *The Life of John Henry Cardinal Newman: Based on His Private Journals and Correspondence* (London: Longmans, Green, 1912), 1:206.

[4] John Henry Newman, *The Mission of St. Philip Neri: An Instruction, Delivered in Substance in the Birmingham Oratory, January, 1850, and at Subsequent Times.* This was published in German in 1922 as John Henry Newman, *St. Philipp Neri*, trans. Maria Knoepfler.

[5] See *Apologia*, 44.

[6] John Henry Newman, "Guardian Angel", in *Verses on Various Occasions* (London: Longmans, Green, 1905), 300–302.

[7] Ward, *The Life*, 2:533.

[8] John Henry Newman, *Meditations and Devotions* (London: Longmans, Green, 1912).

[9] Father Neville in Ward, *The Life*, 2:364n18.

saint's grave seemed too sparse or even monotonous, and he spent many hours with this devotion until his ninetieth year.[10] He also loved the little things of piety, if one may call them so—even what can be described as mundane items and almost as toys for God's children:

> To feel yourself surrounded by all holy arms and defences, with the Sacraments week by week, with the Priests' Benedictions, with crucifixes and rosaries which have been blessed, with holy water, with places or with acts to which Indulgences have been attached, and the "whole Armour of God" . . . to know in short that the Atonement of Christ is not a thing at a distance, or like the sun standing ever against us and separated off from us, but that we are surrounded by an atmosphere and are in a medium, through which His warmth and light flow in upon us on every side, what can one ask, what can one desire, more than this?[11]

In his apologetic work on the veneration of the Mother of God, which emerged from an argument with Pusey, Newman very clearly and resolutely named errors and excesses by name and distanced himself from them, which, then as now, circulated in some circles, determined by unenlightened zeal, confused thinking, and confused sentimentality. But he is generous enough to write to his friend: "Nor do I dispute the right of whoso will to use devotions to the Blessed Virgin which seem to me unnatural and forced. Did authority attempt to put them down *while they do not infringe on the great Catholic verities, I think it would*" *be acting tyrannically.*[12]

---

[10] What Görres means in this sentence by "of the saint's grave" or "of the holy grave" (*des Hl. Grabes*) is unclear. She may be referring to the remains of a martyr named Saint Valentine in a casket under the altar in the chapel of the Oratory. Pope Pius IX gave the remains of this Saint Valentine to Newman with permission to keep his feast on February 21, which is the birthday of Newman. See Henry Tristram, *Cardinal Newman and the Church of the Birmingham Oratory: A History and a Guide* (Gloucester, UK: British Publishing Company, 1934), 58.

[11] Letter to Mrs. Froude, Mary Vale, Perry Bar, June 16, 1848, in Ward, *The Life*, 1:241.

[12] Letter to Pusey, Birmingham, September 5, 1865, in Ward, *The Life*, 2:92. Italics added by Görres. The German text includes "be acting tyrannically" in the quotation. This letter from Pusey, however, actually ends, "I think it would act as the Bishop of London is doing in putting down the devotional observances of the Tractarian party

Some "enlightened Catholics" of his time were downright annoyed by the fact that Newman, without making a fuss, believed in the authenticity of the Holy House of Loretto.

> I went to Loretto with a simple faith, believing what I still more believed when I saw it. I have no doubt now. If you ask me why I believe, it is because *every one* believes it at Rome; cautious as they are and sceptical about some other things—I believe it then as I believe that there is a new planet called Neptune, or that chloroform destroys the sense of pain. *I have no antecedent difficulty in the matter.* He who floated the Ark on the surges of a world-wide sea, and inclosed in it all living things, who has hidden the terrestrial paradise, who said that faith might move mountains, who sustained thousands for forty years in a sterile wilderness, who transported Elias and keeps him hidden till the end, could do this wonder also. . . . In short I feel no *difficulty* in believing it, though it may be often difficult to *realize*.[13]

Let us not forget that this is the same Newman speaking who, in his great speeches on the nature of the university in regard to the natural sciences, which the average cleric then faced with fear and suspicion, called for the greatest freedom to research and to express all their hypotheses!

Poor souls occupy him constantly; he has a character of such loyalty and devotion that this is almost a matter of course. His great poem "The Dream of Gerontius" is perhaps the most beautiful meditation on the departing soul. And he, who with English generosity gave everyone the freedom to choose their own forms of devotion, once said that anyone who generally does not wear a medal, does not avail himself of indulgences, and does not make use of any dispensation has something wrong with his faith.

Newman was such a gentleman that he did not need to demand, as is so often done today, to have the "urbane appearance of the priest", which usually arises from a certain social drive for validation. The sources often talk about the shabbiness and threadbare appearance of his suit—it attracted strangers' attention. Perhaps this peculiar fact hides his deep love for asceticism, which is already so

---

at St. Michael's and elsewhere. He is tender towards freethinkers, and stern towards Romanisers."

[13] Letter to Henry Wilberforce, Maryvale, January 19, 1848, in Ward, *The Life*, 1:198.

clearly evident at Littlemore; even if he later, following the example of his beloved Saint Philip, praises a certain "external secularism with the gentle inward bond of asceticism"[14]—and this trait was an influence in his choice of the Oratory as a way of life. When there was a great need, he spontaneously resorted to great penance: when he was to make a call at the Holy See in Rome because of a conflict with the London Oratory, "on alighting from the *diligence* he walked barefoot to St. Peter's to pray there before going to his hotel."[15]

Any intellectual and cultural snobbery was just as far removed from him. On the occasion of an invitation to the Metaphysical Society in London, he writes: "I have a natural dislike of literary and scientific society *as such*, or what Hurrell Froude, (whom I agreed with in this) used to call 'the aristocracy of talent'; . . . and accordingly it is something of a wonder to me, that a mind so religious as Miss Fox's", who attended the Society, "should feel pleasure in meeting men who either disbelieved the Divine mission or had no love for the person of One she calls '*her* God and *her* Saviour.' "[16]

His charity to the poor was generous, wise, and undisclosed; and when the cholera outbreak occurred in Birmingham, he did not consider himself too precious to provide care in the slums of the factory town.

He hated everything that was theatrical and obtrusive in prayer and worship, and here, too, he was entirely English and gentlemanly; his posture was inconspicuous and deliberately adapted to the ordinary. He used to celebrate Mass quickly;[17] nevertheless, his

---

[14] Letter to Dalgairns, Milan, October 18, 1846, in Ward, *The Life*, 1:144.

[15] Ward, *The Life*, 1:450-51. A "diligence" was a public stagecoach.

[16] Letter to Mr. G. T. Edwards, in Ward, *The Life*, 2:333.

[17] In a footnote in the German edition, Gerl-Falkovitz compares this with the following passage from *Loss and Gain*: "Quickly they go, the whole is quick; for they are all parts of one integral action. Quickly they go; for they are awful words of sacrifice, they are a work too great to delay upon; as when it was said in the beginning: 'What thou doest, do quickly'. Quickly they pass; for the Lord Jesus goes with them, as He passed along the lake in the days of His flesh, quickly calling first one and then another. Quickly they pass; because as the lightning which shineth from one part of heaven unto the other, so is the coming of the Son of Man. Quickly they pass; for they are as the words of Moses, when the Lord came down in the cloud, calling on the Name of the

gaze at the altar—in silent prayer and especially when carrying the monstrance—was unforgettable and moving for those who saw it.

In his estate left behind, there were booklets full of prayer sentiments that testify to his loyalty and responsibility, his love and breadth in equal measure. These prayers were added onto his heart in the long lists of daily and weekly commemorations!

Auld Lang Syne; Dear to me; Kind to me; . . . Faithful women; With claim on me; Loyal to me; Ecclesiastics; The Dead.

1853.

GENERAL OBJECTS.

Friday.

Increase of Priests.
Sanctification of Priests and People.
Spread of Religion.
Conversion of the Nations.
All who befriend or help us.
All who ask my prayers.
All who attend our Church.
All who are in our schools.
Catholic Education . . .
All in England—the Queen.
All I have forgotten.
All who helped me in the Achilli matter.
The Faithful departed.
Opponents and enemies . . .
All whom I have attended on their sick bed.
All whom I ought to have attended and did not.
Any who have died Protestants through me
The Holy Father, for wisdom and fortitude.
The Holy Roman Church . . .
for her success with heathen, infidels, misbelievers,
heretics, schismatics.
For her victory over kings, governments and people.

Lord as He passed by, 'the Lord, the Lord God, merciful and gracious, long-suffering, and abundant in goodness and truth'. And as Moses on the mountain, so we too 'make haste and bow our heads to the earth, and adore.'" John Henry Newman, *Loss and Gain: The Story of a Convert*, rev. ed. (London: Longmans, Green, 1906), 328.

For her confessors, missionaries, apologists,
for her theologians, controversialists, literary men . . .
for the Oratory School with its
matrons, masters, servants, old scholars . . .
MEMENTO VIVORUM.

For all the Fathers and the Brothers,
And our Novices and Scholars,
And the Little Oratory;
And our Friends and Benefactors,
And our Schools for poor and gentle,
And our Parish, past and present,
Harborne, Edgbaston, and Smethwick.
For our preaching and our singing,
For our reading and our writing,
For sufficient worldly goods.
And for all the sacred College,
And the Papal Curia,
And our Bishops and their Clergy,
And St. Philip's London Fathers,
And the University of Ireland,
And for Trinity and Oriel,
And the state of Christendom.
For my private Benefactors,
And my penitents and pupils,
And my kindred and connections,
And my friends and my acquaintance,
And my slanderers and thwarters,
Catholic and Protestant.[18]

As for Newman's death, there is not a lot to say. He died so long before, so much and often, truly "died to the world" (see Gal 6:14)—through countless losses of friends, each of whom took a piece of his heart with him "behind the veil" (see Ex 26:31–35; Heb 10:19–22); with each one his soul went one step further, not to return. He died many times and over long periods of time, in the many serious disappointments in which he truly, painfully, irrevocably buried his hopes for this world—his dreams and plans and wishes.

---

[18] Ward, *The Life*, 2:361–64.

In the end, his years as an elderly man, a patriarch, were a long, physical death; first, he loses his face, then his hearing, the flexibility of his wrist to write—with that he becomes gradually detached from the large group of people around him; he can no longer celebrate Mass, then no longer pray the breviary, finally no longer even the beloved Rosary because even the feeling in his fingertips dies off.[19] Finally, when anyone knocked on his cell door and called his name, he could have answered like Albertus Magnus: "He is no longer here."

The last years are like a long, silent sunset. It was really only the "mortal remainder" that still had to be dissolved. He went over to the beyond on the evening of August 11, 1890, at eight forty-five. "*Ex umbris et imaginibus in veritatem.*"[20]

June 18, 1946,
Ida Friederike Görres[21]

---

[19] See Ward, *The Life*, 2:533.

[20] The words Newman selected to be engraved on his tombstone, that is, "From shadows and images into Truth". Ward, *The Life*, 2:537.

[21] Gerl-Falkovitz writes, "In the manuscript for this book, this section containing chapters 4 to 8 ends with, '18 6 46, I. F. G.,' that is, June 18, 1946, Ida Friederike Görres."

9

TWO POEMS BY NEWMAN

THE TWO WORLDS

Unveil, O Lord, and on us shine
In glory and in grace
This gaudy world grows pale before
The beauty of Thy face.
Till Thou art seen, it seems to be
A sort of fairy ground,
Where suns unsetting light the sky,
And flowers and fruits abound.
But when Thy keener, purer beam
Is pour'd upon our sight
It loses all its power to charm
And what was day is night.
Its noblest toils are then the scourge
Which made Thy blood to flow;
It joys are but the treacherous thorns
Which circled round Thy brow.
And thus, when we renounce for Thee
its restless aims and fears,
The tender memories of the past,
The hopes of coming years,
Poor is our sacrifice, whose eyes
Are lighted from above;
We offer what we cannot keep,
What we have ceased to love.

The Oratory.
1862.[1]

---

[1] "The Two Worlds", in *Verses on Various Occasions* (London: Longmans, Green, 1905), 319–20.

THE DEATH OF MOSES

My Father's hope! my childhood's dream!
The promise from on high!
Long waited for! its glories beam
Now when my death is nigh.
My death is come, but not decay;
Nor eye nor mind is dim;
The keenness of youth's vigorous day
Thrills in each nerve and limb.
Blest scene! thrice welcome after toil—
If no deceit I view;
O might my lips but press the soil,
And prove the vision true!
Its glorious heights, its wealthy plains,
Its many-tinted groves,
They call! but He my steps restrains
Who chastens whom He loves.
Ah! now they melt . . . they are but shades . . .
I die!—yet is no rest,
O Lord! in store, since Canaan fades
But seen, and not possest?

Off Ithaca.
December 30, 1832.[2]

---

[2] "The Death of Moses", *Verses*, 106–7.

II

CONSCIENCE

10

ON CONSCIENCE

The term "freethinker" has gone out of fashion today. It sounds fusty, trite, a little ridiculous. But we who were born around the turn of the [twentieth] century remember the dazzling and disconcerting glow that shone around it in our youth: a freethinker—a term from the late eighteenth century—from the time when "enlightened" reason began to be thought of as maturity, independence, and breaking out of the centuries-old fetters of prejudice and superstition and it viewed itself as the standard by which to judge the world and people. Prejudice and superstition—to those generations, that meant above all dogma. Dogmatic thinking itself was a contradiction: it was viewed as bondage and self-renunciation of the spirit; it was uncreative parroting of a tradition fixed for all time; it was like regurgitated thinking.

Right from the start, the "Truth seeker" was, of course, antithetical to dogma. The "Truth" that he could and had to find was, in any case, beyond dogma, beyond any duty of belief, out in the alluring unknown. Vivacious spirits were seized by a great lust for discovery: in a strange parallel to the urge to discover and innovate in the nineteenth century, that strived for the unknown everywhere, for the sources of the Nile and the Orinoco, for the polar ice caps of the world, for the primeval forests in the interior of foreign continents, for rulership over the hitherto hidden laws and forces of nature—it seemed to the people that the truth that the spirit seeks could not possibly lie in the generally already known realm of the Christian Church. Only those who left the Church behind, like leaving a beloved and respected nursery for the wide world, could be taken seriously as seekers and thinkers.

I still clearly remember the instinctive division that I used to make as a young person. Nobody had told me this; it was just in the air; one simply sensed it: an invisible line separated the intellectual world from that of the pious. On the one side resided the mind, freedom, adventure, the clever, ingenious, and strong people—a glow surrounded them, alluring and dangerous; they had dared to reach for the "Golden Apple" of knowledge, action, enjoyment of life (they were also under its spell). And we resided on the other side—we the believers, small-minded, mediocre, backward, fettered. In exchange, on our side there was the supernatural: grace, the sacraments, the salvation of the soul. One had to choose. "At least in hell one is in good company", scoffed my brothers—and, with melancholy, my sister said: "Well, you see, that's how it is: we have to live among sheep, but in the end, it is worth the effort. In eternity it will be different."

That things were already different in earthly time was seen in the supernatural occurrence of the Youth Movement. Today's youth can no longer imagine what it was like, from the desolate desert of the mind, in which one made reference only to lost centuries, to Dante and Gothic, when names suddenly appeared such as Guardini and Adam, Lippert and Przywara, Herwegen—stars that rose and showed us a new way. By 1920–1930, it was already taken for granted and a matter of course that there was a Catholic intellectual culture that was taken seriously by outsiders with respect and even envy—the mind had returned, and there was great celebration. That belief and understanding have something to do with each other, that thinking does not have to be an enemy, that knowledge does not have to be a danger to belief, that thinking about dogma, from the unshakable rock of what is already established, does not require third-rate, sloppy renunciation of intellectual adventure and, on the contrary, that it requires the highest seriousness in intellectual ventures, that it makes the highest demands on intellectual orderliness, incisiveness, fearless sobriety, and unconditional consistency—all of this opened up for us again, as a surprise, bringing joy, giving purpose to our lives. The halo-like glow of the "freethinker" faded, shrank, and gradually sank into the moth-proof storage chests of half-baked education, slogans, and political propaganda speeches.

Why bring all this up here and now? Because John Henry Newman stood out like a lighthouse in the midst of this development: he is the champion of dogma in the first major attack by liberalism. He was at the start of the great ebb when the tide turned: throughout his entire lifetime, he saw the former high tide fade away. After his death, we saw the tide turn—we saw the waters rush back; they carried us, and they still carry us today.

But a second turning point, it seems to us, is still pending, and Newman has also been its solitary prophet. There is the faith in revealed doctrine and thinking trained in it, knowledge and understanding bestowed by it. There is the faith in revealed law and conscience trained in it, will and action bestowed by it.

Perhaps no other saying by Cardinal Newman is as well-known as this: "Certainly, if I am obliged to bring religion into after-dinner toasts, . . . I shall drink—to the Pope, if you please,—still, to Conscience first."[1] And that other one, though often misquoted: that there are really only two beings in the whole world: God and the soul.[2] For this reason—and for other reasons—the dubious legend that became attached to the great figure of the Church Father of the Twentieth Century was that he was a forerunner and key witness of a certain conception of conscience, which is fashionable even in Catholic circles.

This legend seems to me to be, in essence, nothing more than a transfer of the old "freethinker" to the moral realm. What dogma is to the former, morality is to the latter: the epitome of narrowness, pettiness, submissive bondage, fearful clinging to the crutch of law, prohibition, and literalism, escape from responsibility and confinement to what is traditional.[3] Considered as the opposite of this "moral" attitude stands the free and mature Christian, who is allowed to renounce the law, moral authority, and guidance of the soul because he can. Instead of asking anxiously about prescribed instruction, he regards the law and prohibitions as a preschool for beginners or as prostheses for the intellectual cripple. He stands

---

[1] John Henry Newman, "A Letter Addressed to the Duke of Norfolk", in *Certain Difficulties Felt by Anglicans in Catholic Teaching* (London: Longmans, Green, 1901), 2:261.

[2] Görres may be referring to this passage: "making me rest in the thought of two and two only absolute and luminously self-evident beings, myself and my Creator". John Henry Newman, *Apologia pro Vita Sua*, ed. Ian Ker (London: Penguin Books, 1994), 25. Also, part 3, section 3 of Newman's *Meditations and Devotions* is titled "God and the Soul".

[3] Görres elaborates on this view of morality and how it contrasts with the Catholic view of morality in the chapter "The Nuisance of Morality" in Ida Friederike Görres, *The Church in the Flesh*, trans. Jennifer S. Bryson (Providence: Cluny Media, 2023), 106–47.

above; he judges as lord what is good and bad, what is sin and what is not. An exaggeration? One needs to point out clearly what hangs hazily in the air and is felt by a thousand people even if they do not articulate it.

A German tends to see conscience and law as a pair of opposites. He does not want to reject thinking about the law; surely, he admits, there are always and everywhere people who need it because their consciences are still undeveloped. But the more advanced man demonstrates himself as such precisely by standing *above* the law, and he shows that he is above it by judging it and deciding whether and to what extent it applies to him, whether and to what extent he is bound by it.

The question of conscience, its essence, its meaning, its formation is now on the radar of religious discussion. We must bring the subject into focus here and now. We cannot engage in argument with unbelief about whether conscience even exists as an independent function, whether there is something like a relationship to God, God's voice, God's guidance, or whether there is human free will, which conscience presupposes.

We start with consideration in the Church, and this, in turn, not with a *technical* explanation—an academic one—from theology, philosophy, or psychology but with a practical explanation that moves the mind. And this statement also expresses the way in which an analysis of this kind usually goes on in the average person: not as a thought process, with assertions, conclusions, proofs, all logically structured and examined for validity, but with emotions, with strongly emotional yes and no, with reactions, that is, with responsive movements of the soul and often only of the feelings, with the experiences of being attracted and repelled, with evasive action as well as pushing back, with following and taking sides, and all of this largely dictated from the silent depths of the subconscious. And what we then call theories and principles are often nothing more than the attempt to put this surging confusion into words, to explain it afterward, and often to justify it.

If we want to shed light on this wave today and try to describe the emotional context that surrounds this word "conscience", we will read, for example, that in a thinking mind, if one may say so, conscience triggers a distinct mood of tension: an anticipatory tension, braced for a fight. One gets the feeling that Christian conscience has somehow been given second fiddle up to now; that it is still awaiting its actual liberation, the recognition of its rights, something like its accession to the throne. Germans, in particular, tend to conceive the reality of conscience primarily in opposition, even in contradiction. To whom? To sin? To temptation? To one's own self? Certainly not, but rather to an external opposite, to the law, to the Commandments, to Tradition, to authority in general, to the state, and to the Church. For them, conscience is like the natural opposite of these actual conditions, and in the event of a clash, conscience is always right. Conscience is the fortress to which, in case of doubt, one can withdraw and from which one may—yes, must—assert oneself when confronted with all these claims. The formulation "One enters into agreement with God and from there he masters the situation with confidence" has even become stereotypical—and this plan of action demonstrates his Christian maturity and responsibility. Soon enough, this is no longer a question but a dogma. Whoever has self-awareness exercises his conscience; and in certain circles it works like a shameful testimony to backwardness, narrow-mindedness, and timidity, of having not yet fully "hatched", if one gets a guilty conscience in the face of these assertions or, out of unease, questions oneself and others. Thus, it seems all the more important to clarify again and again what actually applies and what does not among these assertions of greatly varied priority, put forth, marshaled, and championed so indiscriminately regarding what "conscience" actually means.

They are followed by questions in which the word "conscience" is not so clearly in the foreground. But these questions all revolve around issues of conscience formation—namely, what is commonly, as well as in academia, called "Christianity and ethics" and what can be formulated in nonacademic terms like this:

Do you have to be a Christian to be a decent, moral person?

Do you have to be a decent person to be a Christian?

And finally, even: Does one have to be a moral person, in the traditional sense, in order to be a "decent" person, a "valuable" person?

Of course, people do not phrase the last two questions that way; but what they think, feel, and say on this topic pretty much comes down to this.

As for the second question, to what extent a Christian must be a "decent person", there are two important answers. The advocates of them feud with one another, although they basically assume an astonishingly similar starting position. The first ones think that the Christian basically does not need to worry about any "world-centered ethos": namely, one can be a Christian and even pious without being a moral or even a "decent person" by the standards of the world. (From this it can already be seen that this "decent person" is provided with rather shifting considerations for his sense of worth.) In this view, the believing conscience demands submission to and getting in line with a precisely standardized system of Church-prescribed laws, commandments, and prohibitions and regulations: those who live up to these are just and no longer need to strive for other forms of righteousness, virtues, and attitudes.

The second ones think that neither such obedience to law nor "ethics" matters: rather, there are still aspects from pre-Christian times in our religious consciousness that have not yet "hatched" and that have led to serious malformations. So Christian life and the Christian proclamation of the Gospel have been falsified and distorted by the excess of moralizing. Concern about ethics and morals, about virtue and vice, about law and merit is pagan and Jewish, not Christian. Christ redeemed us to freedom; we have outgrown the law, or at least we should have. There are different types of people: ethical and religious; the higher of the two is the second, who is in touch with the supernatural, regardless of whether he forcefully breaks the moral law again and again. If he believes merely in baptism, grace, and the Resurrection, let the bold Lutheran expression apply to him: *Pecca fortiter, sed crede fortius!* "Sin boldly but believe still more greatly!" And true formation of conscience is that which leads people to such freedom, impartiality, and lightheartedness, to take pure and bold individual responsibility and independence seriously.

Did such questions already exist in Newman's time? I think so, even if the third perhaps emerges only veiled within the other two. Each of the three—and their answers—corresponds to a certain cultural niveau and sociological position, and at the same time to an "eternal" attitude, as it were—that is, an attitude that is in itself almost unchangeable regarding human nature.

The question of the "noble pagan" or at least the noble person who does not even need to be a Christian—that is, one having virtue without belief—seems to be one of the favorite topics of the late eighteenth century, the Enlightenment, and the classical court culture in England. This is viewed as an acceptable attitude toward life beyond the turn of the century and, at the same time, far back into the Renaissance, into Late Antiquity: Newman saw its most perfect embodiment in Julian the Apostate. Perhaps this can be described as a typically aristocratic question and response, born of an ethos that is based on honor and beauty and, at its core, knows and recognizes no other values.

In the second question and its first response, we recognize the eternal Pharisee, the "religious hypocrite". This goes back to the Old Testament; it can be found in the late Middle Ages; it emerges strongly in Puritanism and shapes the legalistically focused Catholicism of the past [nineteenth] century: it may perhaps be described as the typical bourgeois attitude, based on an ethos of achievement, sense of duty, and honesty.

In the second response to the second question, and even more so in the third, which is already closely related to it, both earlier accounts merge in a strange way as secondary questions with the main question of the essentially Protestant principle of private judgment and individual responsibility. A certain ethos of social class no longer plays a role here; rather, everything gets lumped together. The individual confronts this in part consciously instead of adapting, but in part he affirms the principle of uprooting, atomization, and above all the notion of general equality from which is derived the idea of the same status and the same rights for all.

Newman did not deal with any of these questions theoretically and systematically; rather, he encountered them just in the air, at work in souls, and as a present hardship. Because he discerned them, accepted them, and offered support in a brotherly, fatherly, priestly manner, he contributed much by way of reflection, scattered in sermons and letters that may plainly have grown out of countless conversations.

The great extent to which the fact of conscience illuminates and dominates throughout his whole life and his fate has been indicated in the preceding chapters. Conscience was the fulcrum of his first conversion to God and his second to the Catholic Church.

For Newman, conscience is the primary, most foundational, and most important proof of God, and that means a lot for someone who is not a skeptic of the usual academic proofs of God but is peculiarly indifferent to and unaffected by them; he knows them and acknowledges them, but they are not meaningful to him. "Were it not for this voice, speaking so clearly in my conscience and my heart, I should be an atheist, or a pantheist, or a polytheist when I looked into the world. I am speaking for myself only; and I am far from denying the real force of the arguments in proof of a God."[4] But: "If I am asked why I believe in a God, I answer that it is because I believe in myself, for I feel it impossible to believe in my own existence (and of that fact I am quite sure) without believing also in the existence of Him, who lives as a Personal, All-seeing, All-judging Being in my conscience."[5] He believes in the "Mystery of His Presence in us",[6] which means conscience. In addition to memory, imagination, and a sense of beauty, man finds in himself a mental faculty that separates his actions into good and bad. It does so not by way of reason, which is also capable of doing this, but in that it extends to all one's actions a palpable echo, happy or painful, both responding, as it were, to the factual and cool previous judgment of reason and confirming it—or, by the same token, denying it. Experience teaches that certain actions set off certain feelings, and by scrutinizing and naming these in myself, I know: this was good, that was bad. The human judgment of reason, like the sense of beauty also, has to do with objects; conscience has to do with persons and with actions only insofar as they are "personal"—though not insofar as they concern *any* persons; rather, my conscience is concerned with me alone and with my actions and with others only insofar as they have something to do with me.[7] I can judge that another is doing good or bad, but I cannot feel remorse or peace of mind for him. Conscience also knows other feelings: awe, hope, and above all fear, in which it again differs from the merely moral judgment of reason. The shame one feels for one's behavior

---

[4] *Apologia*, 216.

[5] *Apologia*, 182.

[6] John Henry Newman, "Sermon 16. Sincerity and Hypocrisy", in *Parochial and Plain Sermons* (London: Longmans, Green, 1906), 235.

[7] See John Henry Newman, *An Essay in Aid of a Grammar of Assent* (London: Longmans, Green, 1903), 126–27.

arouses all sorts of uncomfortable feelings, but not fear, so long as one is not given certain punishments for it. But the guilty person experiences fear and anxiety in his heart even when his evil act is praised and rewarded. This fear implies something: conscience has to do not only with the deed and with the "I" as the perpetrator but with a third party, a living Being, to whom I am responsible for the deed. The fact that besides me there is another participant who has a concern in my behavior is contained in the experience of conscience, and conscience knows that it is dealing with Someone, not something: "We are not affectionate towards a stone, nor do we feel shame before a horse or a dog; we have no remorse or compunction . . . and thus the phenomena of Conscience, as a dictate, avail to impress the imagination with the picture of . . . a just, . . . all-seeing, retributive" person.[8] Because it is the bearer of a message, it has authority. Because it is a judgment of reason, it can be wrong. Our judgments are subject to many influences. The role of conscience as a critic can turn out to be very different in the millions of human hearts; its role as judge remains the same always and everywhere: the testimony that there is good and evil and the sanction that accompanies doing right and wrong.

For Newman, the task of conscience in providing us with the foundations of morality, which the intellect can develop into a moral law, is only secondary: first and foremost, it is "the dictate of an authoritative monitor".[9] Insofar as the appearance of conscience includes the image of a supreme Lord, a Judge who is holy, just, powerful, all-seeing, and retributive, it is the creative principle of religion, just as it is the moral sense of ethics.

That is its first and original aspect. "Moral sense"[10] conjures up an image for only a few people; but everyone knows what a guilty conscience is. "Is there any one who does not know how very painful the feeling of a bad conscience is? . . . What a piercing bitter feeling . . . ? Is not the feeling of a bad conscience different from any other feeling, and more distressing than any other, till we have accustomed ourselves to it? Persons do accustom themselves and

---

[8] *Grammar of Assent*, 110.
[9] *Grammar of Assent*, 106.
[10] See *Grammar of Assent*, chap. 5.

lose this feeling; but till we blunt our conscience, it is very painful. And why? It is the feeling of God's displeasure, and therefore it is so painful."[11] "Conscience is ever forcing on us by threats and by promises that we must follow the right and avoid the wrong; so far it is one and the same in the mind of every one, whatever be its particular errors in particular minds as to the acts which it orders to be done or to be avoided."[12] Conscience is a "calling-by-name" *from outside*; I see it as *interference*, but not unfounded and not open to dispute: "The voice of God in the nature and heart of man, as distinct from the voice of Revelation . . . a principle planted within us, before we have had any training, although training and experience are necessary for its strength, growth, and due formation." Conscience is "the internal witness of both the existence and the law of God. They think it holds of God" and has a duty to Him, "and not of man, as an Angel walking on the earth would be no citizen or dependent of the Civil Power. They would not allow, any more than we do, that it could be resolved into any combination of principles in our nature, more elementary than itself; nay, though it may be called, and is, a law of the mind, they would not grant that it was nothing more; I mean, that it was not a dictate, nor conveyed the notion of responsibility, of duty, of a threat and a promise, with a vividness which discriminated it from all other constituents of our nature."[13] The organ of encountering God is appropriately also the organ for encountering Divine Truth. How much the search for Truth is a matter of conscience has already been discussed in detail [in chapter 4].

What was said there about the knowledge of dogmatic Truth is no less true of moral Truth, thus also of the doctrinal decisions of the Church that confront us in her moral law. Here, too, "a supreme authority" is required, "ruling" the myriad of contradicting individual views "and reconciling individual judgments by a divine right and a recognized wisdom".[14] Here too, "a revelation is not given,

---

[11] "Sermon 14. Religion Pleasant to the Religious", in *Parochial and Plain Sermons*, 7:199–200.

[12] *Grammar of Assent*, 106–7.

[13] "Duke of Norfolk", 2:247–48.

[14] John Henry Newman, *An Essay on the Development of Christian Doctrine* (London: Longmans, Green, 1909), 89.

if there be no authority to decide what it is that is given."[15] Here, too, knowledge and obedience are closely linked. One cannot fully "apprehend" these teachings either, but the Catholic Christian can and must reasonably see that he can believe them, that he must obey them if he wants to belong to the Church. And does the following not also apply here? "A man who fancies he can find out truth by himself, disdains revelation. He who thinks he *has* found it out, is *impatient* of revelation. He fears it will interfere with his own imaginary discoveries, he is unwilling to consult it; and when it does interfere, then he is angry."[16]

The separation of moral reason from obedience to God is the real root of every degeneration of conscience because only both, inseparably united, form a healthy conscience. From this basic understanding, Newman weighs and assesses the three stated attitudes. Basically, they merge into one, and the judgment about them depends on a question about the relationship of each person to God, which is expressed in them. Does conscience need to be formed in a Christian way?

There are people who do not choose to profess a faith, do not recognize a church and perhaps not even Christ, but still recognize an unconditional law over themselves: something that they did not bestow on themselves, did not choose, and did not invent, which also is not simply an embodiment of the will of another person, but something Greater and Other, which demands obedience, from which they do not dare to withdraw, although they do not know how to name the One giving the command: here I stand; I cannot do anything else, even if it were possible for me to do so. This undoubtedly represents a genuine religious bond of conscience, which binds with a sovereignty that cannot be done away with, even in the event of a factual error. Whoever seriously surrenders and submits to this inner light, no matter how foggy and nameless it is for him, will be led, sooner or later, to God. It is *the* experience of God that is offered outside of revelation; indeed, it is inescapable. Of course, such obedience to conscience is only the most basic level,

---

[15] *Christian Doctrine*, 89.
[16] "Sermon 17. The Self-Wise Inquirer", in *Parochial and Plain Sermons*, 1:218.

not the full form; it is the cornerstone, a way station, a first step that requires development.

Everything that is called "formation of conscience", therefore, has a standard: whether one wants to be obedient to it. According to Newman, obedience is the essence of religion; not as if love were absent from it—it is love as obedience, loving obedience, obedient love, which has its law in the will of the beloved Lord.

"Any profession which is disjoined from obedience, is a mere pretence and deceit. . . . You have to seek His face; obedience is the only way of seeking Him."[17] "Obedience to God's command-ments, which implies knowledge of sin and of holiness, and the desire and endeavour to please Him, this is the only practical in-terpreter of Scripture doctrine."[18] Being religious is nothing other than "so placing God's presence and will before us, and so consis-tently acting with a reference to Him, that all we do becomes one body and course of obedience, witnessing without ceasing to Him who made us, and whose servants we are."[19]

For in conscience, the divine law expresses itself, or: "This law, as apprehended in the minds of individual men, is called 'conscience;' and though it may suffer refraction in passing into the intellectual medium of each, it is not therefore so affected as to lose its charac-ter of . . . commanding obedience.["]20 Being able and allowed to obey: for Newman, this is the essence of the task of conscience.

Often and in detail, yes, in long-winded passages, he deals with natural ethics, natural religiosity, the ethos of the *gentleman*, the philosopher—and the Pharisee. It is important that in his reflec-tions, these positions always collapse into one. It is strange that so many of Newman's admirers have come to see him as a bona fide advocate, almost the missionary, of the "ideal of the *gentleman*". That probably comes from the fact that he paints such a benevo-lent, just, winsome, even enchanting picture of purely human per-

---

[17] "Sermon 22. Watching", in *Parochial and Plain Sermons*, 4:332.

[18] "Sermon 4. Secret Faults", in *Parochial and Plain Sermons*, 1:54–55.

[19] "Sermon 15. Mental Prayer", in *Parochial and Plain Sermons*, 7:206.

[20] "Duke of Norfolk", 2:247. In the German text, the quotation begins with "the divine law expresses itself" and ends after "is called 'conscience'". The following sen-tence, however, is clearly a continuation of the quotation from Newman. I have adjusted the closing quotation mark to reflect the quoted passage.

fection, like those famous pages about the *gentleman* in his university lectures.[21] But the surrounding text and many others leave no doubt about how little Newman—in contrast to many Christians today—allows himself to be impressed, how clearly he sees through the questionable nature of this dazzling apparition. He does not need, like some Christian zealots, to deny or degrade the value and charm of what is "only natural" in order to deal with it. But neither does he, *gentleman* that he is, need to gild this picture with the enthusiastic, envious aura of something unattainable. Even so, the austere and melancholy objectivity of his final judgment may alienate some modern readers:

> And such, I say, is the religion of the natural man in every age and place;—often very beautiful on the surface, but worthless in God's sight; good, as far as it goes, but worthless and hopeless, because it does not go further, because it is based on self-sufficiency, and results in self-satisfaction. I grant, it may be beautiful to look at, as in the instance of the young ruler whom our Lord looked at and loved, yet sent away sad; it may have all the delicacy, the amiableness, the tenderness, the religious sentiment, the kindness, which is actually seen . . . in the length and breadth of these kingdoms, in a refined and polished age like this; but still it is rejected by the heart-searching God, because all such persons walk by their own light, not by the True Light of men, because self is their supreme teacher, and because they pace round and round in the small circle of their own thoughts and of their own judgments, careless to know what God says to them, and fearless of being condemned by Him, if only they stand approved in their own sight.[22]

There is a fundamental difference between this spiritual refinement and true religiosity, despite any apparent relationship: one has man as its center, measure, and goal—the other, the Living God. That it falsifies the conscience, yes, alienates it from its nature to the point of reversing its meaning—that is Newman's accusation

---

[21] See *The Idea of a University.*

[22] John Henry Newman, "Sermon 2. The Religion of the Pharisee, the Religion of Mankind", in *Sermons Preached on Various Occasions* (London: Longmans, Green, 1908), 25–26.

against any "autonomous ethics".[23] In terms of content, it may for
a long time demand the same as the Christian moral law, however
much conscience is on the lips: "A false philosophy has misinter-
preted emotions which ought to lead to God".[24]

This is the "besetting sin" of the civilized intellect:[25] "Conscience
tends to become what is called a moral sense; the command of duty
is a sort of taste; sin is not an offence against God, but against human
nature. . . . Their conscience has become a mere self-respect. . . .
When they do wrong, they feel, not contrition, of which God is the
object, but remorse, and a sense of degradation. They call themselves fools, not sinners; they are angry and impatient, not humble."[26]

By eradicating fear, the conscience loses that which is "numi-
nous", the character of being a messenger from the world of that
which is completely different. Newman does not take a minimalist
view of fear in the realm of religious matters, even if it goes without
saying that he does not overestimate or isolate it. He knows that it
does not have to be merely a sign of a lowly and servile mindset,
that it is rather the correct, natural reaction of the guilty person to
the truly fearful holiness of God. True fear of God is a still truer,
higher, and deeper stirring of the soul than the dull and flat calming
of someone who does not know his Counterpart. "Fear carries us
out of ourselves", says Newman in this regard, "whereas shame may
act upon us only within the [limited] round of our own thoughts."[27]
"Had we any real apprehension of God as He is, of ourselves as we
are, we should never dare to serve Him without fear, or to rejoice
unto Him without trembling."[28] The stunting of the image of God
necessarily entails a stunting of conscience, a fading, diminishing,
and trivializing of its claim. Such heresy, as Newman calls it, can, of

---

[23] See, for example, John Henry Newman, *The Idea of a University* (London: Longmans, Green, 1907), 73.

[24] *Idea of a University*, 191.

[25] Newman writes, "Such, I say, is the danger which awaits a civilized age; such is
its besetting sin (not inevitable, God forbid! or we must abandon the use of God's own
gifts), but still the ordinary sin of the Intellect." *Idea of a University*, 191.

[26] *Idea of a University*, 191–92.

[27] *Idea of a University*, 191.

[28] "Religion of the Pharisee", 26.

course, take on very pleasing forms, especially in the case of people with easygoing, flexible, and sympathetic natures who understand virtue as nothing other than what is beautiful in one's way of life, conscience as the aesthetic harmony between themselves and their environment. "Beauty is truth, truth beauty,—that is all / Ye know on earth, and all ye need to know",[29] proclaimed Keats (who would die prematurely, the "Greek" among the English Romantics), and many picked up on the theme. Newman, himself so sensitive to the radiance of beauty, knows that people like this can be enchanting— but a deeper look recognizes them "in the insensibility of conscience, in the ignorance of the very idea of sin, in the contemplation of his own moral consistency, in the simple absence of fear, in the cloudless self-confidence, in the serene self-possession, in the cold self-satisfaction".[30] Does not the shadow of Dorian Gray come into view there?[31]

And how surprised they would be, these preachers of the purely aesthetic freedom from any shackle of conscience, if they found themselves side by side with the same type of men, as a further variety of "Christian" and "Catholic":

They lay no stress on acts of faith, hope, and charity, on simplicity of intention, purity of motive, or mortification of the thoughts; . . . they confine themselves to two or three virtues, superficially practised; . . . they know not the words contrition, penance, and pardon; and . . . they think and argue that, after all, if a man does his duty in the world, according to his vocation, he cannot fail to go to heaven, however little he may do besides, nay, however much, in other matters, he may do that is undeniably unlawful. Thus a soldier's duty is loyalty, obedience, and valour, and he may let other matters take their chance; a trader's duty is honesty; an artisan's duty is industry and contentment; of a gentleman are required veracity, courteousness, and self-respect; of a public man, high-principled ambition; of a woman,

---

[29] John Keats, "Ode on a Grecian Urn", Poetry Foundation, https://www.poetryfoundation.org/poems/44477/ode-on-a-grecian-urn.

[30] *Idea of a University*, 195–96.

[31] Dorian Gray is a fictional character in the novel *The Picture of Dorian Gray* (1890), by Oscar Wilde. Gray was a Victorian man who allowed his selfishness and hedonistic tendencies to corrupt his character over time, though the image he presented to the world remained innocent and pristine.

the domestic virtues; of a minister of religion, decorum, benevolence, and some activity. Now, all these are instances of mere Pharisaical excellence; because there is no apprehension of Almighty God, no insight into His claims on us, . . . no self-condemnation . . . nothing of those deep and sacred feelings which ever characterize the religion of a Christian, and more and more, not less and less, as he mounts up from mere ordinary obedience to the perfection of a saint. . . .

And thus they incur the force of those terrible words, spoken not to a Jewish Ruler, nor to a heathen philosopher, but to a fallen Christian community, to the Christian Pharisees of Laodicea,—"Because thou sayest I am rich, and made wealthy, and have need of nothing; and knowest not that thou art wretched, and miserable, and poor, and blind, and naked."[32]

And beyond this, Newman, with the cautious skepticism of the connoisseur of men, thinks both kinds of "perfection"[33] are not so uncommonly difficult to achieve. The beginning and end of such inner-worldly ethics is "the embellishment of the exterior".[34]

"*Vice lost half its evil by losing all its grossness*", said Burke,[35] unsuspecting that he was evoking praise of the culture of chivalry. The meaning of this, as Newman explained, is this: "It is detection, not the sin, which is the crime; private life is sacred, and inquiry into it is intolerable; and decency is virtue. Scandals, vulgarities, whatever shocks, whatever disgusts, are offences of the first order. . . . Deformity is its abhorrence; accordingly, since it cannot dissuade men from vice, therefore in order to escape the sight of its deformity, it embellishes it. . . . Certainly, it costs little to make men virtuous on conditions such as these; it is like teaching them a language or an accomplishment, to write Latin or to play on an instrument."[36]

With astonishing clarity and sharpness, with calm irony, Newman dissects, in what appears to be very modern psychological analysis, how the mask of the perfect personality builds up step by step, until "it comes to pass that its disciples seem able to fulfil certain pre-

---

[32] "Religion of the Pharisee", 24–26.

[33] *Idea of a University*, 211.

[34] *Idea of a University*, 204.

[35] This quote from Edmund Burke appears in *The Idea of a University*, 201, italics in the original.

[36] *Idea of a University*, 201–4.

cepts of Christianity more readily and exactly than Christians themselves. . . . The school of the world seems to send out living copies of this typical excellence with greater success than the Church."[37]

> Pride, under such training, instead of running to waste in the education of the mind, is turned to account; it gets a new name; it is called self-respect. Though it be the motive principle of the soul, it seldom comes to view; and when it shows itself, then delicacy and gentleness are its attire, and good sense and sense of honour direct its motions. . . . It is directed into the channel of industry, frugality, honesty, and obedience; and it becomes the very staple of the religion and morality held in honour in a day like our own. It becomes the safeguard of chastity, the guarantee of veracity, in high and low. . . . It is the stimulating principle of providence on the one hand . . . and of elegant enjoyment.
>
> Refined by the civilization which has brought it into activity, this self-respect infuses into the mind an intense horror of exposure, and a keen sensitiveness of notoriety and ridicule. It becomes the enemy of extravagances of any kind; it shrinks from what are called scenes; it has no mercy on the mock-heroic, on pretence or egotism. . . . It detests gross adulation . . . but it sees the absurdity of indulging it, it understands the annoyance thereby given to others, and if a tribute must be paid to the wealthy or the powerful, it demands greater subtlety and art in the preparation. Thus vanity is changed into a more dangerous self-conceit, as being checked in its natural eruption. . . . It is from this impatience of the tragic and the bombastic that it is now quietly but energetically opposing itself to the unchristian practice of duelling, which it brands as simply out of taste, and as the remnant of a barbarous age; and certainly it seems likely to effect what Religion has aimed at abolishing in vain.[38]

"The world is content with setting right the surface of things; the Church aims at regenerating the very depths of the heart."

Formation of conscience "begins with the beginning; and, as regards the multitude of her children, is never able to get beyond the beginning, but is continually employed in laying the foundation."[39]

---

[37] *Idea of a University*, 202–3.
[38] *Idea of a University*, 207–8.
[39] *Idea of a University*, 203.

"She is engaged with what is essential, as previous and as introductory to the ornamental and the attractive. She is curing men and keeping them clear of mortal sin. . . . She aims at what is necessary rather than at what is desirable."[40] "The Church aims at realities, the world at decencies. . . . If she can but pull the brands out of the burning, if she can but extract the poisonous root which is the death of the soul, . . . she is content, though she leaves in it lesser maladies, little as she sympathises with them."[41]

"Conscience, too, teaches us, not only that God is, but what He is; it provides for the mind a real image of Him, as a medium of worship; it gives us a rule of right and wrong, as being His rule."[42] In this, "it is a messenger from Him, who, both in nature and in grace, speaks to us behind a veil. . . . Conscience is the aboriginal Vicar of Christ, a prophet in its informations, a monarch in its peremptoriness, a priest in its blessings and anathemas."[43] If so, does the person who has his conscience then need other mediators, teachers, other representatives of God who should make known to him the will of the Most High? Is it not enough?

Certainly not, says Newman. Rather, the reality of the ecclesiastical teaching office—also in questions of morality—is the answer to the complaints of all those who feel the inadequacy of natural light, and the inadequacy of this light is the justification of that office.

Because natural conscience, as it is, is only barely reliable: "All sciences, except the science of Religion, have their certainty in themselves; as far as they are sciences, they consist of necessary conclusions from undeniable premises. . . . But the sense of right and wrong, which is the first element in religion, is so delicate, so fitful, so easily puzzled, obscured, perverted, so subtle in its argumentative methods, so impressible by education, so biassed by pride and passion, so unsteady in its course, that, in the struggle for existence amid the various exercises and triumphs of the human intellect, this sense is at once the highest of all teachers, yet the least luminous."[44]

He urgently needs growth in knowledge of God and human knowledge in order to fulfill his commission: "The natural con-

---

[40] *Idea of a University*, 203. Görres reordered some of the sentences from this passage.
[41] "Duke of Norfolk", 1:252.
[42] *Grammar of Assent*, 390.
[43] "Duke of Norfolk", 2:248–49.
[44] "Duke of Norfolk", 2:253–54.

science of man, if cultivated from within, if"—*if!*—"enlightened by those external aids which in varying degrees are given him in every place and time, would teach him much of his duty to God and man, and would lead him on, by the guidance both of Providence and grace, into the fulness of religious knowledge; but, generally speaking, he is contented that it should tell him very little, and he makes no efforts to gain any juster views than he has at first, of his relations to the world around him and to his Creator. Thus he apprehends part, and part only, of the moral law; has scarcely any idea at all of sanctity."[45]

"We do not know what sin is, because we do not know what God is; we have no standard with which to compare it, till we know what God is . . . and since we do not see God here, till we see Him, we cannot form a just judgment what sin is; till we enter heaven, we must take what God tells us of sin, mainly on faith."[46]

"The Catholic saints alone confess sin, because the Catholic saints alone see God. . . . It is the vision of Him in His infinite gloriousness, the All-holy, the All-beautiful, the All-perfect, which makes us sink into the earth with self-contempt and self-abhorrence. We are contented with ourselves till we contemplate Him."[47] Here lies the secret of Newman's own inscrutable humility: "With the hearing of the ear I have heard Thee . . . but now my eye seeth Thee; therefore I reprove myself, and do penance in dust and ashes", says Job.[48]

The second cornerstone of the formation of conscience is self-knowledge. But, "as well may we suppose, . . . the knowledge of the languages comes by nature"—that is, is present "on its own"—"as that acquaintance with our own heart is natural".[49] "Self-knowledge is a necessary condition for understanding them. . . . The doctrines of the *forgiveness* of sins, and of a *new birth* from sin, cannot be understood without some right knowledge of the *nature* of sin, that is, of our own heart. . . . For it is in proportion as we search our hearts and understand our own nature, that we understand what

---

[45] "Religion of the Pharisee", 20–21.
[46] John Henry Newman, "Discourse 2. Neglect of Divine Calls and Warnings", in *Discourses to Mixed Congregations* (London: Longmans, Green, 1906), 33.
[47] "Religion of the Pharisee", 26–27.
[48] Job 42:5–6, quoted in "Religion of the Pharisee", 28.
[49] "Secret Faults", 1:50.

is meant by an Infinite Governor and Judge. . . . Self-knowledge is
the key to the precepts and doctrines of Scripture."[50] But "no one
perhaps, is entirely ignorant of himself; and even the most advanced
Christian knows himself only 'in part.' "[51]

The conscience, which is always able to "come into agreement
with God and therefore master the situation sovereignly", is rarer
and, above all, more difficult to achieve than is claimed by those who
think that it is a requirement to be "assumed" for every Tom, Dick,
and Harry. "Our reasoning powers are very weak in all inquiries
into moral and religious truth. Clear-sighted as reason is on other
subjects, and trustworthy as a guide, still in questions connected
with our duty to God and man it is very unskilful and equivocating.
After all, it barely reaches the same great truths which are authoritatively set forth by Conscience and by Scripture; and if it be used in
religious inquiries, without reference to these divinely-sanctioned
informants, the probability is, it will miss the Truth altogether";
indeed, the epitome of all "false wisdom . . . is a trusting our own
powers for arriving at religious truth, instead of taking what is di-
vinely provided for us. . . . In the world," which inquires not about
truth but, rather, about gain, "Reason is set against Conscience, and
usurps its power."[52] But where it is genuinely a matter of knowing,
there must be learners and teachers, questions and answers, because
there are beginners and advanced learners, those in development and
those who are mature, the blind and those who see.

Who can say of their conscience that it is really a clear and un-
clouded mirror of the divine celestial script? Who is there whose
heart is so tranquil, his ear so sensitive and so trained that in the
confusing jumble of so many "inner voices" he can at any time
determine with certainty which one is the divine? Newman never
tires of pointing out in many sermons the sources of danger from
which the clouding of conscience arises: "Secret Faults—Neglect of
Divine Calls and Warnings—Moral Consequences of Single Sins",
obedience to "Divine Calls"[53]; such are only a few of them, but
many others continually offer variations on the subject.

---

[50] "Secret Faults", 1:41–43.
[51] "Secret Faults", 1:43.
[52] "Self-wise Inquirer", 1:218–19.
[53] "Secret Faults", "Moral Consequences of Single Sins", "Divine Calls", in *Parochial and Plain Sermons*; "Neglect of Divine Calls and Warnings", in *Discourses*.

With what appears to be a very modern psychological view of depths, Newman takes account of what is nowadays called repression, complexes, and traumas. He knows how the imagination is overwhelmed by curiosity and fear of fellow men, by the sheer force of the impression of what is loud, violent, and sensual; he knows the unconscious long-term and in-depth effects of unacknowledged dreams about oneself and the world, emotional ties and inhibitions—all sources of error for the objective, unbiased view.

For example, he takes children's sins as the forgotten origin of undesirable developments very seriously:

> Sins . . . which we never realized or have altogether forgotten. Ignorant as we may be when children begin to be responsible beings, yet we are ignorant also when they are not so; nor can we assign a date ever so early at which they certainly are not. And even the latest assignable date is very early; and thenceforward, whatever they do exerts, we cannot doubt, a most momentous influence on their character. We know that two lines starting at a small angle, diverge to greater and greater distances, the further they are produced; and surely in like manner a soul living on into eternity may be infinitely changed for the better or the worse by very slight influences exerted on it in the beginning of its course. . . . Yet as sicknesses and accidents then happening permanently affect their body, though they recollect nothing of them, there is no extravagance in the idea that passing sins then contracted and forgotten for ever afterwards, should so affect the soul as to cause those moral differences between man and man which . . . are too clear to be denied . . . and thus the indelible hues of sin and error are imprinted on their souls, and become as really part of their nature as that original sin in which they were born.[54]

And this is half a century before Freud's discovery of the importance of early childhood experiences! These individual, long-forgotten sins are not unlikely to be ascribed to those strange gaps in otherwise good characters that repeatedly leave us in consternation. They are the keys to "defects of character . . . buried"[55] that one day break out and take us and others by surprise.

Newman passes judgment similarly about the importance of the

---

[54] "Sermon 3. Moral Consequences of Single Sins," in *Parochial and Plain Sermons*, 4:39–41.

[55] "Moral Consequences", 4:43.

sins of youth, which are usually weighed so lightly: "The issue of
our youthful trial in good and evil, probably has had somewhat of
a decided character one way or the other; and we may be quite
sure that, if it has issued in evil, we shall not know it. . . . God's
judgments, whether to the world or the individual, are not loudly
spoken. The decree goes forth to build or destroy; Angels hear it;
but we go on in the way of the world as usual, though our souls
may have been, at least for a season, abandoned by God."[56]

And who knows his "sins . . . neglected",[57] which grow under-
ground, as it were, and bring out completely different errors in the
visible, which we may be busy trying to cure but in vain because
we cannot guess the roots? "Softness of mind and manner and false
refinement may sometimes be the result of allowing ourselves in
impure thoughts; or wanderings in prayer may have some subtle
connexion with self-conceit; or passionateness may owe its power
over us to indulgence, though without excess, in eating and drinking."[58] There is that one "indulged" weakness of virtuous people
in particular who do not allow anything else to go through but are
blind to themselves with regard to a favorite mistake and "may in
consequence be producing most distressing effects on his spiritual
state" because this one "neglected" sin lies outside their sight, as it
were, like the treacherously opened gate of a besieged city.[59]

"Alas! who can pretend to estimate the effect of this apparently
slight transgression upon the spiritual state of any one of us? . . .
Alas! what is the real condition of our heart itself?"[60] "Dead bodies keep their warmth a short time; and who can tell but a soul so
circumstanced may be severed from the grace of the Ordinances,
though he partakes them outwardly, and is but existing upon and
exhausting the small treasure of strength and life which is laid up
within him?"[61]

Newman emphasizes in this sermon that conscious and freely
willed sin expels us from the presence of God and obstructs the
channels through which His grace flows to us. But, by far, the greater

---

[56] "Self-wise Inquirer", 1:222–23.
[57] "Moral Consequences", 4:44.
[58] "Moral Consequences", 4:44–45.
[59] "Moral Consequences", 4:44–45.
[60] "Moral Consequences", 4:47.
[61] "Moral Consequences", 4:47–48.

part of this text deals with "secret", that is, unconscious, sins. In this way, he stands in striking contrast to the view, which is very widespread and passionately defended today, that sin is *only* what is committed with full knowledge and will. Newman knows it is otherwise: it is precisely the hidden, unacknowledged missteps that are disastrously potent because people never deal with them properly, never honestly render account. The Church knows why she has us pray: "Cleanse Thou me from hidden faults."[62] We are to blame if we do not know our sins and do not want to know them. The above-mentioned principle can be misused all too easily as a comfortable protective wall behind which we deliberately leave burdensome and worrying things in the twilight, below the threshold of clarity that demands a decision. The depth-psychology and general psychology of our day seem to agree with Newman, as does the ancient ascetic tradition of the Church. He did not speak like this only regarding others; his diary for Keble during his conversion crisis shows how seriously he integrated these insights into his own life.

It is also noticeable that Newman hardly seems to be aware of the fear that is common today of pushing people into the obsessive neurosis of scruples through such formation of conscience. Were people, or at least the English a hundred years ago, still so robust in their mental fabric that this worry was really not called for? Or does Newman demand precisely from the mature and adult conscience that is so often called for today that it should know how to distinguish between severe and slight gradations of sin without overlooking—or withholding—the importance of what is small? Note that Newman never confuses or transposes small and great in either of the texts already cited or the following: he would never have advised a penitent to judge a venial sin as a mortal sin; but he knows what we so often deliberately forget today, namely, that an accumulation of small mistakes results in the most dangerous burdens on the soul, just as a rope made of fine human hair is unbelievably powerful. Newman insists with the greatest emphasis on the incalculable significance of venial sin, like almost all saints, by the

---

[62] As liturgy scholar Matthew Hazell explains, "In the traditional Roman rite (that is, 1962 and before), petitions that we may be 'cleansed from hidden faults' appear in a responsory of the prayers to be said before every Mass, a gradual, a communion antiphon, and several postcommunion prayers. In the Novus Ordo, by contrast, these petitions are almost entirely removed." Correspondence with translator, August 17–18, 2024.

way—and perhaps not least through this consensus he will prove to be one of them.

> If you have triumphed over all mortal sin, as you seem to think, then you must attack your venial sins; there is no help for it; there is nothing else to do. . . . O simple souls! to think you have gained any triumph at all! No: you cannot safely be at peace with any, even the least malignant, of the foes of God; if you are at peace with venial sins, be certain that in their company and under their shadow mortal sins are lurking. Mortal sins are the children of venial, which, though they be not deadly themselves, yet are prolific of death.[63]

In another sermon, he cites negligence in daily prayers, which neither law nor commandment oblige, as an example of such a development:

> He who gives up regularity in prayer has lost a principal means of reminding himself that spiritual life is obedience to a Lawgiver, not a mere feeling or a taste. . . . This is the path which leads to death. Men first leave off private prayer; then they neglect the due observance of the Lord's day (which is a stated service of the same kind); then they gradually let slip from their minds the very idea of obedience to a fixed eternal law; then they actually allow themselves in things which their conscience condemns; then they lose the direction of their conscience, which being ill used, at length refuses to direct them. And thus, being left by their true inward guide, they are obliged to take another guide, their reason, which by itself knows little or nothing about religion; then, this their blind reason forms a system of right or wrong for them, as well as it can, flattering to their own desires, and presumptuous where it is not actually corrupt.[64]

So how can someone who takes small mistakes and venial sins lightly, considering it not worth the effort to pay attention to them, fight, repent, and do penance for them; how can he in any way imagine he has a reliably formed conscience, even a mature and superior conscience?

"Be quite sure, that this apparently small defect will influence your whole spirit and judgment in all things. Be quite sure that

---

[63] "Discourse 6. God's Will the End of Life", in *Discourses*, 120–21.
[64] "Sermon 19. Times of Private Prayer", in *Parochial and Plain Sermons*, 1:253–54.

your judgment of persons, and of events, and of actions, and of doctrines, and your spirit towards God and man, your faith in the high truths of the Gospel, and your knowledge of your duty, all depend in a strange way on this strict endeavour to observe the whole law, on this self-denial in those little things in which obedience *is* a self-denial."[65]

The soul, after all, exists as a whole; it is not a mechanical heap of unrelated acts and thoughts: "But every sin has a history: it is not an accident; it is the fruit of former sins in thought or in deed. . . . Therefore, my brethren, it is but the craft of the devil, which makes you take your sins one by one, while God views them as a whole. . . . They are all connected together; they tend to a whole; they look towards an end, and they hasten on to their fulfilment."[66]

Therefore, no single act of misconduct or omission can be assessed as "only" in and of itself: its place in the fabric proves its role and determines the degree of its disastrous effect unknown to us: "Never think yourself safe because you do your duty in ninety-nine points; it is the hundredth which is to be the ground of your self-denial, which must evidence, or rather instance and realize your faith. . . . Oh, that you may . . . sweep the house diligently to discover what you lack of the *full* measure of obedience!"[67] The full measure of obedience: that alone guarantees us the reliability of the inner light, insofar as a person is allowed to speak of security. But what is to become of a conscience that strives with cunning and diligence to reduce this full measure in all things to a safe minimal norm and calls this striving "generosity and independence"?

No, Newman is not trying to turn us into people with scrupulosity: "I do not wish to sadden you, but to make you cautious; doubt not you will be led on, fear not to fall, provided you do but fear a fall. Fearing will secure you from what you fear."[68]

---

[65] "Sermon 5. Self-Denial the Test of Religious Earnestness", in *Parochial and Plain Sermons*, 1:68–69. In the German edition, Görres has "influence", "in all things", and "the whole law" in italics.

[66] "Neglect of Divine Calls", 27.

[67] "Self-Denial", 1:68.

[68] "Discourse 7. Perseverance in Grace", in *Discourses*, 43.

Does not such a proper, old-style sermon on morality come off as almost startling from the mouth of a man encircled by the extensive glowing aura of being the daring champion of freedom of conscience, which is threatened, and of "modern" Christianity? But should his words here not make us think and shake our premature certainties? "The confession of a good man against himself", he says in another place, "is really a witness against all thoughtless persons who hear it, and a call on them to examine their own hearts."[69] And let us not forget that his words are not just a theory he made up but are drawn from decades of experience as chaplain and confessor.

That is why Newman regards all allegedly "higher" religious education and cultivation of the soul that considers such painstaking work not or no longer necessary, with very skeptical eyes: "Too many men at this time are for raising a high superstructure ere they have laid a deep foundation. . . . The austere doctrines of the Gospel they turn from them. . . . They stumble at the doctrine of post-baptismal sin." Today that means: they deny the danger of sin for the redeemed—"and what part of their creed can be profitable to them, if this is neglected? . . . They scoff at the ascetic life of the Saints as an extravagance or corruption; . . . they would live like the world, yet worship like the Angels."[70]

Whoever neglects or disdains to form his conscience by observing "the whole law",[71] whoever does not strive to be "symmetrical, in the believing mind"[72]—in contrast to one-sided and eclectic—

---

[69] "Secret Faults", 1:48.

[70] John Henry Newman, "Sermon 25. Feasting in Captivity", in *Sermons Bearing on the Subjects of the Day* (London: Longmans, Green, 1902), 392.

[71] James 2:10. The German edition has no citation here, so it is unclear whether Görres is just quoting Scripture or whether she is quoting this phrase from a text by Newman. Newman quotes James 2:10 explicitly or uses the phrase "the whole law" in connection with conscience and obedience in several sermons in his *Parochial and Plain Sermons*; for example, "Sermon 14. Obedience to God the Way to Faith in Christ", 8:204; "Sermon 17. The Testimony of Conscience", 5:240; "Sermon 5. Self-Denial the Test of Religious Earnestness", 1:69; "Sermon 1. The Strictness of the Law of Christ", 4:12; "Sermon 8. God's Commandments Not Grievous", 1:101; and "Sermon 23. Tolerance of Religious Error", 2:286.

[72] "Sermon 10. Faith and Reason, contrasted as Habits of Mind," in *Fifteen Sermons*, 200.

in his inner and outer man, falls only too easily into the bare "dream" of a religiosity that is lived out in religious words, idioms, gestures, and customs without actually being religion. In eerie and disturbing images that are reminiscent of the penitential sermons of earlier centuries, Newman depicts the life, death, and judgment of the "worldly Christian" who lives complacently in the delusion that everything is in order with him while he has long since replaced the Divine Order with a comfortable, thoroughly arbitrary selection of religious individual features that are more pleasing to him and made them harmless, as it were: "To be at ease, is to be unsafe."[73]

Likewise, he has severe and painful words for those who expect everything from grace without wanting to cooperate: "It is the opinion of a large class of religious people, that faith being granted, works follow as a matter of course, without our own trouble. . . . It follows that nothing remains to be done but to bring these sovereign principles before the mind, as a medicine which must work a cure. . . . To care for little duties, to set men right in the details of life, to instruct and refine their conscience, to tutor them in self-denial . . . become superfluous."[74]

By a long shot, knowing does not mean obeying, nor do conscience and reason make repentance easy or tenacious. The Christian must not ask less of himself than the "gentleman" or the noble pagan; and he must not be inferior to the Pharisee in virtue either. More is given to him; more will be demanded. "The day, we know, will come, when every Christian will be judged, not by what God has done for him, but by what he has done for himself: when, of all the varied blessings of Redemption, in which he was clad here, nothing will remain to him, but what he has incorporated in his own moral nature, and made part of himself."[75] Woe to him if "he has rested on the Sacraments, without caring to have the proper dispositions for attending them."[76]

---

[73] "Secret Faults", 1:56.
[74] "Sermon 8. Human Responsibility, as Independent of Circumstances", in *Fifteen Sermons*, 147.
[75] "Sermon 3. Evangelical Sanctity the Completion of Natural Virtue", in *Fifteen Sermons*, 53.
[76] "Neglect of Divine Calls", 37.

This all-encompassing, inconvenient, and unswerving vigilance and self-control are based not least on the knowledge and experience of how delicate, how vulnerable and destructible the gift of conscience is. Everything precious is threatened; it is easier and faster to harm than to cure every living thing: "Beware of trifling with your conscience. It is often said that second thoughts are best; so they are in matters of judgment, but not in matters of conscience. In matters of duty first thoughts are commonly best—they have more in them of the voice of God."[77] "God gives us warnings now and then, but does not repeat them. Balaam's sin consisted in not acting upon what was told him *once for all*."[78]

Here lies the real danger of curiosity, which tempts us to circle around an as-yet-unknown evil at least "from afar", in the opinion that this is not yet serious and therefore harmless: "What must in all cases be the consequence of allowing evil thoughts to be present to us, though we do not actually admit them into our hearts. This, namely,—we shall make ourselves familiar with them."[79] So we are all imperceptibly under its spell, as under the gaze of a snake.

> At first our conscience tells us, in a plain straightforward way, what is right and what is wrong; but when we trifle with this warning, our reason becomes perverted, and comes in aid of our wishes, and deceives us to our ruin. Then we begin to find, that there are arguments available in behalf of bad deeds, and we listen to these till we come to think them true; and then, if perchance better thoughts return, and we make some feeble effort to get at the truth really and sincerely, we find our minds by that time so bewildered that we do not know right from wrong. . . .
>
> Now in all such cases of conduct there is no end of arguing about right or wrong, if we once begin; there are numberless ways of acting, each of which may be speciously defended by argument, but plain, pure-hearted common sense, generally speaking, at the very first sight decides the question for us without argument; but if we do not listen promptly to this secret monitor, its light goes out at once, and we are left to the mercy of mere conjecture, and grope about with but second-best guides. . . . Who can say where we shall stop?[80]

---

[77] "Obedience without Love", 4:36.
[78] "Obedience without Love", 4:35.
[79] "Sermon 5. Curiosity a Temptation to Sin", in *Parochial and Plain Sermons*, 8:66.
[80] "Curiosity", 8:67, 68–69.

Such frequently imperceptible drifting produces something "like the state of men who have undergone some dreadful illness, which changes the constitution of the body. That ready and clear perception of right and wrong, which before directed us, will have disappeared, as beauty of person, or keenness of eyesight in bodily disorders; and when we . . . try to make up our minds which way lies the course of duty on particular trials, we shall bring enfeebled, unsteady powers to the examination; and when we move to act, our limbs (as it were) will move the contrary way, and we shall do wrong when we wish to do right."[81] An uncanny knowledge of oneself and of people speaks from such descriptions.

At last, man falls into a state of hypocrisy—he who with so much fuss elevated truthfulness and loyalty to himself as his guide!—that "Hypocrisy, which we see around us," says Newman, "that state of mind in which the reason, seeing what we should be, and the conscience enjoining it, and the heart being unequal to it, some or other pretence is set up, by way of compromise".[82] "And therefore, he goes about to fortify his position, to explain his conduct, or to excuse himself."[83] We see the examples in Adam, Eve, Cain, Balaam, and the servant who buried his talent. "But it is one thing to have good excuses, another to have good motives."[84]

For Newman, however, the climax of such untruthfulness, untruthfulness of the heart, is this: "They look on themselves, as it were, as independent parties, treating with Almighty God as one of their fellows"—the way a person treats his equal. "They would rather keep their position and stand where they are,—on earth, and so make terms with God in heaven."[85] Here, especially in the mouth of the Christian and those who are religious, not in the mouth of the freethinker, the concept of conscience profoundly turns into its opposite: from being the instrument of submission to God, the mouth has suddenly become the instrument of self-assertion.

With a passionate will to fight, seventy-year-old Newman opposes this fateful mistake:

---

[81] "Curiosity", 8:69.
[82] "Sermon 23. Love, the One Thing Needful", in *Parochial and Plain Sermons*, 5:338.
[83] "Sincerity and Hypocrisy", 5:230.
[84] "Sincerity and Hypocrisy", 5:232.
[85] "Sincerity and Hypocrisy", 5:230.

Let us see what is the notion of conscience in this day in the popular mind. . . . When men advocate the rights of conscience, they in no sense mean the rights of the Creator, nor the duty to Him, in thought and deed, of the creature; but the right of thinking, speaking, writing, and acting, according to their judgment or their humour, without any thought of God at all. . . . They demand . . . for each to be his own master in all things, and to profess what he pleases, asking no one's leave, and accounting priest or preacher . . . unutterably impertinent, who dares to say a word against his going to perdition, if he like it, in his own way. Conscience has rights because it has duties; but in this age, with a large portion of the public, it is the very right and freedom of conscience to dispense with conscience, to ignore a Lawgiver and Judge, to be independent of unseen obligations. It becomes a licence to take up any or no religion, to take up this or that and let it go again, to go to church, to go to chapel, to boast of being above all religions and to be an impartial critic of each of them. Conscience is a stern monitor, but in this century it has been superseded by a counterfeit, which the eighteen centuries prior to it never heard of, and could not have mistaken for it, if they had. It is the right of self-will.[86]

This flaming declaration of war applies, certainly, first of all to what Newman fought all his life in the guise of religious liberalism. Nevertheless, we Catholics of today would do well to measure our fashionable principles of the rights of conscience within the Church honestly against these words. We might be startled.

Here, too, we understand why the conflict between conscience and authority hardly plays a role in Newman's teaching (for us, it is almost *the* issue in conscience formation). We know what a place the painful struggle with authority in the Church actually occupied in his life—one may say, in his entire life, as an Anglican as well as a Catholic. But it was never and nowhere a fundamental conflict, always only a practical one, and after the preceding there is very little to say about it.

"In the case of all of us occasions arise, when practices countenanced by others do not approve themselves to our consciences"[87]—and

---

[86] "Duke of Norfolk", 2:249–50.
[87] "Sermon 4. The Praise of Men", in *Parochial and Plain Sermons*, 7:51.

even if it is not specifically stated in the context, these others can sometimes also be authorities. "If after serious thought we find we cannot acquiesce in them, we must follow our consciences, and stand prepared for the censure of others. We must submit (should it be unavoidable) to appear to those who have no means of understanding us, self-willed, or self-conceited, or obstinate, or eccentric, or headstrong, praying the while that God's mercy may vouchsafe to us, that we be not really what we seem to the world."[88]

As early as the days of the Tractarian Movement, he had written that those who had always given their superiors the respect they were owed were the most devoted servants, but also the most ardent critics. He relished the tragedy that lies in this and that must necessarily follow from such an attitude to the last drop of struggle for the renewal of the Anglican church as in his long Catholic years "under a cloud".[89] But that is why the necessity of such conflicts of conscience never becomes something he asserts; the compatibility of obedience and conscience never becomes a "problem". What he says in the famous public debate with Gladstone about the implications of the Vatican decisions of 1871 in the life of the individual Catholic can, if understood correctly, also apply to this question:

When it [conscience] has the right of opposing the supreme, though not infallible Authority of the Pope, it must be something more than that miserable counterfeit which, as I have said above, now goes by the name. If in a particular case it is to be taken as a sacred and sovereign monitor, its dictate, in order to prevail against the voice of the Pope, must follow upon serious thought, prayer, and all available means of arriving at a right judgment on the matter in question. And further, obedience to the Pope is what is called "in possession"; that is, the *onus probandi* [burden of proof] of establishing a case against him lies, as in all cases of exception, on the side of conscience. Unless a man is able to say to himself, as in the Presence of God, that he must not, and dare not, act upon the Papal injunction, he is bound to obey it, and would commit a great sin in disobeying it. *Primâ facie* it is his bounden duty, even from a sentiment of loyalty, to believe the Pope

---

[88] "Praise of Men", 7:51.
[89] Wilfrid Philip Ward, *The Life of John Henry Cardinal Newman: Based on His Private Journals and Correspondence* (London: Longmans, Green, 1912), 2:151, 152.

right and to act accordingly. He must vanquish that mean, ungenerous, selfish, vulgar spirit of his nature, which, at the very first rumour of a command, places itself in opposition to the Superior who gives it, asks itself whether he is not exceeding his right, and rejoices, in a moral and practical matter to commence with scepticism. He must have no wilful determination to exercise a right of thinking, saying, doing just what he pleases, the question of truth and falsehood, right and wrong, the duty if possible of obedience, the love of speaking as his Head speaks, and of standing in all cases on his Head's side, being simply discarded. If this necessary rule were observed, collisions between the Pope's authority and the authority of conscience would be very rare.[90]

It also belongs here that Newman cites in that profound sermon ["Moral Consequences of Single Sins"] about the remote effect of hidden sins on our conscience and judgment as a particular source of error,

a disobedience in one particular only, which sometimes consists with much excellence in other respects; that of separation or alienation from the Church. . . . We see so much of good principle and right conduct in them, as to be perplexed, and to begin to ask ourselves whether they can be very wrong in their opinions, or whether they themselves gain any harm from them. . . . And though we cannot know who are such . . . yet I would have all those who are thrown with persons who, being separatists, may be such, to bear in mind that their seeming to be holy and religious ever so much, does not prove they are really so, supposing they have this one secret sin chargeable upon them in God's books. . . . Just as a man may be in good health . . . and yet may just have one organ diseased, and the disease not at once appear, but be latent, and yet be mortal, bringing certain death in the event, so may it be with them.[91]

Precisely for this reason, Newman insists on the crispest distinction between what is really a commandment and general obligation in the Church and what is only the private opinion of individuals, even of pious and zealous people: just as with dogma. Just as the way the name of God may not be mentioned in vain or misused,

---

[90] "Duke of Norfolk", 2:257–58.
[91] "Moral Consequences", 4:49–50.

either for educational, activist, or reasons of power politics, so, too, the term "Truth" as well as "holy obedience". Precisely because he obeys God alone, which also means that he obeys God alone in His representatives, Newman knows neither officious subservience nor self-promoting servility and never falls into the yoke of the law, the letter, the paragraphs seen only technically.

From him, we can learn again to recognize the Catholic virtue of obedience. Do we even know what this is? Do we even know anything other than caricatures of this virtue: obedience that is military and cadaver-like, forced, coerced, hypocritical, with gnashing of teeth; conventional obedience of going along and conforming; the hysterical and subservient obedience of emotional bondage? But the obedience of great trust, free and upright, bold and daring, without resentment and suspicion, without reservations and secret rebellion, simple and ardent, confident—how alien it has become to us! When will we find it again? How perfectly did John Henry Newman put it into effect and live it!

He is truly the last person to whom we might dare appeal in order to assert our personal judgment in any matter—our personal benefit, our sympathies or, quite simply, our obstinacy and our fear of uneasy self-conquest against an express command of the Church in the name of conscience.

It goes without saying that such obedience costs a great deal; it cuts to the quick. In a long sermon with the refreshing title "Religion a Weariness to the Natural Man", with a refreshing openness and objectivity, Newman analyzes and describes instinctive resistance that the average as well as the zealous person has at every age against serving God: "It is very wearisome, and very monotonous, to go on day after day watching all we do and think, detecting our secret failings, denying ourselves, creating within us, under God's grace, those parts of the Christian character in which we are deficient." [92] "It is a weariness, a greater weariness than the doing nothing at all." [93]

But in God's name, we should admit, and without further ado,

---

[92] "Sermon 2. Religion a Weariness to the Natural Man", in *Parochial and Plain Sermons*, 7:23.
[93] "A Weariness", 7:19.

"that there is by nature some strange discordance between what we love and what God loves",[94] that it is due to us and not to some nonsense of God's demand advocated by the Church: "The nature of man is flesh, and that which is born of the flesh is flesh. . . . It will occupy itself in various ways, it will take interest in things of sense and time, but it can never be religious. It is at enmity with God."[95]

The practical consequence of Christian faith, he says with indisputable simplicity, is precisely this: we must change. Because we cannot expect that the system of the universe will change for our sake. Fatalism is the dishonest evasion of a guilty conscience that initially proudly demanded its freedom and, after it has gone wrong, begs whiningly that it has never been free because human nature knows no freedom.

"We fear to be too holy. . . . The Church is rising up around us day by day towards heaven, and we do nothing but object, or explain away, or criticise, or make excuses, or wonder."[96] "God has abounded in His mercies to us; we have a depth of power and strength lodged in us; but we have not the heart, we have not the will, we have not the love to use it . . . and it is our own fault that we have it not."[97] "This is the reason why he cannot and does not obey or make progress. . . . We have a power within us to do what we are commanded to do. . . . What we lack is the real, simple, earnest, sincere inclination and aim to use what God has given us. . . . I say, our experience tells us this."[98] It is like one is hearing the *Exercises* of Saint Ignatius.

"O ye men of the world, when ye talk, as ye do, so much of the impossibility . . . are you sure that the impossibility which you insist upon does not lie, not in nature, but in the will? . . . You have never brought yourselves to will it,—you cannot bear to will it. You cannot bear to be other than you are."[99] He has the right to speak like that; he has faithfully walked this path of un-

---

[94] "A Weariness", 7:16.
[95] "A Weariness", 7:23–34.
[96] "Sermon 24. The Power of the Will", in *Parochial and Plain Sermons*, 5:355.
[97] "Power of the Will", 5:343. Görres quotes these phrases out of order.
[98] "Power of the Will", 5:343, 348.
[99] "Power of the Will", 5:350.

speakable hardship, seventy-five out of the ninety years of his life. "Is not holiness the result of many patient, repeated efforts after obedience, gradually working on us, and first modifying and then changing our hearts?"[100] And he learned from it that such a yoke is not slavery, being robbed, and being killed but that it confirms the improbable, the terrifying Master's Word of His burden that is sweet and light.

"Let them not be surprised that *what* the pleasure is cannot be explained to *them*. It is a secret till they try to be religious. Men know what sin is, by experience. They do not know what holiness is; and they cannot obtain the knowledge of its secret pleasure . . . till they 'taste'. . . . This pleasure is as hidden from them, as the pleasures of sin are hidden from the Angels. . . . None other than God the Holy Spirit can help us in this matter, by enlightening and changing our hearts."[101] "Whereby are given unto us exceeding great and precious promises: that by these ye might be partakers of the divine nature."[102]

In what we call conscience, we love to seek the ally of our weakness, the defense attorney of our failure, the writ of protection for our passions, the accomplice of temptation. Newman wants man to find in his conscience the ally of his highest self, the anchor of his decisions, the guardian of his purest possibility, the confidant and guarantor of his destiny: "As the seed has a tree within it, so men have within them Angels."[103]

A teaching that has become foreign and yet is so familiar! His own closing words from his solemn sermon about the procrastinator Balaam are cautionary: "You, my brethren, now hear what you may never hear again, and what perchance in its substance is the word of God. You may never hear it again, though with your

---

[100] "Sermon 1. Holiness Necessary for Future Blessedness", in *Parochial and Plain Sermons*, 1:11.

[101] "Power of the Will", 7:198–99. The German text places the closing quotation mark after "of the divine nature", but the following sentence from 2 Peter 1:4 (here in the King James Version), which Newman quotes in other sermons, does not appear in this sermon. The citation added by Gerl-Falkovitz notes that Görres quotes this "imprecisely".

[102] 2 Peter 1:4.

[103] "Power of the Will", 5:351.

outward ears you hear it a hundred times, because you may be impressed with it now, but never may again . . . but it *may* also arise
from your having heard God's voice and not obeyed it."[104]

---

[104] "Obedience without Love", 4:35–36.

III

ENCORE

A SKETCH OF THE LIFE
OF NEWMAN
1955

Görres published this "Sketch" in her 1955 book Aus der Welt der Heili-gen *(From the world of the saints), which contains profiles of several saints.*[1] *In that book, this "Sketch" belongs to a section titled "Notes and Thoughts". Thus, Görres' style in this chapter reads, at times, more like notes than prose. In keeping with her style of jotting down "notes", I have reformatted the text into a list to help the reader follow the passages that are more like a list of thoughts on various topics rather than continuous prose. The German edition of this chapter has no citations; all citations in this chapter are my own.—TRANS.*

The most important thing for me about Newman's letters is the insight into how far back "our" conflict between modern, in some way "reformist", Catholics and "reactionary" Catholics goes: in fact, a full hundred years. We from the "recent Church" are only the last link in an already quite remarkable chain; we are by no means a "spontaneous awakening", as I previously thought, but rather also heirs to a great, agonizing, invigorating Tradition of which we are unfortunately unaware. Newman is really "our" patron; he has the only possible attitude but thus also the one that is so difficult to implement: the clearest, coolest, critical insight into the thousand grievances and undesirable developments in the Church and the ab-solutely inevitable need for many reforms—*and* the devotion and loyalty to "Rome" (with all the heavy burdens of this term) that is passionate, compelling for the whole human person, and stirring.

~

---

[1] Ida Friederike Görres, "Über J. H. Newman" in *Aus der Welt der Heiligen* (Frankfurt am Main: Josef Knecht, 1955), 54–62. *Aus der Welt der Heiligen* (From the world of the saints) is a collection of essays by Görres on sanctity and the lives of several saints, in-cluding Newman. The book has not yet been translated into English.

In Newman, I also see the peculiar and specifically Catholic mixture of skepticism and trust in religiosity—skepticism and submission, skepticism and obedience to authority. These are not hostile opposites at all, as a simpleton would believe; rather, they complement one another. To a certain extent, nobody keeps tabs on the *real* concerns of all skepticism—the deep, ruthless knowledge of the thousandfold limitations, inadequacy, and fragility of all human knowledge, all human understanding, all human "goodwill"—so frankly, so persistently, not to be deterred, and taken for granted, as we do. And on the other hand, precisely *from* this deep, incurable skepticism about what is merely human, nobody knows so well and thoroughly how we in particular *need* authority, guidance, law, submission—having the inviolably binding decision made for us and removed from us—to be able to exist. And the equally honest skepticism toward the bearers of authority and their limits, in turn, saves us from making them absolute. Newman combines all of this without friction, "naturally", in stride and gracefully, without caving in: how Catholic!

~

Newman: what he was outside of his spiritual formation, who he would have been without it, is an important yet unanswerable question. Would he have been much richer, warmer, more intense, and more versatile, or just a bleak, introverted scholar who aged early? The grace that overtakes him inflicts extreme wounds and brings extreme exaltation at the same time; without "conversion" he might have become "more perfect", but on a lower plane.

It is becoming increasingly clear to me that if I am going to write any book, it will be on *Newman the Saint*. The essential thing about him is that he was a man sacrificed, that is, *une âme détruite* [a shattered soul],[2] someone who was shattered by God in spite of all the humanistic and classical "harmony" and such in him. That is all just part of the foreground. The drama is all inside. His "first conversion" was a lightning strike, which completely and forever destroyed his roots in the earth, and all the subsequent calamities are nothing but the necessary unfolding of this process.

---

[2] For a discussion about how Görres understands the phrase *une âme détruite*, see the first citation in chapter 1 of this volume.

~

Newman thinks about sin and hell with startling harshness. It seems to me that a large number of his admirers here [in Germany] have not yet even noticed this—in this regard he could be considered "unmodern". This is astonishing in that he has lived in an extremely cultivated, proper, unperturbed era, a tame era—not, as we do, in an era in which atrocities and crimes are so blatant in the order of the day; also, he was in quite exclusive circles, in which life was bourgeois, educated, solid, and respectable. So he must have had the worst possible opinion—or experience—of what was going on behind the scenes. He expresses himself quite cautiously and in a Victorian manner, but it is clear enough that he very often means "immorality" in the narrow sense of the word—and he is generally quite skeptical about what is "natural".

Newman's 150th birthday was so long ago! Does he actually belong in the "charismatic century"? Yes and no. On the one hand, he naturally belongs in the flow of the spiritual tide, that is clear; on the other hand, he is the ultimate antithesis of any sort of "mass spirituality", with an almost physical aversion to emotional outbursts, to everything uncontrollable in the religious sphere. Also, he fought on two fronts: against the hubris of "reason" as well as against the fog of "experience". He is the saint of sobriety—which is very rare; namely, as a type of *holiness* that is generally larger than life and enthusiastic, whereas the danger of sobriety lies in shriveling up, being parched, et cetera, and then, because holiness in itself means being spirit-filled, yes, spiritually obsessed, but in a special way.

~

Thoughts on Newman:

The exile, a witness to the invisible—this is his distinction. As intensely as Francis [of Assisi], throughout his whole life Newman was a partner in an inaudible conversation that continually "interrupts" the natural arc of his existence, an existence that was actually made for a solid, firmly rooted life in the best style of the eighteenth century, "classic", as a *scholar* and a *gentleman*.

First conversion: perception of the two invisible poles of existence: *God and myself.*

The saint of discretion—from the beginning that deeply Catholic trait of *inconspicuousness*: with the greatest and most supernatural things and occurrences embedded in everyday life to the point of imperceptibility.

The days of the tracts: he *believes* that he is talking about the very tangible urgent issues of the era, the state church and its problems, and that he is starting a conversation with them. But immediately and increasingly clearly, something uncanny dawns. It is like a ghost; he sees an invisible outline emerge, huge, ancient, nameless, undeniably growing out of it and beyond it, and seeping into his life: the vision of a building in front of which the Anglican church fades more and more into the broken traces of the outlines of a ruin, just a blueprint that got bogged down— a vision that none of his comrades in this fight perceives.

He starts talking to an invisible partner; not his bishops, not the Oxford academic theologians, not the youth around him who are deeply moved. Yes, he addresses them all—and how!—but at the same time and ultimately, they are only masks, transparencies, pretexts. He conjures up before them the Early Church, the Church of the Fathers, the greatest and richest memories of Christianity, the treasure of history from the treasuries of the libraries, unexcavated riches of a forgotten Tradition—but *behind* all this rises again an image, not sought, larger than life: the living Church, not on paper, not sidelined into being just a discussion group, not a mummy to be revived by human zeal, longing, and initiative but, rather, existing *herself* as something alive, demanding, and imperious. And soon she dominates the conversation, takes the lead, asks questions that cannot be avoided.

The arc of his conversion: the deathly fear *it could be true . . . Apologia*: the confrontation, the struggle of Jacob, which results in having a "limp" ever after. Nothing is more erroneous than trying to shift these processes to the level of the pure intellect and deductions or derivations from them. On the contrary. Oh, how important it is that in the end it is *not* theorems but Father Dominic, the simple, uneducated Italian and a missionary to the common people, who is decisive: a trembling challenge of the heart, not of the head, which God accepts and answers in person.[3]

His is a strange, strange conversion: less so a victory and conquest, but rather sublime *failure*, surrender, being taken captive. First came encountering the still invisible but already immensely real Church in the realm of thought, of history. Then she becomes more and more concrete, the experience more drastic, up to and including hierarchy, the temporal body—and what a temporal body!—the one given [at the time], terrible; *nevertheless*, for Newman the vision persists: "like the Cistercians who lived in huts while the construction [of their monastery] was in progress",[4] not *only* in the English diaspora!

A vision that retreats again and again behind a thousand fragmented realities: always just like the ring halves of the two separated royal children, which will be put together as a whole only when they find each other again.[5]

A vision, always a distant and dreamy view: the way one views stories, far, far away from the confident, massive, triumphant Church structure that his contemporaries and fellow believers see—Manning and Ward and so on—whose gaze is firmly and unwaveringly attached to the visible Roman glory.

Newman, however, sees the pilgrim Church, which is transforming and constantly being broken down and reshaped according to secret divine dictate and guidance, up until the threshold of eternity: "One day she will no longer exist."

---

[3] Father, now Blessed, Dominic Barberi, C.P., received Newman into the Church on October 9, 1845. Barberi was beatified in 1963. Also, he is the namesake of the character Father Domenico de Matre Dei in the novel *Loss and Gain*. See John Henry Newman, *Loss and Gain: The Story of a Convert*, rev. ed. (London: Longmans, Green, 1906), 423–24.

[4] Görres may be referring to the Cistercian Abbey of Netley in England, where "a group of monks from Beaulieu Abbey in The New Forest arrived in Netley a year later, in 1239, and probably lived in wooden huts while the Abbey was under construction." Tony Grant, "Netley Abbey and the Gothic", *Jane Austen's World* (blog), January 5, 2018, https://janeaustensworld.com/tag/cistercian-monastic-ruins/.

[5] Görres is referring to a version of the German folk song that begins, "There were two royal children", inspired, in part, by the Greek myth of Hero and Leander. "There Were Two Royal Children", in *German Poetry from the Beginnings to 1750*, ed. and trans. Ingrid Walsøe–Engel (New York: Continuum, 1992), 149.

This relationship is what makes him so inscrutable, suspicious, and eerie to his contemporaries.

Because he, the homeless man of Dublin, is *always* a "visionary": for the Romans, he is a strategic base; for Wiseman, an element of his cunning diplomatic tactics; for the Irish bishops, a piece of tangible, practical usefulness, locally and up to date, to be converted into pounds and shillings. But Newman, the lonely dreamer, sees in this impossible, self-defeating project the idea of the Catholic university; he intuitively sees in it the educational history of the Christian West.

The ecclesiastical era during his life is fearfully defensive, protective, self-segregating—a prohibition of contact with people of other faiths, a taboo against university studies for Catholic youth after the university itself has opened the gates. Only Newman himself sees the "vision" anew, sees the world of the mind—which has dissipated into nothing but hostile or indifferent separate islands—connected by a thousand bridges, according to a mighty plan, a heavenly Venice of mind and trust: *the tide will turn,* and his role is just to pave the way toward that invisible goal:

A voice in the desert, indescribably lonely—*Una Sancta: not* tremendously optimistic and hasty, like Ambrose de Lisle, spun *only* from the threads of the heart for the time being. Ambrose St. John as a "filial descendent" of Oxford, loved as a symbol as much as a person, as a promise, and as an inheritance at the same time. Newman: rationalism of the eighteenth and nineteenth centuries, pride of the human spirit, "positive theology"; everything destines him from the start, as it were, to be a pillar and tower of education, humanities, science—but here, too: how ambivalent is his face, how completely different from his background! A paradox—not banging about and robust, as with Chesterton —silent, though eerily storming like a second face: a silhouette against an endless starry sky of secrets.

A cycle of sermons about the presumptuousness of reason: the boundless resignation of this *man of knowledge,* this prince in the realm of knowledge—the inexpressibly deep insight that "in the beginning, it was not so": not only with the flesh, especially with the mind, with intelligence.

Always in exile, always an exile: who obediently, humbly, without pretense, out of necessity "settles down" in the land of exile—grateful, but not to be deceived.

Waiting: his sermons at St Mary's—in the nineteenth century! "Waiting." Feeling his way for the invisible world ever since he spent time as child in the fairy tales of *A Thousand and One Nights*; and people turned *him* into the herald of the sleekest ideal of a *gentleman*! Nobody knows how to draw the contradiction between the ideal in the foreground and the coming reality as sharply as he does.

A monk: actually a monk (poverty—celibacy—obedience—*stabilitas* [stability]—*nidulum* [nest])—genius of friendship and yet detached; never among his own kind; he had tasted just enough of this (Hurrell Froude!) to miss the real taste for the rest of his life.

"Angelic": a "messenger" from elsewhere—enchanted in the eyes of other people. He never really succeeds in "gaining a foothold", in taking root; all the disappointments are mysterious stamps and signs of this fate.

Outsider: always an *outsider*—too early, too late, longing for home without being able to find it, as only exiles can. The Church once more—an eternal vision, but how humbly he submits to the poor conditions of her reality. He is, in a sense, a spiritualist, if you will, but how much of a contrast to the Fraticelli (the Spiritual Franciscans): how gentle in criticism, how patient in waiting, how heroically docile in listening, how devoted to his so-much-inferior bishop! *O watchmen, how far along is the night?*[6]

Not a mystic: Bremond almost reproaches him for not being a "mystic"; oh no, much more likely, he too, trapped in the "rabbit hut"

---

[6] Görres may be suggesting a comparison between the bishops of Newman's era and the corrupt leaders of Israel during the time of Isaiah, as in Isaiah 56:10:

His watchmen are blind,
they are all without knowledge;
they are all dumb dogs,
they cannot bark;
dreaming, lying down,
loving to slumber.

of drought and darkness—also here in *exile* and on the move—
"*and I am far from home.*"[7]

Church Father of the Twentieth Century: explicitly the twentieth,
that is, a lighthouse in the rotation of the stars, strangely having
two faces—one is the familiar one that is already fading; the other
is only beginning to reveal itself and to shine like a rising star in
our great darkness.

Morning star: not the evening star of a cherished but sinking culture,
humanism, et cetera; rather, the morning star of a free, lonely,
believing spirituality.[8]

---

[7] John Henry Newman, "The Pillar of the Cloud", in *Verses on Various Occasions*
(London: Longmans, Green, 1905), 156.

[8] Görres expressed a somewhat similar sentiment in her journals in the 1950s: "Newman, too, had to descend into the 'cave', dwelling in obscurity, oblivion, inactivity, so as
to 'lay the ground' for the century to come, to be himself the foundation, cornerstone,
basis of a new future". Görres, *Broken Lights: Diaries and Letters 1951–1959*, trans. Barbara Waldstein-Wartburg (London: Burns and Oates, 1964), 119.

APPENDIX A

Timeline of the Life of John Henry Newman

1801	February 21	Born in Old Broad Street, London, the eldest of six children.
	April 9	Baptized in the Anglican Church of St Benet Fink.
1808	May 1	Starts school in Ealing.
1816	March 8	His father's bank closes.
	August–December	Newman's first conversion.
	December 14	Enters Trinity College, Oxford, as a commoner.
1817	June 8	Comes into residence at Trinity College.
	November 30	First Communion in the Church of England.
1818	May 18	Elected scholar of Trinity College.
	November 4	Together with his friend J. W. Bowden, publishes *St. Bartholomew's Eve*.
1820	December 5	B.A. degree.
1821	May	Letter to the editor of the *British Critic*, on the analogue difficulties in mathematics and religion.
	November 1	Newman's father is declared bankrupt.
1822	January 11	Newman decides to take orders in the Church of England.
	April 12	Elected fellow of Oriel College, Oxford.
	July 1	Whately gets Newman to assist him in preparing his articles on logic for the *Encyclopaedia Metropolitana*.
1824	May 31	Finishes his articles on Cicero.
	June 13	Ordained a deacon in Christ Church, Oxford.
	June 23	First sermon in Over Worton.
	July 3	Interested in becoming a foreign missionary.
	July 4	Starts pastoral work in St Clement's, Oxford.
	September 29	His father dies.

Chronology prepared by the International Centre of Newman Friends. Used with permission.

1825	March 26	Becomes vice principal of St Alban's Hall, Oxford, under R. Whately.
	May 29	Ordained priest of the Church of England in Christ Church, Oxford.
	August 15	Starts his article "Miracles".
	September 9	Starts his article "Apollonius".
1826	February 21	Resigns as curate of St Clement's and as vice principal of St Alban's in order to start as tutor of Oriel College after Easter.
	March 31	R. H. Froude, R. I. Wilberforce elected fellows of Oriel College.
	May	Opposition to Dr. Hampden.
	May 1	Decides to read the Fathers of the Church systematically.
	July 2	First university sermon.
1828	January 5	Youngest sister, Mary, dies.
	February 2	Becomes vicar of the University Church of St Mary the Virgin, Oxford. Hawkins is elected provost of Oriel College.
1829		First disagreements with Hawkins and Whately about the reelection of Peel in Parliament.
1830		Newman resigns his tutorship at Oriel College due to differences with Hawkins concerning principles.
1831		Newman gives more time to his duties as vicar of St Mary's.
1832		Concludes his first book, *The Arians of the Fourth Century*.
	December	Travels to the Mediterranean with R. H. Froude and his father, Archdeacon Froude.
1833	April 19	Returns to Sicily by himself and nearly dies of fever.
	June 16	Writes "Lead, Kindly Light" ("The Pillar of the Cloud") on the boat from Palermo to Marseilles.
	July 9	Returns to England.
	July 14	Keble preaches the Assize Sermon on "National Apostasy" at St Mary's, Oxford. This Newman always considered to be the beginning of the Oxford Movement.
	September 9	Publishes the first of the Tracts for the Times, which spread the ideas of the Oxford Movement.

		Newman wrote twenty-nine Tracts in all between this time and February 1841.
1834	March	First volume of *Parochial Sermons* published.
		Five more volumes published by the end of February 1842. Newman begins work on an edition of St. Dionysius of Alexandria—never published.
1835		*Parochial and Plain Sermons*, volume 2, published.
1836		*Parochial and Plain Sermons*, volume 3.
	February 28	Newman's closest friend, R. H. Froude, dies of consumption.
		Newman begins to have a church built in Littlemore.
	April 27	Marriage of his sister Jemima to J. Mozley.
	May 17	Newman's mother dies.
	September 27	Marriage of his sister Harriett to T. Mozley.
1838		Newman becomes editor of *British Critic*, a post that he holds until July 1841.
1839		*Parochial and Plain Sermons*, volume 4.
	Summer	Completes his reading on the Monophysites and is unsettled by what he reads.
1840	January	*Parochial and Plain Sermons*, volume 5.
1841	January 25	Tract 90 published.
	September	Newman moves to Littlemore, where he remains until February 1846.
1842		Letter to Robert Wilberforce about his doubts.
		Second essay on miracles, as preface to the translation of Fleury's *Church History*.
1843	Summer	Newman's doubt about the Church of England is greater than his doubt about the Roman Church.
	September 18	Newman resigns St Mary's.
	September 25	Preaches his last Anglican sermon, "The Parting of Friends", at Littlemore.
		Publishes sermons bearing on subjects of the day.
1844		Finishes the translation of the *Select Treatises of St. Athanasius* in controversy with the Arians.
	September	Newman's first friend in Oxford, John Bowden, dies.
1845	February 13	Ward is condemned by the university because of his tendency toward Rome. Newman's Tract 90 escapes condemnation. Newman begins writing his *Essay on the Development of Christian Doctrine*.

	October 3	Newman resigns from his fellowship at Oriel College.
1845 October 9		Newman is received into the "one true fold of Christ", the Roman Catholic Church, by Dominic Barberi in Littlemore.
	November 1	Confirmed by Dr. Wiseman in Oscott.
1846	February 22	Newman leaves Littlemore for Maryvale, Old Oscott, offered to him by Dr. Wiseman.
	September	Leaves England for Rome, where he will prepare for the priesthood.
1847	January	Decides to become an Oratorian.
	May 30	Ordination to the priesthood.
1848	February 1	Foundation of the first Oratory in England, Maryvale. The novel *Loss and Gain* published.
1849	February 2	Opens the Oratory in Alcester Street, Birmingham.
	June	Foundation of the Oratory in London.
	November	Publishes *Discourses to Mixed Congregations*.
1850	August 22	Pope Pius IX awards the honorary degree of divinity to Newman.
	Summer	Lectures in London: *Certain Difficulties Felt by Anglicans in Submitting to the Catholic Church*.
	October	Wiseman announces the restoration of the Catholic ecclesiastical hierarchy in England, which causes a strong reaction among Anglicans.
1851		Lectures in Birmingham: *On the Present Position of Catholics in England*. In the fifth lecture, he denounces the ex-priest Achilli and, as a consequence, is sued for libel.
	November 5	The long Achilli trial starts.
	November 12	Newman is nominated the first rector of the Catholic University of Ireland.
1852	January	Difficulties in the London Oratory.
	February	The Oratorians in Birmingham move from Alcester Street to Edgbaston.
	May 10	Newman delivers his first university lecture in Dublin, later in the year published together with others as *Discourses on the Nature and Scope of University Education*.
	July 13	Newman preaches "The Second Spring" for the first synod since the restoration of the Catholic hierarchy in England.

1853	January 31	The end of the Achilli trial: Newman loses it and is fined one hundred pounds.
	November 22	The Oratory Church in Birmingham opened.
1854	November 3	The Catholic University of Ireland opened in Dublin, with Newman as rector.
1855	Summer	Newman publishes his second novel, *Callista*.
	Autumn	The difficulties with the London Oratory result in a separation of both houses.
1856	May 1	The University Church in Dublin, dedicated to the apostles Peter and Paul, opened.
1857	March	Newman informs the Irish bishops that he wants to resign as rector of the university, effective November 14. They ask him to remain for another year as nonresiding rector.
	July	He publishes *Sermons Preached on Various Occasions*.
	August	Wiseman informs Newman that the supervision of a new translation of the Bible is to be entrusted to him. The plan, however, was not to be realized.
1859	March 21	Newman takes over as editor of the *Rambler* in order to prevent a censure by the hierarchy. After the July issue with his article "On Consulting the Faithful in Matters of Doctrine", he is requested to resign.
	May 2	Foundation of the Oratory School.
1864	January	Charles Kingsley states in an article that truth for its own sake had never been a virtue with the Catholic clergy and refers to Newman as having affirmed this. Newman starts a correspondence with Charles Kingsley.
	April–June	Newman's answer to Kingsley: *Apologia pro vita sua*.
1865	May–June	*The Dream of Gerontius*.
1866	January	*A Letter to Pusey on Occasion of His Recent Eirenicon* published.
	December 25	Propaganda Fide gives permission to found an Oratory at Oxford; a *post scriptum*, however, mentions that Newman should not take residence there. The Oxford plan is dropped.
1870	March 15	*An Essay in Aid of a Grammar of Assent*.

1871		Publication of *Sermons Preached before the University of Oxford* and *Essays Critical and Historical* (essays dating back to the Anglican period of Newman's life).
1872		Publication of *Discussions and Arguments* and *Historical Sketches*, volumes 1, 2, and 3.
1875	January 14	Publication of *A Letter to the Duke of Norfolk* in answer to Gladstone's accusation that Catholics are not loyal subjects of the state.
	May 24	Death of Ambrose St. John, Newman's most faithful friend.
1877		*Via Media*, volume 1, 3rd edition, with the important preface.
		Honorary fellow of Trinity College, Oxford.
1879	January 31	Newman receives through Cardinal Manning and Bishop Ullathorne the news that the cardinalate is offered to him.
	March 15	The cardinal secretary of state sends Newman the official announcement of his elevation to the cardinalate.
	April 16	Newman starts his journey to Rome.
	April 27	Newman has his first audience with Pope Leo XIII.
	May 12	Newman receives the "biglietto" of the cardinal secretary of state in which it is communicated to him that that same morning, during a secret consistory, he had been elevated to the cardinalate. Newman answers, giving his "Biglietto Speech".
	May 13	Newman goes to the Vatican in order to receive the cardinal's biretta from Pope Leo XIII.
	May 15	During the public consistory, Newman receives, together with the other newly nominated cardinals, the red hat.
	July 1	Newman returns to Birmingham.
1880	May	Newman visits Oxford and Trinity College again. Two sermons preached in the Church of St. Aloysius, Oxford, on Trinity Sunday, 1880, and printed for private circulation.
1881	February	*Select Treatises of St. Athanasius in Controversy with the Arians*, 2nd edition, published.

	June 26	Cardinal Newman preaches at the London Oratory.
1882		*Prologue to the "Andria" of Terence* (Latin).
		Notes of a Visit to the Russian Church, by William Palmer, selected and arranged by Cardinal Newman.
1883		*Via Media*, volume 2, 3rd edition.
1884	February	"What Is a Catholic Obliged to Believe Concerning the Inspiration of the Canonical Scripture? Being a Pro-script to an Article in the *Nineteenth Century Review*", in answer to Professor Healy (*Stray Essays*).
1885	October	"The Development of Religious Error" in the *Contemporary Review*.
1886		Newman's health begins to fail.
1889	December 25	Newman celebrates Holy Mass for the last time. According to Father Neville, when Newman found himself unable to celebrate Mass anymore, he learned by heart a Mass of the Blessed Virgin and a Mass of the Dead. One or the other of these Masses he repeated daily, whole or in part, and with the due ceremonies, for the chance that he hoped for, since his sight and strength varied: that, with the brighter sunlight of the spring, he might someday find himself in condition to say Mass once again. He was determined, he said, that no want of readiness on his part should cause him to miss the opportunity, should it occur. He continued this preparation until within two or three days of his death.
1890	August 10	He receives the last sacraments.
	August 11	Death of Newman.
	August 19	Newman is buried in Rednal near Birmingham, in the Oratorian graveyard.

APPENDIX B

Timeline of the Life of Ida Friederike Görres

1901	December 2	Born at Schloss Ronsperg in Bohemia; née Friederike Maria Anna von Coudenhove-Kalergi.[1] Father: Heinrich Count/Reichsgraf von Coudenhove-Kalergi (1856–1906), Diplomat in Japan and elsewhere; Mother: Mitsuko Countess von Coudenhove-Kalergi, née Aoyama (1871–1941); brothers Johann, Richard, Gerolf, Karl-Heinrich; sisters: Elsa, Olga.
	December 4	Baptized by Father Josef Mauritz.
1913–1916		Educated at Sacre Coeur School in Pressbaum near Vienna, Austria.
1916–1918		Educated at the Mary Ward School of the "Maria Ward Sisters", known in German as the "Englische Fräulein", in St. Pölten, Austria.
early 1920s		Encounter with the Catholic Youth Movement in Germany and the Neuland Movement in Austria.
1923–1925		Novitiate with the Mary Ward Sisters in St. Pölten, Austria.
1925–1931		Study of history at the University of Vienna, Austria and social work at the women's social college in Freiburg, Germany; leader for Girls and Young Women with Quickborn at Burg Rothenfels, Germany; contributor to the journal *Die Schildgenossen* at Burg Rothenfels.

---

[1] Prior to her marriage in 1935, Görres generally used only Coudenhove as her last name, not Coudenhove-Kalergi, and she did not use the indications of her noble lineage "von" or "Countess" with her name. Gerl-Falkovitz, email to the translator, July 26, 2022. For example, she published her essays and books prior to 1935 under the names "Ida Coudenhove" and "Ida Friederike Coudenhove." Ida was a shortened form of Friederike that she added to her name.

1932–1935		Ministry work for the Diocese of Meissen, Germany.
Easter 1935		Marriage to Carl-Josef Görres (1903–1973).
1935–1939		Lives in Chemnitz, Berlin, and Leipzig, Germany.
1939		Moves to Stuttgart-Degerloch, Germany.
1942		Begin periods of severe illness.
1944		Bombed out in 1944, moves to Kirchheim unter Teck, Germany.
1945		Moves back to Stuttgart-Degerloch.
1946		"Letter on the Church" in the journal *Frankfurter Hefte*
1950		Begin severe illness (brain spasms).
1962		Moves to Freiburg, Germany.
1969		Called to participate in the Synod of Würzburg, Germany.
1971	May 14	Collapses after delivering a speech at the Synod of Würzburg.
	May 15	Death in Frankfurt Marian Hospital.
	May 18	Burial at the Bergäcker Cemetery in Freiburg.
	May 19	Requiem Mass at the cathedral, Freiburg with eulogy delivered by Father Joseph Ratzinger (later Pope Benedict XVI).[2]

---

[2] Joseph Ratzinger, "Eulogy for Ida Friederike Görres", trans. Jennifer S. Bryson, *Logos* 23, no. 4 (Fall 2020): 148–55.

REGISTER OF PERSONS

Abbreviations

C.O.   Congregatio Oratorii (Congregation of the Oratory, Oratorian)

C.Ss.R. Congregatio Sanctissimi Redemptoris (Redemptorist)

O.F.M.   Ordo Fratrum Minorum (Order of Friars Minor, Franciscan)

O.S.B.   Ordo Sancti Benedicti (Order of Saint Benedict, Benedictine)

S.J.   Societas Iesu (Society of Jesus, Jesuit)

V.H.M. Visitation of Holy Mary (Sisters of the Visitation)

Acton, Lord John (1834–1902): English Catholic historian and politician.

Adam, Karl (1876–1966): German Catholic theologian.

Alfred (848/849–899): king of the West Saxons (871–ca. 886) and king of the Anglo-Saxons (ca. 886–899).

Arnold, Thomas (1795–1842): British educator and historian, Anglican clergyman.

Artz, Johannes (1936–2016): German scholar of Newman.

Asmussen, Hans (1898–1968): German Lutheran pastor, friend of Ida Görres.

This register of persons was added for the English edition of this book. The German edition contains several paragraph-length biographical notes about a few key English men and women in Newman's life who may not be familiar to German readers. Instead, for this English edition, I have prepared short biographical notes on most of the individuals mentioned in this book—not only some of the English figures but also many of the Germans and Austrians who may not be familiar to modern English readers. In the draft manuscript for this book, Görres often refers to individuals only by last name, occasionally only by first name. I have done my best to identify the full names.—Trans.

Barberi, Blessed Dominic, C.P. (1792–1849): Italian Passionist priest, missionary to England; he received Newman into the Church.

Becker, Werner, C.O. (1904–1981): German Catholic priest, Oratorian, scholar of Newman.

Bellasis, Edward (1800–1873): English Catholic convert involved in the Oxford Movement.

Benedict XVI (1927–2022): né Joseph Ratzinger (1927–2022), German priest, cardinal, pope (2005–2013), pope emeritus (2013–2022), correspondent of Ida Görres; he gave the eulogy at her funeral.

Benson, Edward Frederic (1867–1940): British author; wrote a book on Victorian England.

Berdyaev, Nikolai (1874–1948): Russian philosopher, theologian.

Bergengruen, Werner (1892–1964): German born in Estonia, Catholic convert, poet, novelist, friend of Ida Görres.

Biemer, Günter (1929–2019): German scholar of Newman, founder of the German Newman Society, an editor of *Internationale Cardinal-Newman-Studien*.

Blennerhassett, Lady Charlotte (1843–1917): née Countess Charlotte Julia von Leyden, German Catholic writer, author of a 1904 biography of Newman in German.

Bodelschwingh, Friedrich von (1831–1910): German Protestant theologian and politician; established charitable foundations.

Borromeo, Saint Charles (1538–1584): Italian archbishop of Milan, cardinal, a leading figure in the Counter-Reformation.

Bowden, John William (1798–1844): English Anglican, friend of Newman; involved in the Tractarian Movement.

Brémond, Henri (1865–1933): French Catholic priest, author of a book on the psychology of Newman.

Brentano, Clemens (1778–1842): German poet and novelist of the German Romantic period.

Breucha, Hermann (1902–1972): German Catholic parish priest and friend of Ida Görres after World War II.

Brown, Thomas Joseph, O.S.B. (1796–1880): English Catholic, bishop of Newport and Menevia (1850–1880).

Bunsen, Christian Karl Josias von (1791–1860): German diplomat; involved in the king of Prussia's effort to establish a Prusso-Anglican bishopric in Jerusalem, to which Newman objected.

Caswall, Edward, C.O. (1814–1878): English Catholic convert, Oratorian priest, friend of Newman.

Church, Richard William (aka Dean) (1815–1890): English Anglican, friend of Newman; involved in the Tractarian Movement.

Chardin, Teilhard de, S.J. (1881–1955): French Jesuit priest, controversial Catholic intellectual.

Cisneros, Francisco Jiménez de, O.F.M. (1436–1517): Spanish cardinal, archbishop of Toledo (1495–1517), religious reformer.

Coleridge, Samuel Taylor (1772–1834): English poet in the Romantic movement.

Combes, André (1899–1969): French Catholic priest; corresponded with Görres regarding his study of Saint Thérèse of Lisieux.

Copeland, William John (1804–1885): English Anglican clergyman, friend of Newman.

Coudenhove-Kalergi, Gerolf Josef Benedikt Graf von (1896–1978): brother of Ida Görres, lawyer, scholar of Japanese studies.

Coudenhove-Kalergi, Johann Graf von (1893–1965): brother of Ida Görres.

Coudenhove-Kalergi, Elisabeth Maria Anna Gräfin von (1898–1936): sister of Ida Görres; known as Elsa.

Coudenhove-Kalergi, Heinrich Reichsgraf von (1856–1906): father of Ida Görres, Habsburg empire diplomat.

Coudenhove-Kalergi, Karl Heinrich Graf von (1903–1987): brother of Ida Görres.

Coudenhove-Kalergi, Mitsuko Maria Thekla Gräfin von (1871 Japan–1941 Austria): née Aoyama, mother of Ida Görres.

Coudenhove-Kalergi, Olga Marietta Henriette Maria Gräfin von (1900–1976): sister of Ida Görres.

Coudenhove-Kalergi, Richard Nikolaus Graf von (1894–1972): brother of Ida Görres, founder of the Pan-Europa Movement.

Cullen, Paul (1803–1878): Irish Catholic, archbishop of Dublin (1852–1878); cardinal (1866–1878).

Dalgairns, John (1818–1876): English Catholic convert, priest, friend of Newman.

Dark, Sidney (1874–1947): English journalist, author; wrote a short biography of Newman.

de Vere, Aubrey (1814–1902): Irish Catholic convert, poet, writer, correspondent of Newman.

Dodsworth, William (1789–1861): English, involved in the Tractarian Movement, opponent of liberalism, convert to Catholicism, correspondent of Newman.

Döllinger, Johann Joseph Ignaz (1799–1890): German Catholic priest; met Newman, excommunicated in 1871.

Domenico de Mater Dei: Catholic priest known as Father Domenico in Newman's novel *Loss and Gain*.

Dreves, Guido Maria, S.J. (1854–1909): German Catholic priest; translated some of Newman's sermons into German.

Droste-Hülshoff, Annette von (1797–1848): German Catholic poet, novelist, composer.

Duke of Norfolk, aka Henry Fitzalan-Howard, fifteenth Duke of Norfolk (1847–1917): English Catholic, addressee of Newman's "Letter to the Duke of Norfolk" in 1875.

Edward IV (1442–1483): king of England (1461–1470, 1471–1483).

Edward VI (1537–1553): king of England and Ireland (1547–1553), son of King Henry VIII.

Eichendorff, Joseph Freiherr von (1788–1857): German writer of the German Romantic period.

Faber, Frederick William, C.O. (1814–1863): English Catholic convert, Oratorian priest, colleague of Newman.

Findl-Ludescher, Anna (b. 1965): Austrian author of a dissertation (later published as a book) about Ida Friederike Görres.

Fischer, Josepha (1934–2021): German friend of Ida Görres.

Friedrich, Caspar David (1774–1840): German painter of the Romantic era.

Frederick William IV (1795–1861): king of Prussia (1840–1861); sought to establish a Prusso-Anglican bishopric in Jerusalem, to which Newman objected.

Fries, Heinrich (1911–1998): German Catholic theologian.

Froude, Catherine: née Holdsworth, English, wife of William Froude.

Froude, Isy (short for Eliza) (1839–1931): English, daughter of William Froude, Catholic convert; married Anatole von Hügel in 1880.

Froude, James Anthony (1818–1894): English historian, novelist, magazine editor, brother of Richard Hurrell and William Froude.

Froude, Richard Hurrell (1803–1836): English Anglican, leader in the Oxford Movement, friend of Newman, brother of James Anthony and William Froude.

Froude, William (1810–1879): English, friend of Newman, brother of James Anthony and Richard Hurrell Froude.

Fry, Elizabeth (1780–1845): English social reformer, Quaker.

Gallitzin, Adelheid Amalie (1748–1806): German princess, intellectual salon figure.

Garibaldi, Giuseppe (1807–1882): Italian general, politician.

Gautier, Lucien Marcelin (1850–1924): Swiss Protestant theologian.

Gerl-Falkovitz, Hanna-Barbara (1945–): German philosopher, professor, scholar of Romano Guardini, Edith Stein, and Ida Friederike Görres.

Giberne, Maria Pia, V.H.M. (1802–1885): née Maria Rosina Giberne, French-English convert to Catholicism, artist, entered convent of Sisters of the Visitation in Autun, France, friend of Newman.

Gladstone, William Ewart (1809–1898): British statesman, liberal politician.

Glaser-Fürst, Maria Theresia (1917–2004): German, administrator of the estate of Father Hermann Breucha.

Goethe, Johann Wolfgang (1749–1832): German novelist, poet, playwright, Romantic era.

Goldsmith, Oliver (1728–1774): Anglo-Irish novelist, playwright, poet.

Gordan, Paulus, O.S.B. (1912–1999): né Günther Gordan, German Jewish Catholic convert, priest at the Benedictine archabbey of Beuron, Germany, friend of Ida Görres.

Gordon, Joseph, C.O. (1813–1853): né John Gordon, English Catholic convert.

Gordon, William Philip, C.O. (1827–1900): Catholic priest, London Oratory, correspondent of Newman; known as Philip Gordon.

Görres, Albert (1918–1996): brother of Carl-Josef Görres, brother-in-law of Ida Görres, husband of Silvia Görres, Catholic psychologist.

Görres, Carl-Josef (1903–1973): husband of Ida Görres, brother of Albert Görres, engineer.

Görres, Silvia (1925–2015): née Volkart, wife of Albert Görres, sister-in-law of Ida Görres.

Gray, Dorian: fictional character in the novel *The Picture of Dorian Gray* (1890) by Oscar Wilde; Gray is a Victorian man who allows his selfishness and hedonistic tendencies to corrupt his character over time.

Gregory XVI (1831–1846), né Bartolomeo Alberto Cappellari, Italian, pope (1831–1846)

Grosche, Robert (1888–1967): German Catholic theologian, priest.

Guardini, Romano (1885–1968): German Catholic theologian, priest, key figure in the Catholic Youth Movement in Germany.

Gulde, Wilhelm (1903–1998): German scholar of Newman.

Günther, Anton (1783–1863): Austrian Catholic philosopher and theologian, priest.

Gurwood, John (1788–1845): British career officer in the British army, author.

Gwynn, Denis (1893–1973): Irish writer, scholar of modern history, editor of the *Dublin Review*.

Haecker, Theodor (1879–1945): German Catholic convert, translator of works by Newman into German.

Harper, Gordon Huntington (1904–1934): American, wrote his dissertation on the Froude family in the Oxford Movement.

Herwegen, Ildefons, O.S.B. (1874–1946): German Catholic priest, abbot of the Benedictine Maria Laach Abbey, Germany.

Hirscher, Johann Baptist von (1788–1865): German Catholic theologian, priest.

Hofbauer, Saint Clement Maria, C.Ss.R. (1751–1820): Austrian Catholic priest, particularly influential among Catholics in Vienna.

Holmes, Mary (1815–1878): English Catholic convert, friend of Newman.

Hume, David (1711–1776): Scottish Enlightenment philosopher.

Hutton, Arthur Wollaston (1848–1912): English Catholic convert, Oratorian (1876–1883); later left the Catholic faith but on his deathbed asked to be received back into the Church.

Irvine, J. W. (d. 1906): English clergymen, rector of St Mary the Virgin at the Walls, Colchester, UK, later at St Mary's vicarage in Littlemore; appointed an honorary canon in 1890.[1]

Julian the Apostate (fourth century), Roman emperor (361–363), apostate from Christianity, promoter of Neoplatonic philosophy.

Kahlefeld, Heinrich, C.O. (1903–1980): German Catholic priest, theologian, friend of Ida Görres.

Karrer, Otto (1888–1976): German (later Swiss) Catholic priest, early scholar of Newman in Germany.

Keats, John (1795–1821): English Romantic-era poet.

Keble, John (1792–1866): English Anglican, a leader of the Oxford Movement, friend of Newman.

Ken, Thomas (1637–1711): English Anglican bishop.

Ketteler, Wilhelm von (1811–1877): German Catholic, bishop of Mainz (1850–1877); known for his social teachings.

Kierkegaard, Søren (1813–1855): Danish philosopher, poet, religious author.

Klaiber, Beatrix (1929–2020): German, executor of the estate of Ida Görres in Freiburg, Germany, responsible for unpublished papers Görres left behind.[2]

Kleinert, Michael (b. 1965): German Catholic priest; wrote a dissertation (later published as a book) on Ida Görres.

Knoepfler, Maria (1881–1927): German Catholic, translator of works by Newman into German.

Kolping, Blessed Adolph (1813–1865): German Catholic priest; initiated the organization of social aid for workers.

Kolb, Annette (1870–1967): German author, Catholic.

Kopisch, August (1799–1853): German inventor, artist, writer.

---

[1] "Obituaries," *Gentleman's Magazine* 301 (July–December 1906), 220. He is identified only as "Canon Irvine" in this volume. I believe this refers to J. W. Irvine.

[2] Some of the unpublished papers Görres left with Beatrix Klaiber are now in the Archive of the Archdiocese of Freiburg, Germany.

Kuehnelt-Leddihn, Erik von (1909–1999): Austrian political author, friend of Ida Görres.

Lacordaire, Jean-Baptiste Henri, O.P. (1802–1861): French Catholic priest, intellectual, political activist; reestablished the Dominican Order in France after the French Revolution.

Lake, William (1817–1897): English Anglican clergyman, dean of Durham Cathedral, UK.

Lamennais, Félicité Robert de (1782–1854): French Catholic priest, liberal Catholic intellectual.

Laros, Matthias (1882–1965): German Catholic priest, editor of a multivolume set of selected works of Newman in German.

Laud, William (1573–1645): English Anglican bishop.

le Fort, Gertrud von (1876–1971): German Catholic convert, writer, poet.

Leo XII (1760–1829): né Annibale Francesco Clemente Melchiorre Girolamo Nicola della Genga, Italian pope (1823–1829).

Leo XIII (1810–1903): né Vincenzo Gioacchino Raffaele Luigi Pecci, Italian pope (1878–1903).

Lessing, Gotthold Ephraim (1729–1781): German Enlightenment philosopher, playwright.

Lippert, Peter, S.J. (1879–1936): German Catholic priest; involved in the Catholic revival in Germany in the 1920s.

Lisle, Ambrose de (1809–1878): English Catholic convert.

Lutz, Joseph A.: German biographer of Newman in 1948.

Manning, Henry Edward (1808–1892): English Catholic convert, archbishop of Westminster (1865–1892), cardinal.

Maria Pia, Sister: *See* Maria Rosina Giberne.

Mauritz, Josef (dates unknown): Catholic priest in Bohemia who baptized Ida Görres in Ronsperg, Bohemia.

Mayers, Walter (1790–1828): English, Evangelical clergyman, schoolteacher of Newman, brother-in-law of Maria Rosina Giberne.

Meynell, Wilfrid (1852–1948): British newspaper publisher, author, Catholic convert; wrote biographies of Newman and Cardinal Manning.

Milner, Joseph (1852–1948): English Catholic convert, newspaper writer.

Möhler, Johann Adam (1796–1838): German Catholic theologian, Church historian.

Mörike, Eduard Friedrich (1804–1875): German Lutheran pastor, Romantic-era author.

Mozley, Anne (1809–1891): English, editor of Newman's letters and diaries, sister-in-law of Newman's sister Jemima.

Mozley, Thomas (1806–1893): English Anglican clergyman, involved in the Oxford Movement, brother-in-law of Newman.

Müller, Adam Heinrich (1779–1829): German, Romantic-era author, political theorist.

Münster, Maria Birgitta zu, O.S.B. (1908–1988): née Ursula zu Münster, German Catholic convert, nun at the Abbey of Saint Walburga in Eichstätt, Germany, friend of Ida Görres; translated into German a selection of Newman's works on St Mary and work by Réginald Garrigou-Lagrange.

Neville, William Paine, C.O. (1824–1905): English, Catholic convert, priest, aide to Newman at the Oratory in Birmingham, Newman's literary executor.

Newman, Harriett (1803–1852): English, sister of John Henry Newman, wife of Thomas Mozley.

Newman, Jemima (1772–1836): née Jemima Fourdrinier, English, mother of John Henry Newman.

Newman, Jemima Charlotte (1807–1879): English, sister of John Henry Newman, wife of John Mozley.

Newman, Mary (1809–1828): English, sister of John Henry Newman.

Nigg, Walter (1903–1988): Swiss Reformed theologian, scholar of hagiography, friend of Ida Görres.

O'Connell, Daniel (1775–1847): Irish politician, advocate for the interests of Catholics.

Ollard, Sidney L. (1875–1949): Anglican priest, author of a short history of the Oxford Movement.

Overbeck, Johann Friedrich (1789–1869): German painter.

Ozanam, Blessed Antoine Frédéric (1813–1853): French scholar, lawyer, a co-founder of the charitable Society of Saint Vincent de Paul.

Palmer, William (1803–1885): English Anglican, lay theologian, early supporter of (but later distant from) the Oxford Movement.

Pascal, Blaise (1623–1662): French Catholic mathematician, philosopher theologian.

Pattison, Mark (1813–1884): English Anglican clergyman.

Pecham, Sir Robert (d. 1569): English, buried in the Church of San Gregorio in Rome;[3] one account of an inscription there reads: "Here lies Robert Pecham, an English Catholic, who, after the disruption of England and the Church, quitted his country, unable to endure life there without the Church, and who, coming to Rome, died, unable to endure life here without his country."[4]

Pius VII (1742–1823): né Barnaba Niccolò Maria Luigi Chiaramonti, Italian pope (1800–1823).

Pius IX (1792–1878): né Giovanni Maria Mastai-Ferretti, Italian pope (1846–1878).

Poole, Imelda (1815–1881): née Maria Spencer Ruscombe Poole, English Catholic convert, friend of Newman; entered a convent of a third-order English Dominican Congregation of St Catherine of Siena in Clifton (which later relocated to Stone), England.

Pugin, Augustus (1812–1852): English architect of Gothic Revival style.

---

[3] Florens Deuchler, Jeffrey Hoffeld, and Helmut Nickel, *The Cloisters Apocalypse: Commentaries on an Early Fourteenth-Century Manuscript* (New York: Metropolitan Museum of Art, 1971), 2:31.

[4] Bernard Holland, "Patriotism", *Dublin Review* 162, no. 325 (April–June 1918): 213.

Purcell, Edmund Sheridan (1824?–1899): English, author of a book about Cardinal Manning.

Pusey, Edward (1800–1882): English Anglican, a leader in the Oxford Movement, friend of Newman.

Ratzinger, Joseph / Benedict XVI (1927–2022): German, pope (2005–2013), pope emeritus (2013–2022), correspondent with Ida Görres; gave the eulogy at her funeral.

Reding, Charles: the lead character in John Henry Newman's semi-autobiographical novel *Loss and Gain*, thought to be fashioned after Newman himself.

Rickards, Samuel (1796–1865): English Anglican clergyman, opponent of the Oxford Movement.

Rose, Hugh James (1795–1838): English Anglican clergyman.

Rosenberg, Alfons (1902–1985): German Jewish convert to Catholicism, scholar, friend of Ida Görres.

Rosmini, Blessed Antonio (1797–1855): Italian Catholic priest; his book *Of the Five Wounds of the Church* was placed on the *Index Librorum Prohibitorum* (*Index of Prohibited Books*) in 1849.

Ryder, Henry Ignatius Dudley, C.O. (1837–1907): English Catholic priest of the Birmingham Oratory.

Sailer, Johann Michael, S.J. (1751–1832): German Catholic priest, bishop (1822–1832), promoter of the Catholic Enlightenment.

Sauer: It is unclear which Sauer Görres is referring to. Perhaps Joseph Sauer (1803–1868): German Catholic priest involved with several Catholic newspapers.

Schlegel, Friedrich von (1772–1829): German intellectual of the early Romantic era.

Schmidlin, Josef (1876–1944): German Catholic priest, author of a multivolume history of the popes.

Schneider, Reinhold (1903–1958): German Catholic author.

Scott, Sir Walter (1771–1832): Scottish novelist and poet.

Shairp, John Campbell (1819–1885): Scottish Presbyterian, had an interest in the Oxford Movement but remained Protestant.

Shelley, Percy Bysshe (1792–1822): English Romantic-era poet.

Siebenrock, Roman (b. 1957): German Catholic scholar of Newman.

Siewerth, Gustav (1903–1963): German Catholic philosopher, scholar of Aquinas and Thomist philosophy, friend of Ida Görres.

Simon, Paul (1882–1946): German Catholic priest, theologian; involved in the 1946 conference on Newman in Cologne, Germany.

Spülbeck, Otto (1904–1970): German Catholic priest, bishop of Meissen in the German Democratic Republic (1955–1977), friend of Ida Görres.

Stein, Edith (1891–1942): German Jewish Catholic convert, Carmelite nun, philosopher, translator of some works by Newman into German; also known as Saint Teresa Benedicta of the Cross.

St. John, Ambrose, C.O. (1815–1875): English Catholic convert, priest, friend of Newman.

Stolberg, Friedrich Graf zu (1750–1819): German poet of the early Romantic era.

Strachey, Lytton (1880–1932): English writer, author of biographies of prominent Victorian-era figures.

Sugg, Joyce (1923–2008): English, scholar of Newman, Catholic convert from Anglicanism, author of a book about Newman's relationship with women.

Teilhard de Chardin, Pierre, S.J. (1881–1955): French Jesuit priest, controversial Catholic intellectual.

Teresa Benedicta of the Cross, Saint: *See* Stein, Edith.

Theis, Nicolas (1911–1985): Catholic priest, scholar of Newman, born in Germany; ordained and lived in Luxembourg.

Thérèse of Lisieux, Saint (1873–1897): French Carmelite nun, subject of Görres' most famous work, *The Hidden Face*.

Thorvaldsen, Bertel (1770–1844): Danish-Icelandic sculptor.

Tristram, Henry, C.O. (d. 1955): English Catholic priest, Birmingham Oratory, editor of a book on Newman.

Ullathorne, William, O.S.B. (1806–1889): English Catholic, bishop of Birmingham (1850–1888).

Undset, Sigrid (1882–1949): Norwegian Catholic convert, novelist.

Valentine, Saint (dates unknown): martyr whose remains were found in the catacombs and given to the Oratory in Birmingham by Pope Pius IX.[5]

Veith, Johann Emanuel (1787–1876): Austrian Catholic priest, doctor, poet.

Victoria, Queen (1819–1901): English, queen of the United Kingdom of Great Britain and Ireland (1837–1901).

Waldmüller, Ferdinand Georg (1793–1865): Austrian painter and writer.

Ward, Mary Venerable (1585–1645): English Catholic nun, founder of two women's orders; Ida Görres wrote a book about her, was educated at a school run by Mary Ward Sisters, and for two years was a novice in an order of nuns founded by her.

Ward, Wilfrid Philip (1856–1916): English Catholic, author of a biography of Newman, son of W. G. Ward.

Ward, William George (1812–1882): English Catholic convert, in Newman's circles, father of W. P. Ward.

Weiger, Josef (1883–1966): German Catholic priest, early scholar of Newman in Germany.

Werner, Zacharias (1768–1823): German Catholic convert, priest, writer, influential preacher in Vienna.

---

[5] Henry Tristram, *Cardinal Newman and the Church of the Birmingham Oratory* (Gloucester, UK: British Publishing Company, 1934), 58. (This Saint Valentine is not the same as the famous Saint Valentine, whose feast is February 14.)

Whateley, Richard (1787–1863): Irish, Church of Ireland Anglican and archbishop of Dublin.

Wilberforce, Henry (1807–1873): English Catholic convert; involved in the Tractarian Movement, writer.

Willam, Franz Michel (1894–1981): Austrian Catholic priest, Newman scholar.

Williams, Isaac (1802–1865): Welsh, Anglican clergyman; involved in the Tractarian Movement.

Wiseman, Nicholas (1802–1865): Irish Catholic priest, bishop (1840–1865), cardinal (1850–1865).

Wood, Samuel Francis (1809–1843): English, friend of Newman; studied at Oxford.

Wooten, Frances (d. 1876): English, wife of a doctor at Oxford in the Tractarian Movement, Catholic convert received into the Church by Newman; as a widow, she became the housemother, the "Dame", for the boys' boarding school run by the Oratory in Birmingham.[6]

Wordsworth, William (1770–1850): English poet, Romantic era.

Ximenes: *See* Cisneros, Francisco Jiménez de.

---

[6] See Edmund Campion, "Newman's Female Friends: Celebrating John Henry Newman's Canonisation", *Australian Catholic Historical Society Journal* 40 (2019), 145; James Tolhurst, introduction to John Henry Newman, *Discussions and Arguments on Various Subjects* (Leominster, Herefordshire, UK: Gracewing, 2004), xlix.

BIBLIOGRAPHY

Aquinas, Thomas. *The Summa Theologiæ of St. Thomas Aquinas*. Translated by the Fathers of the English Dominican Province. 2nd edition. London: Burns Oates and Washbourne, 1920. New Advent. https://www.newadvent.org/summa/.

Arnold, Claus. "Newman's Reception in Germany: From Döllinger to Ratzinger". *Newman Studies Journal* 18, no. 1 (2021): 5–23.

Batlogg, Andreas. "Zwischen Pietät und Revolution: Neuentdeckung von Ida Friederike Görres?" *Stimmen der Zeit* 219, no. 12 (2001): 857–60.

Becker, Werner. "Chronologie von Übersetzungen der Werke Newmans". In *Newman Studien* 1, edited by Heinrich Fries and Werner Becker, 295–300. Nuremberg: Glock und Lutz, 1948.

Benson, Edward Frederic. *As We Were: A Victorian Peep Show*. London: Longmans, Green, 1930.

Biemer, Günter. Letter to Hanna-Barbara Gerl-Falkovitz. June 19, 2002. Gerl-Falkovitz Private Archive, Erlangen, Germany.

Blehl, Vincent Ferrer. *Pilgrim Journey: John Henry Newman 1801–1845*. London: Burns and Oates, 2001.

Blennerhassett, Charlotte. *John Henry Kardinal Newman: Ein Beitrag zur religiösen Entwicklungsgeschichte der Gegenwart*. Berlin: Verlag Gebrüder Paetel, 1904.

Bremond, Henri. *The Mystery of Newman*. Translated by H. C. Corrance. London: Williams and Norgate, 1907.

Bremond, Henri. *Newman: Essai de biographie psychologique*. Paris: Bloud, 1906.

Breucha, Hermann. *Hoffnung auf das Ewige: Ausgewählte Predigten.* Weissenhorn, Germany: Konrad Verlag, 1983.

Breucha, Hermann. "Newman als Prediger." In *Newman Studien 1.* Edited by Heinrich Fries and Werner Becker, 157–77. Nuremberg, Germany: Glock und Lutz, 1948.

Burgbrief Burg Rothenfels 3 (1980). [This issue is a report about a conference on Ida Friederike Görres, held in May 1980 at Burg Rothenfels, Germany.]

Campion, Edmund. "Newman's Female Friends: Celebrating John Henry Newman's Canonisation". *Australian Catholic Historical Society Journal* 40 (2019): 144–54.

Church, Richard W. *The Oxford Movement: Twelve Years, 1833–1845.* London: Macmillan, 1891.

Dark, Sidney. *Newman.* Vol. 36 of Great Lives. London: Duckworth, 1934.

Deuchler, Florens, Jeffrey Hoffeld, and Helmut Nickel. *The Cloisters Apocalypse: Commentaries on an Early Fourteenth-Century Manuscript.* Vol. 2. New York: Metropolitan Museum of Art, 1971.

Eliot, T. S. "Weinachtspredigt des Thomas Beckett". Translated by Ida Friederike Görres. *Werkblätter. Bundesrundbrief des Quickborn* 1, no. 12 (December 1948).

Findl-Ludescher, Anna. *"Stützen kann nur, was widersteht": Ida Friederike Görres—ihr Leben und ihre Kirchenschriften.* Salzburger Theologische Studien 9. Innsbruck, Austria: Tyrolia, 1999.

Fries, Heinrich. *Die Religionsphilosophie Newmans.* Stuttgart, Germany: Schwabenverlag, 1948.

Gerl-Falkovitz, Hanna-Barbara. Email to the translator. July 26, 2022.

———. "Die Newman-Rezeption in den 20er Jahren in Deutschland: Edith Stein im Umkreis von Maria Knoepfler, Romano Guardini und Erich Przywara". *Communio* 5 (2001): 434–49.

————. "Görres, Ida Friederike". In *Baden-Württembergische Biographien*, edited by B. Ottnad, 2:161–63. Stuttgart: Kohlhammer, 1999.

————. " 'Only the Lover Discerns': A Brief Introduction to Ida Friederike Görres". Translated by Jennifer S. Bryson. *Logos* 23, no. 4 (September 9, 2020): 117–22.

————. "Zwischen den Zeiten: Ida Friederike Görres (1901–1971)". In *Freundinnen: Christliche Frauen aus zwei Jahrtausenden*, 121–32. Munich: Pfeiffer, 1994.

Glaser-Fürst, Maria. *Franziska Werfer 1906–1985: Die erste katholische Theologin und Religionslehrerin im Dienst der Kirche in der Diözese Rottenburg. Zeugnis eines Lebens aus Glaube, Wahrheit, Liebe.* Weißenhorn, Germany: Konrad Verlag, 2001.

————. Letter to Hanna Barbara Gerl-Falkovitz, March 6, 2002. Gerl-Falkovitz Private Archive, Erlangen, Germany.

Goethe, Johann Wolfgang von. *103 Great Poems: A Dual-Language Book = 103 Meistergedichte.* Translated and edited by Stanley Applebaum. Mineola, N.Y.: Dover Publications, 1999.

————. *Elective Affinities.* Translated by David Constantine. Oxford, UK: Oxford University Press, 1994.

————. *Faust. A Tragedy: In a Modern Translation.* Translated by Alice Raphael. New York: Heritage Press, 1932.

————. "The Sorcerer's Apprentice". In *103 Great Poems: A Dual Language Book = 103 Meistergedichte.*

————. *Die Wahlverwandtschaften: Ein Roman.* Munich: Anaconda Verlag, 2008. First published 1809 by Cotta (Tübingen).

Görres, Carl-Josef. Letter to Klara and Hilde Neles. November 20, 1948. Gerl-Falkovitz Private Archive, Erlangen, Germany.

Görres, Ida Friederike. *Aus der Welt der Heiligen.* Frankfurt am Main: Josef Knecht, 1955.

————. *Bread Grows in Winter.* Translated by Jennifer S. Bryson. San Francisco: Ignatius Press, forthcoming.

————. "Brief über die Kirche". *Frankfurter Hefte* 1, no. 8 (November 1946): 716–33. [New, full translation into English by Bryson completed; forthcoming.]

————. *Broken Lights: Diaries and Letters 1951–1959.* Translated by Barbara Waldstein-Wartburg. London: Burns and Oates, 1964.

————. *The Church in the Flesh.* Translated by Jennifer S. Bryson. Providence: Cluny Media, 2023.

————. "Demolition Troops in the Church". In *Bread Grows in Winter.* Translated by Jennifer S. Bryson. San Francisco: Ignatius Press, forthcoming.

————. *Gedichte.* Edited and with an introduction by Hanna-Barbara Gerl-Falkovitz. 3rd ed. Dresden: Thelem, 2008.

————. *The Hidden Face: A Study of St. Thérèse of Lisieux.* Translated by Richard Winston and Clara Winston. San Francisco: Ignatius Press, 2003. First published 1959 by Burns and Oates (London).

————. *John Henry Newman—der Geopferte: ein anderer Blick auf ein großes Leben.* Edited by Hanna-Barbara Gerl-Falkovitz. Vallendar-Schönstatt, Germany: Patris Verlag, 2015. First published 2004 as *Der Geopferte: Ein anderer Blick auf John Henry Newman.*

————., ed. *Kristall: Bild und Ebenbild. Werkheft für Mädchen.* Frankfurt am Main: Josef Knecht, 1947. First edition 1935, edited by Ida Friederike Coudenhove.

————. *Die leibhaftige Kirche: Gespräch unter Laien.* Frankfurt am Main: J. Knecht Verlag, 1950.

————. "A Letter on the Church (1946)". Translated by Ida Friederike Görres. *Dublin Review* 223 (Winter 1949): 71–89.

————. Letter to Annalies Stiglocher. September 7, 1949. Archive of the Archdiocese of Freiburg im Breisgau, Germany.

————. Letter to Hermann Stenger. March 29, 1955. [Held privately by Herman Stenger at the time Gerl-Falkovitz published this book. Stenger died in 2016. Location of the letter as of 2022 is unknown.]

————. *Mary Ward*. Translated by Elise Codd. London: Longmans, Green, 1939.

————. *Nocturnen: Tagebuch und Aufzeichnungen*. Frankfurt am Main: Knecht, 1949.

————. *On Marriage and on Being Single*. Translated by Jennifer S. Bryson. San Francisco: Ignatius Press, forthcoming.

————. "Reinhold Schneiders 'Unglaube' oder die negative Mystik". In *Der göttliche Bettler*, 122–29. Frankfurt am Main: Josef Knecht, 1959. [Translation into English by Bryson completed; forthcoming.]

————. *Das Senfkorn von Lisieux: Das verborgene Antlitz: Neue Deutungen*. 8th ed. Freiburg im Breisgau: Herder, 1958.

————. *Eine Studie über Therese von Lisieux:* Freiburg im Breisgau: Herder, 1943.

————. "Trusting the Church". In *Bread Grows in Winter*. Translated by Jennifer S. Bryson. Forthcoming. San Francisco: Ignatius Press, forthcoming.

————. "Über J. H. Newman." In *Aus der Welt der Heiligen*, 54–62. Frankfurt am Main: Josef Knecht, 1955. [This essay is included in this volume as chapter 11.]

————. *Das verborgene Antlitz. Eine Studie über Therese von Lisieux*. 2nd ed. Freiburg im Breisgau, Germany: Herder, 1946.

————. *Der verborgene Schatz*. Frankfurt am Main: Josef Knecht, 1949.

————. "Vertrauen zur Kirche." In *Winter Wächst das Brot*, 103–31. Einsiedeln, Switzerland: Johannes Verlag, 1970.

————. *Von Ehe und von Einsamkeit*. Donauworth, Germany: Auer Verlag, 1949.

————. "Vom Optimismus Zur Hoffnung." In *Aus christlichem Denken in der Neuheit der Tage*, edited by Karl Rudolf, 267–79. Freiburg im Breisgau, Germany and Vienna, Austria: Verlag Herder, 1941. [Translation into English by Bryson completed; forthcoming.]

————. *Was Ehe auf immer bindet: Unsystematische Meditation zur Unlös-barkeit der Ehe, anthropologisch betrachtet.* Berlin: Morus Verlag, 1971.

————., ed. "Was wir wollen." In *Kristall. Bild und Ebenbild. Werkheft für Mädchen,* 4–7. Frankfurt am Main: Josef Knecht, 1947.

————. *Weltfrömmigkeit.* Edited by Beatrix Klaiber. Frankfurt am Main: Josef Knecht, 1975.

————. *What Binds Marriage Forever: Reflections on the Indissolubility of Marriage.* Introduction by Jonathan Bieler. Translated by Jennifer S. Bryson. [Washington D.C.: Catholic University of America Press. Forthcoming.]

————. *"Wirklich die neue Phönixgestalt?" Ida Friederike Görres über Kirche und Konzil: Unbekannte Briefe 1962–1971 an Paulus Gordan.* Edited by Hanna-Barbara Gerl-Falkovitz. Heiligenkreuz, Austria: Be+Be Verlag, 2015.

————. *Zwischen den Zeiten; aus meinen Tagebüchern, 1951 bis 1959.* Olten, Germany: Walter-Verlag, 1960.

Govaert, Sister Lutgard, F.S.O. Letter to Hanna-Barbara Gerl-Falkovitz. March 23, 2002. Gerl-Falkovitz Private Archive, Erlangen, Germany.

Grant, Tony. "Netley Abbey and the Gothic". *Jane Austen's World* (blog), January 5, 2018. https://janeaustensworld.com/tag/cistercian-monastic-ruins/.

Gregory XVI, Pope. Encyclical letter *Mirari vos.* August 15, 1832. Papal Encyclicals. https://www.papalencyclicals.net/greg16/g16mirar.htm.

Gwynn, Denis. "John Henry Newman, 1801–1890". In *John Henry Newman: Centenary Essays,* edited by Henry Tristram, 16–35. London: Burns, Oates and Washbourne, 1945.

Harper, Gordon Huntington. *Cardinal Newman and William Froude, F.R.S.: A Correspondence.* Baltimore: Johns Hopkins Press, 1933.

Holland, Bernard. "Patriotism". *Dublin Review* 162, no. 325 (April–June 1918): 205–23.

Irenaeus, *Against Heresies*. Translated by Alexander Roberts and William Rambaut. In *Ante-Nicene Fathers*, vol. 1, edited by Alexander Roberts, James Donaldson, and A. Cleveland Coxe. Buffalo: Christian Literature Publishing, 1885. Revised and edited for New Advent by Kevin Knight. https://www.newadvent.org/fathers/0103303.htm.

Karrer, Otto, ed. *Kardinal John Henry Newman, Die Kirche*. Einsiedeln: Benziger, 1945.

Keats, John. "Ode on a Grecian Urn". Poetry Foundation. https://www.poetryfoundation.org/poems/44477/ode-on-a-grecian-urn.

Kleinert, Michael. *Es wächst viel Brot in der Winternacht. Theologische Grundlinien im Werk von Ida Friederike Görres*. Studien zur systematischen und spirituellen Theologie 36. Würzburg, Germany: Echter Verlag, 2002.

Kuehnelt-Leddihn, Erik von. *Weltweite Kirche, Begegnungen und Erfahrungen in sechs Kontinenten 1909-1999*. Stein am Rhein, Germany: Christiana, 2000.

Langgässer, Elisabeth. "Die Welt vor den Toren der Kirche." In *Elisabeth Langgässer: eine biographische Skizze* by Karlheinz Müller. Darmstadt, Germany: Gesellschaft Hessischer Literaturfreunde, 1990.

Lessing, Gotthold Ephraim. *Lessings ausgewählte Werke*. Leipzig, Germany: G. J. Göschen, 1867.

Lewis, C. S. *Letters to Malcolm: Chiefly on Prayer*. New York: Harcourt, Brace and World, 1963.

Lounsbury, Thomas Raynesford. *James Fenimore Cooper*. Boston: Houghton, Mifflin, 1882.

Lutz, Joseph A. *Kardinal John Henry Newman: Ein Zeit- und Lebensbild*. Einsiedeln, Switzerland: Benziger, 1948.

Middleton, R. D. "The Vicar of St. Mary's". In *John Henry Newman: Centenary Essays*, edited by Henry Tristram, 127-38. London: Burns, Oates and Washbourne, 1945.

Milner, Joseph. *The History of the Church of Christ*. 6 vols. London: T. Cadell, 1827-1833. Revised by George Stokes, ca. 1880.

Mozley, Anne, ed. *Letters and Correspondence of John Henry Newman during His Life in the English Church: With a Brief Autobiography*. Vols. 1 and 2. Longmans, Green, 1903.

New World Encyclopedia contributors. "Ethical Culture". *New World Encyclopedia*. https://www.newworldencyclopedia.org/p/index.php?title=Ethical_Culture&oldid=1139299.

Newman, Johann Heinrich [*sic*]. *Ausgewählte Predigten auf alle Sonntage des Kirchenjahres und für die Feste des Herrn von Johann Heinrich Kardinal Newman*. Translated by Guido Maria Dreves. Kempten and Munich: Kösel Verlag, 1907.

Newman, John Henry. *Apologia Pro Vita Sua*. Edited by Ian Ker. London: Penguin Books, 1994.

———. *Betrachtungen und Gebete*. Translated by Maria Knoepfler. Munich: Theatiner, 1924.

———. *Callista: A Tale of the Third Century*. London: Longmans, Green, 1901.

———. *Certain Difficulties Felt by Anglicans in Catholic Teaching*. Vols. 1 and 2. London: Longmans, Green, 1901.

———. *Christentum: Ein Aufbau*. Vols. 1–8. Translated by Otto Karrer. Edited by Erich Przywara. Freiburg im Breisgau: Herder, 1922.

———. *Correspondence of John Henry Newman with John Keble and Others, 1839–1845*. London: Longmans, Green, 1917.

———. "The Death of Moses." In *Verses on Various Occasions*, 106–7. London: Longmans, Green, 1905.

———. *Discourses to Mixed Congregations*. London: Longmans, Green, 1906.

———. "The Dream of Gerontius". In *Verses on Various Occasions*, 323–70. London: Longmans, Green, 1905.

———. *An Essay in Aid of a Grammar of Assent*. London: Longmans, Green, 1903.

———. *An Essay on the Development of Christian Doctrine*. London: Longmans, Green, 1909.

————. *Fifteen Sermons Preached before the University of Oxford between A.D. 1826 and 1843*. London: Longmans, Green, 1909.

————. "Führ, liebes Licht". In Ida Friederike Görres, *Der verborgene Schatz*, translated by Ida Friederike Görres, 93. Frankfurt am Main: Josef Knecht, 1949.

————. "Der Gentleman." Translated by William Gulde. *Frankfurter Hefte* 1, no. 1 (1946): 89–90. [This is an excerpt from *The Idea of a University*.]

————. *Gespräche mit Gott: Ausgewählte Worte*. Stuttgart-Degerloch: Vita Nova Verlag, 1946.

————. *The Idea of a University*. London: Longmans, Green, 1907.

————. *Lectures on the Present Position of Catholics in England: Addressed to the Brothers of the Oratory in the Summer of 1851*. London: Longmans, Green, 1908.

————. "A Letter Addressed to the Duke of Norfolk". In *Certain Difficulties Felt by Anglicans in Catholic Teaching*, 2:246–61. London: Longmans, Green, 1901.

————. *The Letters and Diaries of John Henry Newman*. 32 vols. Edited by various. Oxford, UK: Oxford University Press and the Birmingham Oratory, 1961–2008.

————. *Loss and Gain: The Story of a Convert*. Rev. ed. London: Longmans, Green, 1906.

————. *Maria im Heilsplan*. Translated and with an introduction by Birgitta zu Münster, O.S.B. Freiburg im Breisgau, Germany: Herder, 1953.

————. *Meditations and Devotions*. London: Longmans, Green, 1912.

————. *The Mission of St. Philip Neri: An Instruction, Delivered in Substance in the Birmingham Oratory, January, 1850, and at Subsequent Times*. Rome: Cuggiani, 1901.

————. *Parochial and Plain Sermons*. 8 vols. London: Longmans, Green, 1906.

————. *Philosophie des Glaubens (Grammar of Assent)*. Translated by Theodor Haecker. Munich: Hermann A. Wiechmann, 1921.

———. "The Pillar of the Cloud". In *Verses on Various Occasions*, 156–57. London: Longmans, Green, 1905.

———. *Philipp Neri*. Translated by Maria Knoepfler. Munich: Theatiner, 1922.

———. *Predigten: Gesamtausgabe*. Stuttgart 1948–1962. DP I–VIII: *Pfarr- und Volkspredigten*; DP IX: *Predigten zu Tagesfragen*; DP X: *Predigten zu verschiedenen Anlässen*; DP XI: *Predigten vor Katholiken und Andersgläubigen*; DP XII: *Der Anruf Gottes. Neun bisher unveröffentlichte Predigten aus der katholischen Zeit*. Stuttgart, Germany 1965.

———. *Sermons Bearing on the Subjects of the Day*. London: Longmans, Green, 1902.

———. *Sermons Preached on Various Occasions*. London: Longmans, Green, 1908.

———. *Tracts for the Times*. Edited by James Tolhurst. Vol. 10 of *The Works of Cardinal Newman: Birmingham Oratory Millennium Edition*. Leominster, Herefordshire, UK: Gracewing, 2013.

———. *Verses on Various Occasions*. London: Longmans, Green, 1905.

———. *The Via Media of the Anglican Church*. London: Basil Montagu Pickering, 1877.

Nigg, Walter. "Eine unter tausend: Ida Friederike Görres". In *Heilige und Dichter*, 227–49. Freiburg im Breisgau, Germany: Olten Verlag, 1982.

"Obituaries", *Gentleman's Magazine* 301 (July–December 1906), 220.

Ollard, Sidney Leslie. *A Short History of the Oxford Movement*. London: Mowbray, 1983.

Paraïso, Jean-Yves, ed. *"Brief über die Kirche." Die Kontroverse um Ida Friederike Görres Aufsatz-Ein Dokumentationsband*. Cologne, Germany: Böhlau Verlag, 2005.

Purcell, Edmund Sheridan. *Life of Cardinal Manning, Archbishop of Westminster*. Vol. 2. London: Macmillan, 1896.

Ratzinger, Joseph. "Eulogy for Ida Friederike Görres". Translated by Jennifer S. Bryson. *Logos* 23, no. 4 (Fall 2020): 148–55.

Rosmini, Antonio. *Of the Five Wounds of the Holy Church*. Edited by Henry Parry Liddon. London: Rivingtons, 1883.

Schamoni, Wilhelm. *The Face of the Saints*. Translated by Anne Fremantle. Freeport, N.Y.: Books for Libraries Press, 1947.

Scheler, Max. *Über Ressentiment und moralisches Wertgefühl*. Leipzig, Germany: Verlag von Wilhelm Engelmann, 1912.

Schiffers, Norbert. *Die Einheit der Kirche nach John Henry Newman*. Düsseldorf: Patmos Verlag, 1956.

Schmidlin, Josef. *Papstgeschichte der neuesten Zeit: Papsttum und Päpste im Zeitalter der Restauration (1800–1846)*. Munich: Josef Kösel and Friedrich Pustet, 1933.

Schmidt, Susanna. "Ida Friederike Görres (1901–1971)". In *Zeitgeschichte in Lebensbildern: Aus dem deutschen Katholizismus des 19. und 20. Jahrhunderts*, edited by Jürgen Aretz, Rudolf Morsey, and Anton Rauscher. 10:179–90. Münster, Germany: Aschendorff Verlag, 2001.

Schneider, Reinhold. *Das Inselreich: Gesetz und Größe der britischen Macht*. In *Gesammelte Werke*, edited by Edwin Maria Landau, 2. Frankfurt am Main: Insel Verlag, 1979.

———. *Das Unzerstörbare: Religiöse Schriften*. In *Gesammelte Werke*, edited by Edwin Maria Landau, 9. Frankfurt am Main: Insel Verlag, 1978.

Siebenrock, Roman. "Wahrheit, Gewissen und Geschichte: Eine systematisch-theologische Rekonstruktion des Wirkens John Henry Kardinal Newmans". In *Internationale Cardinal-Newman-Studien* 15. Sigmaringendorf, Germany: Regio-Verlag Glock und Lutz, 1996.

Simon, Paul. "Newman und der englische Katholizismus". In *Newman Studien* 1, 13–28. Nuremberg, Germany: Glock and Lutz, 1948.

"Sodom apple." In *Oxford English Dictionary*. oed.com.

Stephens, James. *Fionn, der Held und andere irische Sagen und Märchen*. Translated by Ida Friederike Görres. Freiburg im Breisgau, Germany: Herder, 1936 [and Heiligenkreuz, Austria: Be+Be Verlag, 2017, with an introduction by Hanna-Barbara Gerl-Falkovitz].

Strachey, Lytton. *Eminent Victorians*. New York: Modern Library, 1918.

Sugg, Joyce. *Ever Yours Affly. John Henry Newman and His Female Circle*. Leominster, Herefordshire, UK: Gracewing, 1996.

"There Were Two Royal Children". In *German Poetry from the Beginnings to 1750*. Edited and translated by Ingrid Walsøe–Engel, 149. New York: Continuum, 1992.

Thérèse of Lisieux. *Story of a Soul: The Autobiography of St. Thérèse of Lisieux*. Translated by John Clarke. Washington, D.C.: Institute of Carmelite Studies, 1996.

Thomas of Celano, Brother. *The Lives of Saint Francis of Assisi*. Translated by A. G. Ferrers Howell. London: Methuen, 1908.

Tolhurst, James. Introduction to *John Henry Newman, Discussions and Arguments on Various Subjects*, vii–xlix. Leominster, Herefordshire, UK: Gracewing, 2004.

Trevor, Meriol. *Newman: Light in Winter*. Garden City, N.Y.: Doubleday, 1963.

Tristram, Henry, ed. *John Henry Newman: Centenary Essays*. London: Burns, Oates and Washbourne, 1945.

———. *Cardinal Newman and the Church of the Birmingham Oratory: A History and a Guide*. Gloucester, UK: British Publishing Company, 1934.

———. "On Reading Newman". In *John Henry Newman: Centenary Essays*, edited by Henry Tristram, 223–41. London: Burns, Oates and Washbourne, 1945.

———. "With Newman at Prayer". In *John Henry Newman: Centenary Essays*, edited by Henry Tristram, 101–26. London: Burns, Oates and Washbourne, 1945.

Ward, Wilfrid Philip. *Aubrey de Vere: A Memoir, Based on His Unpublished Diaries and Correspondence*. London: Longmans, Green, 1904.

———. *The Life of John Henry Cardinal Newman: Based on His Private Journals and Correspondence*. Vols. 1 and 2. London: Longmans, Green, 1912.

Werfer, Franziska. *Hermann Breucha (1902–1972): Aufbruch der Kirche im Bild eines Priesters*. Weissenhorn, Germany: Konrad Verlag, 1982.

Wintersinger, Bärbel. Letter to Hanna-Barbara Gerl-Falkovitz, March 11, 1991. Gerl–Falkovitz Private Archive, Erlangen, Germany.

INDEX